BURT FRANKLIN: BIBLIOGRAPHY & REFERENCE SERIES 257

ARCHBISHOP LAUD COMMEMORATION

1895.

FROM A PICTURE BY MYTTENS, IN
THE POSSESSION OF CHARLES W. WOOD, ESQ.
On the front of the picture is the following inscription:

LAUD: L. BYSHOP LONDON 1631
ÆTATIS SUÆ 58

Archbishop Laud Commemoration, 1895.

——✠——

Lectures on Archbishop Laud

TOGETHER WITH A

Bibliography of Laudian Literature

AND THE

Laudian Exhibition Catalogue

ETC.

EDITED BY

WILLIAM EDWARD COLLINS, M.A.

Professor of Ecclesiastical History at King's College, London.

BURT FRANKLIN
NEW YORK

Prejudged by foes determined not to spare,
An old weak Man for vengeance thrown aside,
LAUD "in the painful art of dying" tried,
(Like a poor bird entangled in a snare
Whose heart still flutters, though his wings forbear
To stir in useless struggle) hath relied
On hope that conscious innocence supplied,
And in his prison breathes celestial air.
Why tarries then thy chariot ? Wherefore stay,
O Death ! the ensanguined yet triumphant wheels,
Which thou prepar'st, full often, to convey
(What time a State with madding faction reels)
The Saint or Patriot to the world that heals
All wounds, all perturbations doth allay ?

WILLIAM WORDSWORTH.

Published by BURT FRANKLIN
235 East 44th St., New York, N.Y. 10017
Originally Published: 1895
Reprinted: 1969
Printed in the U.S.A.

Library of Congress Card Catalog No.: 68-58472
Burt Franklin: Bibliography and Reference Series 257

TABLE OF CONTENTS.

INTRODUCTION.

I. THE MEMORY OF ARCHBISHOP LAUD.

Two hundred and fifty years have elapsed since Archbishop Laud laid down his life upon the scaffold. During this period his personal character, his principles, and his work in Church and State, have been viewed in nearly every light that indifference, prejudice, or partisanship could throw upon them. He has been pursued from his own day to the present (as was perhaps only to be expected) by the unfriendly criticism of non-conformists, and enjoys a reputation as a persecutor which he shared only with Bishop Bonner and Bloody Mary. But apart from this perpetual under-current, many stages of opinion can be clearly traced. The nearly indiscriminate eulogy of Heylin and the constitutional Churchmen of the later Stuart reigns gave place in time to the colder and less appreciative tones of the latitudinarian divines, who looked upon him, with Burnet, as " hot and indiscreet. eagerly pursuing such matters as were either very inconsiderable or mischievous," or thought with Hacket that although " there were very good things to be found in the Lord Archbishop," yet there was much more which " was unpardonable." The former view revived under Queen Anne, and never died out. It is to be found now and again throughout the eighteenth century, and especially, for instance, in the pages of the *European Magazine* of a hundred years ago (see p. 269) ; but more and more it came to be identified with high Toryism ; often with Jacobitism. The estimate of Burnet and Hacket came to be generally accepted, and has become more and more exaggerated in the process, until at length the climax was reached in the bitter and strangely distorted estimate of Lord Macaulay.

The natural result of the Tractarian movement was to revive and popularise a presentment which erred quite as much on the other side. This, however, can scarcely be said to have held its ground against that of Macaulay, which has continued to be the prevalent view among uninformed people down to the present day, as will be at once realised by anyone who has followed the utterances of provincial newspapers and Nonconformist preachers on the subject during the last few months.

At length, however, the prospect is becoming clearer. No doubt there will always be two or more views held as to the man and his work. But there is at least a tendency to base these views upon a study of the facts of the case, rather than upon certain pre-conceived ideas. Something, at any rate, of the rancour of partisanship has passed away. And whilst lapse of time is doubtless one great factor in this change, it is due, far more largely than to any other single event, to the publication of Dr. S. R. Gardiner's great *History of England.* We are better able now to see how much there was of good in the principles and aims of the noblest spirits on both sides. And many have been found to do honour to Archbishop Laud's courage, zeal, personal piety, and love of learning, who sympathise very little, or not at all, with the political principles which he deemed it almost part of his religion to uphold. But after all, his work on behalf of the English Church is that by which, in the long run, he must stand or fall. It is here, for good or for evil, hat his influence has been most manifest. And the voice of those who best represent the mind of that Church has gone forth with no uncertain sound. Whatever he may be to other men, to us at least he is an apostle. There can surely be no doubt that the whole course of our history since then has been, in the main, in accordance with the great aims which, however imperfectly, Archbishop Laud strove to carry out. Failures in judgment, in humility, in charity, there may have been ; but the broad fact remains that to him, more perhaps than to any other man, the Church of England owes her present shape.

But although there has been a great and growing recognition of the debt which we owe to him, no adequate attempt has been made to commemorate his services. After the Restoration a medal was indeed struck in his honour, many copies of which still exist, in silver or in brass : but this was no more than might have been done to commemorate a great victory or to inaugurate a mayoralty. His body was translated to Oxford in 1663, and buried in solemn state in the Chapel of S. John's College, Oxford, between the founder and Juxon : but by his own express direction it was done privately, and at night. (See the details in Hutton's *William Laud*, p. 228). It may perhaps have been no more than an accidental coincidence, but the two hundredth anniversary of his death was marked by the appearance, in the *Christian Remembrancer* for January 1845, of Mozley's memorable article. But this was all. The completion of a quarter of a millenium from the date of his death seemed, therefore, a fitting opportunity for bringing before the public mind one whose significance to our own day is illustrated by the fact that, within a few months, three such lives of him have appeared as those by "A Romish Recusant," Mr. Simpkinson, and Mr. Hutton. And the Archbishop Laud Commemoration of 1895 is the result.

II. THE ARCHBISHOP LAUD COMMEMORATION, 1895.

It is not necessary here to tell the story of the Commemoration at any length. The idea originated in the Church of Allhallows

Barking, "a Church," as Heylin says, "of Laud's own Patronage and Jurisdiction"; there the Commemoration was carried out; and it was from the first intended that if there were any proceeds after paying expenses, they should go to the Restoration Fund of this Church.* With the co-operation of an influential Committee, whose names will be found at the beginning of the revised Exhibition Catalogue (p. 281), the following scheme was drawn up, and was carried out in its entirety:—

1. Services in Allhallows Barking Church, E.C.

> *Thursday, Jan. 10th* (Beheading of Archbishop Laud).
>
>> 7.0 a.m.—Holy Eucharist.
>>
>> 7.30 a.m.—Mattins.
>>
>> 1.5 p.m.—*Te Deum* on the site of the Scaffold in Trinity Square, with the reading of the account of the death of the Archbishop.
>>
>> 5.0 p.m.—Evensong (Choral).

> *Friday, Jan. 11th* (Deposition of Archbishop Laud).
>
>> 8.0 a.m.—Holy Eucharist (Choral).
>>
>> 11.0 a.m.—Mattins.
>>
>> 8.0 p.m.—Evensong.

2. Exhibition of Laudian Relics.

This was held in the handsome Schoolroom adjoining the Church (designed by Mr. J. L. Pearson, R.A., and given to the Parish by the Rev. A. J. Mason, D.D., the Vicar). It was declared open after the Service at 1.5 p.m. on Jan. 10, and remained open daily (Sundays excepted) from 11 a.m. to 5 p.m. until the end of the month, and on Tuesdays and Thursdays from 7.30 p.m. to 9.30 p.m. also. A charge of One Shilling was in general made for admittance.

---

* This has been done. After paying all expenses there remained a small balance: and the proceeds of the present volume, if any, will be devoted to the same good object.

3. A Course of Lectures was delivered in the Church, at 3.30 p.m. on the following days : Thursday Jan. 10th, Thursday Jan. 17th, Monday Jan. 21st, Thursday Jan. 24th, and Thursday Jan. 31st. The subjects and names of lecturers will be found in the Table of Contents.

The Commemoration was an unqualified success. Thursday Jan. 10th was clear, but piercingly cold : but long before one o'clock there was a very large concourse of people, all (or nearly all) evidently sympathetic, upon Tower Hill and about the site of the Scaffold (in the garden of Trinity Square). At 1.5 a procession left the Church, consisting of the choir of Allhallows Barking, augmented by members of several other neighbouring choirs, in cassock and surplice, and the clergy. And although no effort had been made to attract numbers (in fact no general invitation was issued) a considerable body of clergy took part, in addition to those serving the Church of Allhallows. At the site the Te Deum was sung, and Dr. Mason read the account of the Archbishop's death, from Heylin, in a voice that could be heard far and wide : and then, after prayer, the procession returned to the Church. The proceedings were, as the *Times* said, simple and dignified throughout.

The Exhibition was not less successful. It was crowded throughout the first day, and the attendance during the rest of the time that it remained open was very satisfactory, especially when the bad weather is taken into account. In all, over two thousand persons paid it a visit : and it was evidently greatly appreciated, being small enough to be studied in detail, and yet very representative.

Long before 3.30 p.m. on Jan. 10th the Church was crowded in every part to hear the Bishop of Peterborough's lecture : the greater part of the congregation consisting of men. At the time appointed his lordship, who wore his violet cassock, with his pectoral cross and black academical gown, was conducted to the pulpit by the vicar. Dr. Mason, from his stall, gave out the hymn

"O God, our help in ages past," which was sung unaccompanied. Then the Bishop, having said the Collect for SS. Simon and Jude, and the Lord's Prayer, began his lecture, which was listened to with rapt attention. After the Benediction the large congregation left the Church, many of them proceeding at once to the Exhibition.

The other services, and the lectures, were very well attended; and the interest remained unimpaired to the end of the Commemoration.

The Commemoration received a very considerable share of public attention. All the London daily newspapers, and most of the chief provincial ones, had leading articles on the subject, some of them on Jan. 10th or 11th, and some a little before or after. The best of these, from the *Times* of Jan. 11th, is reprinted in this volume (at p. 157 f.); but many more were of no small permanent value. Moreover, a very large number of newspapers and magazines, home and colonial and foreign, dealt with the subject at greater or less length, many of them giving illustrations of the exhibits, or other illustrations in connection with the Commemoration. And as Secretary I received a very large number of letters, some of them of the most touching character, which seemed to show that thought had been quickened and interest roused, and that much good had been done in many ways.

Naturally too, it came in for no small share of adverse criticism. Much of this was very welcome, not only as showing "How it strikes a Contemporary," and not only for its own intrinsic value, but because in many cases there was an evident and progressive appreciation of the fact that those who were concerned in the matter were not necessarily either bigoted fanatics or crack-brained enthusiasts. On the other hand, there was much that could easily have been spared. The amazingly wild statements of some newspapers—naturally, provincial ones above all—showed that, though truth may be stronger than falsehood, yet at least falsehood is very strong. Thus a quotation from Macaulay was (of course) always treated as final and conclusive. Charles I. was again and again confused with

Charles II, and spoken of accordingly. The statement that Laud was Archbishop in the reign of Queen Elizabeth was made without hesitation and (apparently) received without contradiction. It seemed to be a permissible opinion that his name might be spelled Lund, or Lord, or Loud. That he made use of the thumb-screw and the Scavenger's Daughter and the fire and stake was as indisputable a fact of history as that he was a Jesuit in disguise. A great London daily newspaper accepted and made use of (though it did not originate) the statement that he was mainly responsible for the ejection of the ministers in 1662 ; and it need hardly be said that numbers of small fry followed in its wake. After this it would be superfluous to mention any of the vast number of smaller mistakes which were made.

Perhaps even more remarkable (not to say deplorable) was the intolerant tone of certain pronouncements on the subject. Thus there was a characteristic effusion in the *Daily News;* and a small section of the so-called "religious" newspapers distinguished themselves by their acerbity. And the Commemoration called forth a number of anonymous communications (mostly on postcards) which strangely recall the kind of thing with which Archbishop Laud had to deal; and show that the spirit which animated the fanatic of his day is by no means extinct. A few of these are printed here on account of their historical interest; and nobody who is acquainted with such "libels" as are preserved in the Record Office or in Lambeth Palace Library will have any difficulty in recognising the resemblance :—

1. "There will be another anniversary of a socalled Martyr on the 30th. The tricky Ch 1st. You and your colleagues, can go through some more mumby jumby in pseudo religiosity What an outcome of medevial (*sic*) legerdemain and fireworks. Poor fellows your minds seem incapable of understanding progress, but ever harping on the past. all such frauds as Ch 1st Laud, Strafford, C 2nd James 2nd were a disgrace to our Nation and all you parrotters (*sic*) of the 19th centy ought to be

sent to the Tower or Treadmill. You are dispensers of the husks and Chaff There is no sense in your patter."

2. "Archbishop Laud, the man whom you delight to honor but of whom the Lord hath said 'this man draweth near unto Me with his lips but his heart is far from Me.' The man who sought to deprive the Church of God of all real inward and spiritual grace and substitute in its stead an unreal external sin (*sic*), as though the Lord took pleasure in gorgeous apparel and lighted candles. The man who sought to propagate his hollow forms by persecutions and cruelties of the most atrocious character, throwing into prison slitting and cutting off noses and ears of those who believed and realised that religion was a thing of the heart. This is the man whom you delight to honor!"

3. "You are doing the work of the great Whore of Babylon and leading them to the Pope as your Laud did. And you deserve the same recompense as he received from his righteous judges. Curse you."

There are others even grosser ; but they cannot be quoted here. The writers of communications such as these may be compared with, *e.g.*, the authors of some of the tracts in the Bibliography. And perhaps it may be pointed out here, more suitably than elsewhere, that one of the latter would seem to have predicted the actual year of the Laud Commemoration, MDCCCXCV. * (See Laudian Bibliography No. 135). Such, at any rate is the least unintelligible meaning which can be twisted out of the latter part of Richard Newrobe's title.† And perhaps it might not yet be too late to prove that "the 12. day of the moneth Tridemiter, according to the Infernall collateration. peccandi" stands for the 10th day of January. The suggestion is given for what it is worth, to all whom it may concern!

* I could scarcely believe my eyes when I first saw this tract in the Reading Room of the British Museum.

† There is no reference of any kind to the year 1895 in the body of the pamphlet, nor anything to explain the latter part of the title. But in this it by no means stands alone.

III. THE MEMORIAL VOLUME.

From the first the announcement had been made that the lectures &c. would be published in a permanent form ; but the work of preparation has proved to be so much more than was at first expected, and has been so much interrupted by other duties, that a certain amount of delay has been unavoidable. It is hoped that this may be to some extent compensated for by the fact that the Bibliography is more complete than it otherwise could have been.

It remains to speak in detail of the contents of the volume.

a. The Portrait.—Some days after the Exhibition was opened, it was enriched, through the great kindness of Mrs. Davis Cooper, by the addition of a miniature of Archbishop Laud on ivory (Laudian Exhibition Catalogue No. 74). It had been painted by herself in 1858, from a portrait by Myttens, which was then in her husband's hands for the purpose of being used in the preparation of a large engraving containing many figures. The miniature not only formed an additional feature of great interest in the Exhibition, throwing light upon the mutual relations of the Vandyck portraits, the bust, and the engravings, but it opened up also an important question as to the present whereabouts of the Myttens portrait, of which nothing was known. A letter to the *Times* on the subject, however, at once brought an answer from the present owner, Charles W. Wood, Esq., of 1, Gloucester Place, W., who not only allowed Dr. Mason and myself to see the picture, but in the kindest manner possible consented that an autotype reproduction should form the frontispiece to this volume. And all who possess it will see at once how great is their debt to him for allowing the reproduction of this magnificent portrait, which must surely be allowed to rank even above those by Vandyck.

b. The Lectures.—These are printed exactly as they were delivered, a few references being added in one or two cases only.

The first, by the Bishop of Peterborough, has already been printed *verbatim* in the *Guardian* for Jan. 16: the others are now printed for the first time, although parts of some of them have been reported and printed nearly in full.

c. The Laudian Bibliography.—This has involved a considerable amount of labour of a rather perplexing kind, especially as it had to be carried out by one who was a novice at the work, and could only give to it spare hours which were all too few. Omissions there probably are: a first bibliography is hardly ever final, and indeed it is one of the functions of such a work to be the means of enabling the learned to find out its own imperfections. But both omissions and other errors might have been fewer ˌhad it been possible to begin with the method which was only learned little by little in the school of experience.

Excepting in one or two instances, no attempt has been made to reproduce the typography of the original titlepages; and in some cases it has not seemed necessary to give the entire text; but the practice in this matter can hardly be considered uniform. In general, too, a reference is given (in the case of rare books), to some library &c. in which a copy is to be found; but this has not been possible in every instance.

In the case of one who occupied so large a place in the history of his time, the difficulty has often been rather what to leave out than what to include: for almost every satire of the time brings in his name in some form or other. On the other hand the lists of satirical portraits, of books dedicated to the Archbishop, and of foreign pamphlets will all probably prove to be incomplete. Books or collections, too, in which one or more of Laud's letters first appeared in print—such as the Strafford Letters, Vossii Epistolæ, or the Gentleman's Magazine—are purposely omitted from the list: but under No. 75 will be found a reference to the works in which all the letters hitherto printed first appeared.

The classification of the books included, moreover, has often proved no easy **matter**; but the system which has been adopted has been explained at the beginning of the Bibliography. New editions of any work are placed in order of their date, immediately after the first edition, and are distinguished by being somewhat indented. Translations have been placed in the same class as the works which they represent: thus for instance a translation of a letter of Laud's will be found classified under the heading of Laud's Works : this seemed inevitable because, in the case of some of the letters which exist in English translations only (such as No. 39), it is really impossible to say whether the translation is his or not. And where there are a large number of works in any one year (as in 1641), they are arranged in order of subjects (as far as possible) and not alphabetically. The latter plan has its advantages, but the fatal objection is the fact that the *Mercurie* letters (Nos. 148-152), for instance, would have been separated entirely from one another. The former plan doubtless has its disadvantages; but they will to some extent be obviated by the fulness of the index. And as the numbering is, after all, only made for convenient reference, there seemed to be no reason against inserting, with numbers but within brackets, several works which may in fact never have appeared (such as No. 18) or may have nothing to do with Laud (such as No. 37).

Several interesting points may be noticed, which have been unearthed during the preparation of the Bibliography. There is for instance the very curious incomplete and unpublished pamphlet (No. 93) which has apparently been overlooked hitherto in connection with Laud, and which tells its own tale so clearly. There is, again, the curious reference to the year MDCCCXCV, which has been already noticed (No. 135). A flood of light, too, is thrown on the closeness of the relations between England and Holland, by the fact that so large a number of translations appeared, and so quickly. of the publications on behalf of and against the Archbishop. It illustrates, moreover, the character of the two peoples; for although a considerable number of tracts appeared in England dealing with the affairs of the Low Countries, there are very few translations; and the total number of such tracts certainly cannot compare with the number published abroad relating to England. And, although the fact is already well known, it is worth noticing how many English books in this list either really were, or professed to be, printed abroad. We see, too, that the printers of that century (as is shown, for example, in Nos. 177 and 207, and Laudian Exhibition Catalogue No. 81) used to employ the same wood block over and over again to represent different people, with a boldness which has only survived in a very small degree in these degenerate days. And once again, it is interesting to find that the last edition of Heylin's *Cyprianus Anglicus*, and the last two editions of White's *Answer to Fisher* (which includes Laud's *Third Conference*) appeared in Dublin.

d. Newly published writings of Laud.—It formed no part of the present scheme to collect together everything of Archbishop Laud's which had not appeared in the collected edition of his works. Had this been intended, the State Paper Office would have supplied many formal documents, and a great number of short notes by the Archbishop upon speeches or despatches—most of which are to be found described or transcribed in the published Calendars. And a few things are to be found elsewhere, *e.g.* one letter (to the City of Edinburgh) in the *English Historical Review*, and various papers in the different volumes published by the *Historical MSS. Commission.*

But although this was not intended, the case is different with writings which are otherwise inaccessible. Laud's Instrument of Resignation of the Chancellorship of Oxford is here published for the first time, from the original in the Bodleian Library, of which a photograph was included in the magnificent collection lent by Professor Margoliouth to the Laudian Exhibition (*Catalogue* No. 54). Three curious and interesting sets of Latin verses, written by Laud on public occasions while he was President of S. John's College, are reprinted *verbatim* from the very rare volumes (see Bibliography Nos. 1-3) in the British Museum.

e. The Laudian Exhibition Catalogue.—This has been subjected to a certain amount of revision and correction, though not such as to alter its form in any way. The original Catalogue was necessarily prepared very hastily, and a few errors which occurred in consequence have now been corrected; whilst descriptions have been inserted of exhibits which appeared too late to be catalogued, and the numbers are altered accordingly.

Something may be added here as to the Exhibition itself. It would seem to have been very fairly complete. In fact, I am only aware of five *desiderata* of any importace.

(i) There is in Lambeth Palace Library, as was pointed out by the writer of an able article in the *Illustrated London News*, a lozenge-shaped pane of glass from a window of the old Croydon Palace, upon which Laud has written with a diamond. Of this nothing was known until it was too late to apply for the loan of it. (ii) The Committee had not discovered the whereabouts of the magnificent portrait of Laud by Myttens until the last week in January. (iii) There are at Ickwell-Bury in Bedfordshire, a large silver Monteith (or punch-bowl) and several pairs of silver candlesticks bearing the Laud and Robinson arms, and a Vandyck portrait of Laud, in which the "drooping eye" is especially noticeable. These were the gift of the Archbishop to his grand-niece Sarah, the daughter of Sir John Robinson, who became the wife of John Harvey of Ickwell-Bury, Esq. Owing to serious illness, their present owner, Mrs. Harvey of Ickwell-Bury, did not know of the Exhibition in time to lend these, as she would otherwise gladly have done. (iv) There is a copy of the first edition of Bellarmine's *Disputationes*, in three volumes, Lugdunum, 1596,-9,-6. folio, in Archbishop Marsh's Library* at Dublin, with copious (and very interesting) annotations in Laud's handwriting : but unfortu-

---

* This Library originally belonged to Bishop Stillingfleet, of Worcester, and was purchased from his executors by Abp. Marsh, for public use in the diocese of Dublin. The copy of Bellarmine may therefore have been used in the preparation of Stillingfleet's *Rational Account.* (*Bibliography* No. 231).

nately nothing was known of this until the Exhibition was already
open. Its absence is, however, of less consequence owing to the
fact that the notes have already been printed in Laud's *Works*
VI. 607-708. (v) His Grace the Duke of Buccleuch was unable to
lend to the Exhibition a miniature portrait of Archbishop Laud in
his possession.

In order that this list may not seem incomplete, mention must
be made here of two other Laudian relics which I have been quite
unable to trace. (i) A copy of Andrewes's *Tortura Torti* (1609)
with numerous MS notes by Laud, was advertised for sale, as I am
informed by Professor Mayor, in the book catalogue of Mr. T.
Kerslake (of Bristol) for October 1859 (No. 52). The comments of
the scholar upon the famous work of his illustrious master in the
art of controversy should be very valuable ; but so far I have failed
to trace the book. (ii) The same thing is true of a MS by Laud
upon Church Government, which was sold for £21 at Dawson
Turner's in 1859 [Lowndes *Bibl. Manual*, p. 1318]. It should also
be mentioned that there is a very beautiful ivory drinking-cup in
private hands, which was exhibited at Harrow many years ago,
and of which a drawing was given in the *Illustrated London News* at
the time, as Archbishop Laud's Chalice. But there seems to be
no sufficient reason for describing it as a chalice, nor for ascribing
it to Archbishop Laud ; and consequently the present owners felt
that it ought not to have a place in the Laudian Exhibition.

f. Conclusion.—It remains only, in conclusion, to return thanks
to a large number of friends who have helped me in the preparation of this volume. Mr. F. A. Hyett, who, with the Rev. W.
Bazeley, is engaged upon a *Gloucestershire Bibliography*, most generously placed at my disposal his collections in relation to Archbishop
Laud; and the Rev. W. C. Boulter lent me a large collection of
cuttings from book-catalogues having reference to him: both of
these have been useful. My debt to Mr. Charles W. Wood has
been already acknowledged. And for kind help of various sorts
I am indebted to the Bishop of Edinburgh Lord Northbourne,

Mr. C. H. Firth, the Rev. J. L. Fish, the Rev. Dr. J. T. Fowler, Mr. Hubert Hall (of the Record Office), Mrs. Harvey of Ickwell-Bury, the Rev. W. H. Hutton, Mr. Falconer Madan, Professor Margoliouth, the Rev. Dr. Mason, the Rev. Professor J. E. B. Mayor, Mr. H. C. Richards, the Rev. Dr. Sparrow-Simpson, the Rev. Professor G. T. Stokes, and the late Rev. Precentor Venables; and above all, to Miss Mary Sterland, for much help in correction of proofs and in many other ways.

W. E. C.

Morwenstow,

S. Bartholomew's Day 1895.

ERRATA.

p. 186. No. 68. *For Bp.* read *David.*

p. 197. No. 94. *The letter* is *by Bishop Hall, as I ought to have remembered. It occurs as* No. 4 *in his third* Decade of Epistles, *first published in 1611, as a* Letter to Mr. W. L. *(always supposed to be William Laud.) But of course he had no hand in this republication.*

I.

LAUD'S POSITION IN THE HISTORY OF THE ENGLISH CHURCH.

THE RIGHT REV. MANDELL CREIGHTON, D.D.,
LORD BISHOP OF PETERBOROUGH.

LAUD'S POSITION IN THE HISTORY OF THE ENGLISH CHURCH.

WE turn to the records of the past with a desire to escape from the perplexities which beset our judgment of the present. We long to find principles, clearly marked, working themselves out to a triumphant end. We pine for characters of majestic simplicity, whose integrity and wisdom are alike beyond dispute. It is sad to confess that the search for heroes is fruitless ; that there are few characters which defy criticism ; that the forms of controversy have changed rather than their nature ; that men and women are still sons and daughters of debate ; that the issues of the activity of those who played a great part in affairs are strangely complicated, and still make demands on our charity in judging them.

It is not my purpose to-day to eulogise the character of him whose memory we are met to celebrate. My object is to put before you the task which he undertook, and the difficulties which beset him. The judgment of history is necessarily stern : it can make no allowance for good intentions : it must pass beyond immediate success or failure. and must estimate all the results of action which it has the penetration to perceive. First, then, I should say that William Laud has an unfailing claim upon the homage of English Churchmen, because he did much to fix the character of the system of the English Church. Some explanation is necessary to

show how and why such a task devolved on him; and
for this purpose I must ask you to follow me in a brief
survey of the actual conditions which Laud had to face.
The great religious movement of the sixteenth century
produced a universal change, which affected all countries
alike.   It marshalled into opposite camps tendencies of
thought which had long been antagonistic, though the
antagonism had been humoured or suppressed.   It swept
away the dominant theology which had formed the
groundwork for the abuses which provoked revolt.
Post-Tridentine theology in the Roman Church owes
more to Luther than to his scholastic predecessors of
the fifteenth century.   Everywhere there were changes,
and it was difficult to foresee the final settlement in any
quarter.

In England the limitations of change were at first
clearly defined.   They were—abolition of the Papal
jurisdiction, remedy of abuses in the organisation of the
Church which were due to that jurisdiction, greater
simplicity and intelligibility in public worship.   These
corresponded with the fuller development of that
national consciousness whose watchword has always
been " England for the English."   They corresponded
with the political ideal of England's position, which first
took a definite shape in the hands of Wolsey, and has
ever since prevailed—that England should use its
natural advantages and its large resources to act as an
independent arbitrator in European affairs.   The conception of an English patriarchate, *quasi alterius orbis papa*,
was as old as Anselm, and was almost realised by

Wolsey.   It seemed no great innovation to give it practical effect.

But when change is in the air it is impossible to erect barriers beyond which it may not pass.   The reigns of Edward VI. and Mary witnessed two forms of re-action, both of them worked by a small party from above, neither of them according with the wishes of the English people.   One thing only was obvious to the statesmen of Elizabeth's reign—that Romanism meant the loss of English liberty and England's subjection to the overwhelming influence of the Spanish monarchy. But in England itself men's minds had been stirred by alternate persecutions, and partisanship had arisen on both sides.   Parties had unconsciously formed them-selves, and corresponded with parties existing on the Continent, where national and social antagonisms had assumed a religious garb.   It was difficult to see how the conception which lay at the root of the English Reformation was to be realised, an independent and united England, strong in its union, and able through its strength to mediate in the struggles on the Continent and produce peace by the example of its own moderating influence.

We miss the whole point of what actually occurred if we do not recognise the existence of this ideal, which was the result of England's past experience.   England united was safe, and could impose its will gradually but decisively on the Continent ; England disunited was helpless, and became the scene of plots, intrigues, and passionate animosities, which would drag it into Continental warfare as a feeble ally to one or other of the contending powers. Religious unity was felt by the wisest to be a political necessity ; no sacrifice was too great to obtain it. The best hope was that the English people would accept the spirit of the changes made under Henry VIII., and forget after a little time the spirit displayed under Edward VI. and Mary. If the framework was securely erected, things might slowly adjust themselves. Hot blood would cool ; opinions would modify one another ; the general forms of public worship were such as all men might readily agree to accept ; on doubtful points of practice and belief there was large latitude.

Such were the hopes of the wise and prudent ; but it requires little knowledge of history to know that wisdom and prudence play a very slight part in directing human affairs. The motive power in all things is generally the passionate resolve of small bodies of men to have their own way because it is their own. There was a sufficient number of adherents of the Marian Church to form a party, which intrigued abroad for Elizabeth's downfall and the subjection of England to Spain. This party had little hold in England itself, where Romanism might have speedily been absorbed if the religious settlement had prospered as it was hoped. But the returned exiles from Geneva had adopted the views of the French reformer, and strove to give them practical effect. The theology of Calvin was a weighty contribution towards many questions which had been brought into prominence in recent controversy. The rulers of the English Church regarded it with sympathy, and had no desire to prevent its free discussion or to limit arbitrarily its acceptance. But Calvin was not only the author of a system of theology, but of a new system of Church government and of public worship. His English adherents were not content to hold his theological opinions; they strove to impose his system of worship and government. They denounced Episcopacy; they discarded surplices; they objected to the Liturgy; they steadily worked for the purpose of imposing upon England the Genevan system of discipline.

The immediate result of their action was to give force and vitality to the old form of worship. Men were not unwilling to exchange the old services in Latin for those modelled on them which were contained in the Prayer-book. But in the face of the agitation set on foot by the adherents of Geneva, what security had they that these would be decently performed or permanently retained? If England was after all to submit to a foreign yoke, Rome was preferable to Geneva. So some argued; and the pardonable hesitation of many who were not interested in religious controversy deepened into a quiet adherence to the old system, which at least was definite when all else seemed shifting. Thus a Romanist party grew up in England, which was dangerous, not on religious grounds, but because it gave an opportunity for political interference from without.

Thus the prospect of a united England faded away on one side. The question still remained, How could it best be maintained on the other? There can be little

doubt that the mass of the people were satisfied with the
Prayer-book. But there was a minority who favoured
a more radical change. This minority was at first not
so much strong in numbers as in resoluteness. It did
not represent popular feeling, but consisted of earnest
men, many of whom had been in exile, men who took
orders in the Church, and claimed to work for the public
good according to their own convictions. This body
ound a home in the desolate Universities, where they
influenced the minds of the young and built up adherents. To them the Prayer-book was merely a temporary
makeshift—a halfway house between the Romanism
which they detested and the Calvinism which they soon
hoped to establish.

For an understanding of the course of events it is
necessary to remember two things which are generally
overlooked or misrepresented. First of all, the Puritan
party were not struggling for toleration, but for mastery.
They did not ask for wider option within the system of
the Church, but they wished to substitute another
system for it. Every point of concession gained was
but a step towards a new demand. Objections were
made first to the use of the surplice, then to the liturgy,
then to Episcopacy. The aim of the objectors was
gradually to introduce the Presbyterian system. The
minister was to be approved by the *classis ;* ceremonies
were to be gradually dropped ; churchwardens and over-
seers were to be turned into elders ; the Church was to
be administered by classical, provincial, and general
assemblies ; Bishops might remain as chairmen of these

meetings till the time came for their disappearance; the liturgy was to be slurred over, and the congregation invited only to a sermon prefaced by a long extempore prayer. By a judicious perseverance in this policy the Church was to be transformed into Presbyterianism. This was the persistent endeavour of the Puritans; it was consistent and intelligible.

A second point to notice is that the leaders in this movement were found amongst the clergy, particularly in the Universities. The Romanists manifested their hostility by withdrawing from the Church, organising themselves apart, and looking for help from abroad to bring back England to their way of thinking. The Puritans entered into the organisation of the Church and strove to change it from within. The first Nonconformists were clergy who refused to conduct their services according to the Prayer-book.

It was this fact which constituted the great difficulty in the way of uniting religious feeling in England on a basis which would give unity and strength. Religious questions were unfortunately also political questions. England, united either with Romanism or with foreign Protestantism, would have sacrificed its independent position and would never have emerged into the England of to-day. If the reign of Elizabeth was the great period in the making of modern England, it was because Elizabeth always aimed at holding a mediating position abroad, and husbanded England's resources while other countries were squandering theirs in warfare. Had the Puritans prevailed, this advantage would have been lost.

Taking the largest historical view, I think it must be admitted that England owes a debt of gratitude to those who upheld its struggling Church. We may admire the zeal and the conscientiousness of the Puritans ; we may own that they contributed valuable elements to the national character, and largely influenced for good England's subsequent development. But we must say in all fairness that they were not patriotic in their early days, and that their endeavours to make England Calvinistic did not correspond to the best interests of the nation. We may regret that their excellent qualities were deprived of their full influence because they were expressed mainly in resolute antagonism.

Thus the English Church was identified with the English nation alike in its strength and in its weakness. The Church was surrounded by powerful foes, organised on a definite basis, and it seemed almost impossible for it to make good its mediate position. The English State was in a similar position ; no statesman, except Elizabeth herself, thought it possible for England to stand alone. Yet Elizabeth succeeded, in spite of overwhelming difficulties. Church and State alike grew into a consciousness of their mission, of their capacities, and of their inherent strength.

It is enough for me to suggest the close connection between the two. I am concerned only with the Church. There was the system corresponding truly to the needs of the nation's life, and generally accepted ; but the difficulty was in working it efficiently. There was no desire on the part of the authorities of the Church to check prematurely theological controversies. Many of the Bishops were strongly imbued with Calvin's teaching. But it was necessary to have an orderly and decent service, in which all might join. To this the Puritans objected : they would have no remnants of the past ; they could not work in fetters ; they would be content with nothing less than the system of Geneva. Episcopal visitations, admonitions, and injunctions were powerless. Ecclesiastical authority was set at nought. Attempts were made again and again to meet the demands of the Nonconformists : ceremonies were explained, ritual was simplified, trivial matters were allowed to assume importance. Every effort was made to procure peace, but was made in vain.

This period of experiment to discover a basis of unity compatible with the maintenance of the ecclesiastical system was not favourable for the definite exhibition of the system itself. Many Bishops were themselves uncertain how far they might go in their concessions. The country parishes were often ill manned ; the ecclesiastical organisation was defective ; there was much disorder. It required time for a sense of loyalty to the Church to gather round a genuine appreciation of its system. For this purpose thought and knowledge were necessary. Amid the violent utterances of partisans the real issue was obscured ; and the lofty aims of cultivated piety were not immediately attractive in a time of discord. But it was through controversy that opinion developed, and the position of the Church became better defined. First Jewel stated its difference from the Roman system ; then Hooker, with still more massive learning, fortified it against the attacks of the Puritans, and indicated the limits of possible concession.

The onslaught of Calvinism gradually died away before the appeal to Christian antiquity and the history of the Christian Church. Whitgift, as Archbishop, could exercise stronger discipline over the clergy than Parker had ventured on. Yet Whitgift was content with demanding an acknowledgment that the Prayer-book was unobjectionable. He asked only for outward uniformity and obedience to the law. It was unfortunate that the last demand was so convenient in its form ; for it suggested a mass of enlightened opinion, which was not convinced by argument or by reference to strictly ecclesiastical principles, but was suppressed by a system imposed from motives of public policy. However, the influence of Calvinism as a system of Church Government and discipline, gradually waned. When it assumed a merely doctrinal aspect Whitgift was willing to make large concessions. It was for wiser heads than his to see that the theology of Calvin had already exercised its due influence on the English Church, and that further definition on the dubious points contained in the Lambeth articles was not desirable. The Hampton Court Conference emphasised the fact that Calvinism was not to change the system of the Church ; that the Prayer-book stood the test of Scripture interpreted by primitive usage ; and that this interpretation was not to be set aside in favour of the private judgment of the most eminent theologians of the sixteenth century.

During this period the system of the Church was constantly on the defensive, and so had little opportunity of putting forth its full strength. There was a genuine desire to make it suitable for the whole mass of the English people. Suggestions for this purpose had been freely made and fully considered. From a period of controversy emerged the conviction of essential principles. It was the old Church, freed from accretions, brought back to its primitive form, recognising individual liberty and consequent responsibility, appealing to the head as well at to the heart, with Scriptural reasons for what it did and what it omitted. All this became increasingly apparent to the new generation which had grown up under the influence of its services, and had caught their meaning.

This developed consciousness found its fitting expression in the formation of characters, which were avowedly built on the system of the Church, and which set forth its distinctive features. Controversy, alas! is sometimes inevitable; but, like any other form of warfare, it is in itself unlovely, and is only valued for the peace which follows upon it. Pious lives are more effective than learned disputations; the still, small voice of devotion penetrates farther than the keenest arguments. Bishop Andrewes was the type of a temper which was powerful among the clergy; George Herbert and Nicholas Ferrar were examples of its influence among the laity. Herbert was led to take orders at the age of thirty-seven, and during his brief pastorate of three years was a model of devotion to the duties of his office. Ferrar withdrew from public life that he might live with his family and friends in an atmosphere of quiet and educated piety. These men had common characteristics : they were lovers of peace, they were men of learning, they strove to form their lives by the practice of orderly devotion, they loved the Church, and strove to make its meaning clear by scrupulous care for everything which could make its services intelligible and attractive. Cultured devotion and spiritual sweetness have perhaps never been set forth more cogently and persuasively than in their lives, their characters, and their writings. They indicated splendid possibilities of a religious future, which had been the dream of thinking minds during the weary century of debate through which Europe had disconsolately passed.

For it is well to abandon all illusions about the sixteenth century. There were strong men ; there were powerful minds ; but there was a dearth of beautiful characters. A time of revolt and upheaval is a time of one-sided energy, and of moral uncertainty, of hardness, of unsound argument, of imperfect self-control, of vacillation, of self-seeking. It is difficult in such a time to find heroes, to discover a man whom we can unreservedly admire. The Church of Rome had fortified itself against attack by the Inquisition, and by the passionate zeal of the Society of Jesus, which soon degenerated into unprincipled intrigue. Calvin raised against it a massive system, which bound together the members of his com-

munity by an overpowering sense of their direct depend-
ence on God through His particular election of each
individual soul. Beside these two great systems all else
seemed inconclusive, poor, feeble, and doomed to failure.
Yet where in either of them was there place for the aspi-
rations of the devout scholar, of the man who reverenced
liberty, who believed in progressive enlightenment, who
longed for an intelligent order of things in which the
Christian consciousness should seek for spiritual truth?
It was not merely by accident that the great scholar
Isaac Casaubon ended his days in England, made happy
by the society of Andrewes. It is significant of the
temper of the times that the Puritans pelted him with
stones in the street when they found that he was not a
partisan on their side. Still, despite this, Casaubon,
with his vast learning and his wide experience of the
Continent, found peace for his soul in England, which
he called "the isle of the blessed." In it, despite all
drawbacks, still lingered a reverence for knowledge, a
love of truth, and a sense of the problems of the future.

Now, herein lies Laud's claim to greatness, that he
recognised the possibilities of the English Church, not
merely for England itself, but as the guardian of all that
was best and most fruitful for the future of religious progress. "This poor Church of England," he said in his
speech upon the scaffold, "hath flourished, and hath
been a shelter to other neighbouring Churches when
storms have driven upon them." Laud had at heart
the ideal of a united England, with a Church at once
Catholic, Scriptural, Apostolic, free from superstition,

yet reverently retaining all that was primitive ; a resting-
place for all men of enlightenment ; a model of piety and
devotion to a distracted world ; strong in its capacity for
mediating between opposing systems ; full of the zeal
which comes from knowledge and largeheartedness. He
saw the value of the qualities which Andrewes had
quietly and patiently expressed, and he longed to set
them forth universally and unmistakably that they might
do their work in the hearts and consciences of men. He
had a clear conception of the mission of the English
Church, and his one aim was to embody that conception
in its system with clearness and definitenesss which
could not fail to be convincing. Hitherto this conception
had been blurred and obscured, had slowly found its way
into shape, and had remained in the background amid
the din of contending parties. Laud wished to make it
positive, to set it in the forefront, and rally England
round it.

There are two things which must be kept distinct—
Laud's conception of the Church of England, and the
means which he took to embody this conception. I am
endeavouring to judge it strictly on historical grounds.
The questions which agitated Laud's time still agitate
in some degree our own day also. But we must not
suppose that they wore the same appearance then,
or had the same meaning. What Laud had before
him was briefly this : the attempt to substitute the
system of Calvin for the system of the Church had
failed ; but Calvinism was still strong ; and there was a
desire on the part of politicians to make such a religious

settlement in England as suited general convenience. Why, it is often asked, did not James I., Laud, and Charles I. fall in with this suggestion of obvious utility, and allow a Church which had room for all?

There is, of course, the answer that an institution must after all be something, and that there are limits to latitude of opinion which no institution can transcend. But this does not, I think, account for Laud's attitude. He was a statesman, and not merely a politician. He recognised that England had a part to play in the world, a duty which it could not refuse to fulfil. He saw that that duty was one of composing differences, of mediating, pacifying, and influencing. It seems to me that this has been, and still is, England's great contribution to European progress. Sufficiently isolated to be able to stand aloof from foreign politics and solve her own problems, she is yet sufficiently near to be receptive of all foreign movements, and to deal with them, both practically and speculatively, in a wise and deliberate way. But it is hard for any nation consistently to hold such an attitude, which, indeed, can only be realised in great crises by great statesmen. Elizabeth in a time of great danger and difficulty stood alone among her Ministers, and directed England's course, against their judgment of temporary expediency, steadily in this direction. For some time she alone understood the difference between an English Church and an Anglican Church. Owing to her resoluteness, there was time for the lesson to be learned; and Laud was the first who fully apprehended its full significance. To him the

Church of England was not, as it had been to his predecessors, an arrangement for expressing the religious
consciousness of the English people.   It was a system,
instinct with life, full of mighty possibilities, with a
world-wide mission, peculiarly its own.   He asked
England to take this view, to recognise its achievements,
to value its great possession, to sink minor differences,
and put forth its united power for God's glory.   The
services of the Church, he thought, were intelligible in
their simplicity, and had suffered in the past because
they had never been suitably displayed.   Let them only
be fully and fairly performed, and they would of themselves attract and convince.   Men would soon understand
and love them.

So Laud began his ecclesiastical revival with care
for outward things.   It was not that he put principles in
the background, but he thought that the worship of the
Church was the best form of teaching.   Argument and
controversy had done little; let the voice of devotion
be heard, and it would prevail :—

I laboured (he says) that the external worship of God in this
Church might be kept up in uniformity and decency and in some
beauty of holiness. And this the rather because, first, I found that
with the contempt of outward worship of God the inward fell away
apace, and profaneness began boldly to show itself.

There was a second reason which weighed strongly with
Laud.   The strength of Romanism in England lay in
the divided condition of the Church :—

I could speak (Laud goes on) with no conscientious person
almost that were wavering in religion, but the great motive which
wrought upon them to disaffect or think meanly of the Church of

England, was that the external worship of God was so lost, and the churches themselves suffered to lie in such a base and slovenly fashion in most places of the kingdom.

So Laud's desire was to teach men by the eye and by the heart ; to set before them the quiet dignity of an orderly system, and let its teaching gradually sink into their minds. He enforced uniformity, not because uniformity was convenient for the nation, nor because it was enacted by law, but because it was necessary to set forth the strength and beauty of the devotional system of the Church of England. Within that system he was prepared to allow large latitude for difference of opinion. He had no wish to curb liberty of thought, but he aimed at checking what he held to be disorderly and disloyal action. There was the Prayer-book. Let men reverently perform the services therein prescribed, and let them discuss temperately and charitably theological questions in a scholarly spirit. Laud was always anxious to remove difficulties which prevented thoughtful men from taking holy orders. He was satisfied that Chillingworth should subscribe the Thirty-nine Articles as being articles of peace—*i.e.*, " as containing no errors which may necessitate or warrant any man to disturb the peace or renounce the communion of it." He had no fear of the results of free inquiry, if devotion and reverence held the first place. The system of the Church was to be definite, but it was to be large, sympathetic, and liberal.

This in outline was Laud's ideal. Even those who do not agree with it may at least admit its nobility, and confess that it was a worthy object to absorb the energies of an ecclesiastical statesman. But even those who agree with it most entirely must recognise that Laud was wrong in the means by which he tried to accomplish his end. Indeed it may be doubted if he possessed that first great quality for a practical statesman—instinctive sympathy for the conditions under which his work has to be done. Laud knew what he wanted—that in itself gives a certain claim to greatness—but he took the readiest, the most obvious way to gain his end, and scarcely stopped to consider how he could work most acceptably. His training was academic, his mind was logical; he had all the defects of a purely academic character. He lacked personal dignity and geniality. He did not recognise the large part which is played in popular opinion by prejudice. He thought that, if a thing was reasonable, the only way of proving its reasonableness was by enforcing it. He was conscious of his personal limitations, and the consciousness seems to have depressed him instead of spurring him to self-discipline and self-improvement. Rarely has a man displayed so much activity with so little hopefulness. He does not seem to have felt the need for enthusiasm, and he did not kindle it in others. His plans came before men's eyes in a mass of details which were not irradiated by an intelligible principle. He treated mankind as if they were children, and he their schoolmaster. " Do this because I tell you, and you will see its use in time," is not a command which is readily obeyed by Englishmen. He did not draw the line between what was of primary importance and what was trivial, between regulating the services of the Church and the demeanour of the worshippers. Men might recognise the desirability of the orderly and decent performance of the service, of the restoration of churches, of guarding the Communion-table from profane uses by removing it from the body of the church to the east end. But it was a most undesirable extension of authority to prescribe specific acts of reverence as equally applicable to all. He was over-hasty, over-punctilious. He was proud of his prodigious activity, which sometimes degenerated into fussiness. He made men feel unquiet, because they did not know how much farther he was going. He was not content with laying down great lines which could be quietly filled in afterwards.

But more than this, he completely identified the Church with the State. He knew, to quote his own words, " that my order as a Bishop, and my power of jurisdiction, is by Divine apostolical right, and unalterable (for aught I know) in the Church of Christ;" but he took no other view of his right to exercise his office, either of power or jurisdiction, than as derived from the Crown, and exercisable according to law. He does not seem to have thought of the paternal jurisdiction inherent in his office, and independent of anything that the State could confer. The loss of this conception did more to confuse men's minds about the nature of the Church than any of Laud's measures did to make it clear. His action did much to stereotype the view of a Bishop's office, as an executor of national laws, passed through

motives of expediency, and founded on other than
theological reasons. This was the view which rendered
Episcopacy unpopular, which gave strength to Nonconformity, and involved the system of the Church in
current politics. If Laud had conferred with his clergy,
and striven to guide and influence them by the authority
of his episcopal office, if he had exhorted his suffragans
to do the same, his revival might not have gone so far,
but it would assuredly have rested on a firmer basis. It
would have been ecclesiastical in a true sense, and would
have associated discipline with the system of the Church
rather than the laws of the State. If the Church of
England claimed to refer to primitive antiquity for its
belief and practice, surely its Episcopal government
should be carried on with reference to primitive methods.
As it was, Laud's exercise of authority was an anomaly.

But Laud not only exercised his office as deriving
its power from the State, but further held secular office
in the State. This was one of the great evils of the
mediæval Church, a fertile source of abuses. Yet Laud
shut his eyes to its obvious dangers, and believed that
civil power was best in the hands of Churchmen.
Moreover, the work which Laud had set himself in the
Church was more than enough for any man's energies.
He could not carry the burden which he placed upon
his shoulders. When much work has to be done a man
is bound to be niggardly of his time ; he becomes
impatient of details ; he delegates business which
he considers unimportant. But spiritual work is all
concerned with details ; and he who would work for

God must learn never to be in a hurry, must curb his natural impatience, must remember how tenderly God has dealt with him, must regard no time wasted which composes differences, or removes scruples, or resolves doubts, which cheers, consoles or convinces. Laud's visitations and injunctions depended for their effect on the manner in which they were carried out. If their execution was committed to an official, who was only concerned with results, they were sure to give grievous offence. If they were done hurriedly, fretfully, peevishly, they were not likely to be understood. It is impossible not to admit that, as years went on, and the burden of work increased, Laud failed in temper and discretion, grew more arbitrary and less hopeful. He was grimly doing his duty, sensitive to the dislike which he felt to be growing around him, unable to avert the danger which he felt to be impending.

But besides its effect on Laud's own character, his position as a State Official identified the Church with a policy which more and more ran counter to the wishes of the nation, and strove to maintain itself by methods which raised serious opposition. The Church under his guidance lost all chance of exercising a mediating influence ; it seemed to be an integral part of a particular system of government. Opposition to the Government implied opposition to the Church, and the Bishops were regarded as the mainstays of a royal dictatorship.

We know the disasters that followed. It is needless to speculate if they could have been averted. So far as Laud is concerned, they only emphasised the truth that

he who undertakes to do God's work with the world's
weapons will stand or fall according to his worldly
prudence, and not according to the excellence of his
intentions. Laud chose to work through power rather
than influence ; his power failed him, and he fell before
his foes. That they were relentless and pursued their
triumph to the utmost we can only regret for their own
sakes.

You may think that I have dwelt unduly on Laud's
errors and shortcomings, that I have not made allowances
for the difficulties of the time, that I have applied too
high a standard. We learn more, I think, from considering the causes of men's failure than of their
success. The great question about great men is not
" Why did they accomplish so much ? " but " Why did
they not accomplish more ? " Is not that the question
which we need to ask most diligently about ourselves ?
It is not so hard to have a noble end ; the difficulty lies
in working it out by worthy means. We can never
learn this lesson enough. It is the great moral lesson
which history teaches, and only when this lesson is
clearly taught does history teach aright. Laud's conception of the Church was sounder, larger, more
practical than that of his opponents. Events justified
his wisdom. Presbyterianism was tried and failed ;
independency was tried and failed ; efforts at ecclesiastical combination proved to be impossible. When
England again had to consider the matter, nothing was
vital except the system of Laud, which was practically
accepted at the Restoration. It was after all the most

possible, because it was the most intelligible. Laud
had laid down its main lines. The Church of England
was part of the Catholic Church, holding the Catholic
faith, maintaining the historic Episcopacy, dispensing
the sacraments according to primitive ordinance. " I
die," said Laud in his will, " I die as I have lived, in
the true orthodox profession of the Catholic faith of
Christ, a true member of His Catholic Church, within the
communion of a living part thereof, the present Church
of England." This was the position of the English
Church, and nothing subsequently altered it. Com-
promises might be urged by politicians, but nothing
could be accepted which threatened to destroy the order
of the English Church as a part of the continuous
Church of Christ. This was the original basis of the
English Church. It had been passionately attacked
from the beginning. It had been inadequately expressed
in practice. Laud asserted it clearly and definitely, and
showed how it was to be set forth and what it involved.
He won for it deep reverence and profound conviction,
which were conspicuously shown by Charles I. Had
Charles been willing to abandon the Church, and give
up Episcopacy, he might have saved his throne and his
life. But on this point Charles stood firm ; for this he
died, and by dying saved it for the future.

Men may differ in their opinions about the form of
the Church, or even if any particular form is necessary.
But amid the differences which they see around them,
they may at least, if they are fair-minded, agree on this—
that the Church of England has discharged a special

duty in the Christian commonwealth, and has done a
work which no other organisation could have done. We
who are its faithful children have boundless hopes of its
future possibilities for doing God's work in the world.
All may combine, without any sacrifice of their own
convictions, in recognising what Laud did, and in
admitting the services rendered since to God and man
by the Church which he maintained at a crisis of its
existence. None of us, however much we may be
devoted to that Church, can wish to be mere eulogists,
or even apologists, of Laud's policy and actions. The
cause for which Laud contended is too precious in our
eyes for us to associate it with human frailty and want
of judgment. We accept Laud's teaching with
gratitude ; we admire his zeal, his devotion, his courage,
his conscientiousness. We commemorate to-day all
that was great and noble, all that was lasting, in his life
and character. We seek the heart and the head of the
man, and rejoice in the clear vision and enlightened
insight which saw and claimed the fair heritage which
is ours to-day.

II.

LAUD AS A STATESMAN.

THE REV. W. E. COLLINS, M.A., PROFESSOR OF ECCLESIASTICAL HISTORY AT KING'S COLLEGE, LONDON.

LAUD AS A STATESMAN.

" LET us now praise famous men, and our fathers that
begat us, ... such as did bear rule in their kingdom,
men renowned for their power, giving counsel by their
understanding." Such is the text which Heylin places
on the title page of his famous life of the great prelate
to whom he had once been chaplain. Not even Heylin
himself would have ventured to apply to him the words
that follow, and to number him among "leaders of the
people by their counsels;" but perhaps the majority of
Englishmen in Heylin's own day would have felt that
the preceding words were eminently applicable to him,
and the great bulk of English Churchmen continued to
do so for many years afterwards. Whereas at the
present day they are probably few who would be willing
to reckon Laud among really great statesmen.

And yet no view of the man which fails to consider
him in this aspect can be more than a very partial one.
Certainly statecraft occupied a very large place in his
thoughts; few men of his day gave it a greater share of
attention than he. It is true that he was nearly fifty
years of age before we hear of his being employed in
any business of state; but in the years that followed
he, if ever any man, "fulfilled a long time." It is true
that the period during which he was actually in power
was less than twelve years on the largest estimate; but
no mistake could be greater than to measure his influence
by this period alone, important though it was. For in
those days far more than now, he who would guide the

conscience of princes was bound to be ready, not merely
to inculcate abstract principles and to regulate private
conduct, but to give definite and practical advice at
every emergency. And from the first moment that he
set foot at Court, if not before, Laud gave himself to
the study of affairs of state, being resolved to use his
influence with those in power to good purpose. And he
did so. There might be cases, no doubt, when he was
not consulted; very important affairs were at times
transacted without his knowledge, such as the journey
to Spain and the treatment of the troubles in Scotland;
but from the first, and in a rapidly increasing degree after
the accession of Charles I., his hand is again and again
·to be seen behind the acts of those in power. Now, as
the Diary informs us, it is by his advice that action is
taken in some matter having momentous consequences
in the State; now, as the papers in the Record Office
reveal to us, the first draft of a Royal Speech, or the
reply to a Parliamentary remonstrance, is by him, or
some important minute, or report, or pamphlet, is found
to be sharply and carefully annotated in his familiar
handwriting. The dislike of the Court party for him, the
personal enmity of the Queen and the Papists about
her, or the spasmodic activity and constitutional reserve
of the King, might keep him in the dark at times; but
even if his influence is not always present it is never entirely absent from the government of Charles I. After
the suspension of Archbishop Abbot, and still more after
his death, all this was emphasized by another consideration. It was by no mere convention that the Archbishop

of Canterbury was called the first subject of the realm, for he was in truth something more. He had been from the very earliest times—from, and even before, the time that there *was* an united England—the Spiritual Father of the King and of the Kingdom, with an authority and weight all the greater because it was undefined and irreducible to any mere sequence of powers. As Archbishop, William Laud never lost sight of the unique character of his position in the State; and whether for good or for evil, whether he exercised it well or ill, no Archbishop since Cranmer, at any rate, has realised and magnified his office in this direction in anything like the same degree. We may regard the character as beneficial or the reverse—and the irresistible logic of events showed that it was rapidly becoming a thing of the past—but Laud must take his place in the line, and at the end of the line, of great political primates. He ranks with Dunstan and Lanfranc, with Thomas Becket and Hubert Walter, with Langton and Winchelsea and Wolsey and Cranmer; for Wolsey must not be left out, although he never occupied the throne of Canterbury.

The Bishop of Peterborough told us last week, that if we would understand Laud's position in the history of the English Church, we must begin by realising the circumstances of the Church as he found it. So, too, if we would understand his political position, we must begin by realising the circumstances of the State. In the latter, as in the former, an unavoidable period of crisis had come, in ways which we must now trace.

The early Stuart kings had received from the Tudors a heritage of power which was quite out of keeping with the earlier development of constitutional government in England. This had arisen from a variety of causes. The fall of the old baronage in the Wars of the Roses had removed the chief counterpoise to the authority of the King, while it had left him richer by far than before. And the new nobility which arose in their place consisted of men who, for the most part, depended entirely upon the King for their positions, had received most of their estates from him, and were subservient in proportion. A new mercantile class was arising under the royal protection, which was soon to be almost the centre of gravity of the nation; but it was too young as yet, and too dependent upon the King, to be really powerful. Accordingly the King grew greatly in power and prestige, and was king *over* these estates in a sense more absolute, perhaps, than ever before. Then came the religious revolution of the sixteenth century; the clergy proved to be powerless, parliament was powerless, to liberate us from the tyrannous domination of the Pope in matters ecclesiastical; and the whole nation gathered round the one power which was strong enough to do what was necessary.

The abolition of the papal authority in England meant the culmination of the royal power; and seeing that they were a line of kings as masterful as any which ever sat upon the English throne, it is little wonder that, until the end of the century, the Tudors were able to do practically as they pleased, so long as they com-

plied more or less with constitutional forms. Arbitrary
control of the ecclesiastical order, arbitrary ways of
obtaining money, of enforcing the royal will, of doing by
letters patent what would naturally have been done
by parliamentary authority, all these became more
and more prevalent. When, in the latter years of
Elizabeth's reign, the Commons became stronger, the
Queen always knew just when it was necessary to give
way; and owing to the national confidence in her
wisdom, her power was really increased rather than
diminished by her timely concessions. So that when
she died, she left to the Stuarts as a heritage the
tradition of almost absolute power. Meanwhile, with
the prevalent reverence for things un-English came the
study of foreign theories of government, and men began
to regard the King of England as theoretically above
the law, and to impute to him powers and privileges
which might be inherent in a King of France, but were
entirely foreign to a King of England. After this it
was merely a question of growth. A noisy, but comparatively small band of learned men began to declare,
from their study of foreign theories of government and
sixteenth-century theories of the relation of the King to
the Church, that the King was King by unique Divine
right, and that he, and he alone among laymen, derived
his power directly from God.

Now, Laud was no theoretical politician of this
stamp. Others might prate volubly of the Right Divine;
Cowell might speak of the King's absolute power to
make laws without the consent of Parliament; Main-

waring might say that " if any King shall command that
which stands not in any opposition to the original laws
of God, nature, nations, and the Gospel (though it be
not correspondent in every circumstance to laws national
and municipal), no subject may, without hazard of his
own damnation in rebelling against God, question or
disobey the will and pleasure of his Sovereign." Laud
was far too practical to lay much stress upon anything
of the kind. It may be too much to say, with Mr.
Gardiner, that the Divine right of Kings never assumed
prominence in his mind; for we shall be brought up
suddenly by Laud's own words in the Sermon at the
opening of Charles's second Parliament : " The King
is God's immediate lieutenant upon earth ; and therefore
one and the same action is God's by ordinance, and the
King's by execution. And the power which resides in
the King is not any assuming to himself, nor any gift
from the people, but God's power, as well in, as over,
him." Or again, "The King's power, that is from God;
the judge's and subordinate magistrate's power, that is
from the King. . . . All judges, and courts of justice,
even this great congregation, this great council now
ready to sit [meaning Parliament], receive influence and
power from the King, and are dispensers of his justice,
as well as their own, both in the laws they make and in
the laws they execute : in the causes which they hear
and in the sentences which they give : the King, God's
High Steward, and they stewards under him." * Thus
he was far too much a man of his time to be otherwise

---

* Sermon IV. (*Works*, vol. i, pp. 94, 100).

than profoundly influenced by the prevalent political
theories. Still he was quite content to accept whatever
there was precedent for, and never to go beyond it. On
no single occasion, probably, did he consciously act
against good Tudor precedent, or what the judges
assured him was such ; not only so, but no man was so
careful as he to search out and analyse the records, that
he might confine his action on the King's behalf scru-
pulously within the limits which this authority seemed
to allow of.

But it is precisely at this point that Laud came into
hostile conflict with a political tendency nobler than his
own. The absolutism of Tudor Kings was nothing less
than providential for England; it did for us what nothing
else could have done. But none the less, it ran directly
counter to the whole course of the natural development
of our constitution. If a constitution is a living thing,
as it should be, it must have a certain natural growth
or development. For a constitution to remain absolutely
stereotyped while man, civilization, time, all advance,
is a sign of decadence, if not death : here as elsewhere,
to stand still while all else is moving, is to go backward.
And, in a word, the development which came naturally
in our constitution involved the gradual restriction of
prerogative by law. In early days, comparatively few
matters were the subject of law, while most were
within the sphere of prerogative. The way of progress for
us—the way of God's guidance, as shown by the course of
our history, if we believe that God shows us His presence
in history—was by the gradual increase of the sphere of

orderly law, side by side with the restriction of arbitrary prerogative. And this development involved something more. At first the "residuary authority," so to speak, was in the King; when circumstances arose which the law did not seem to provide for, the King was the natural person to make what provision seemed necessary. Gradually, however—by steps often incapable of being traced, with occasional reactions, yet with a continuous course which is now obvious to all who have eyes to see —gradually the prerogative came to be the limited thing. What was not explicitly included within the royal prerogative came to be regarded as within the control of Parliament. And a change had passed over Parliament too: the Commons, who voted supplies, had grown all unconsciously to be the most important part of Parliament. It was this which Selden meant when he said in his pithy way, " The House of Commons is called the Lower House in twenty Acts of Parliament; but what are twenty Acts of Parliament among friends? "*
It was this which Pym meant when, in ever-memorable words, he called the House of Commons " the soul of the body politic." Of course it is very true that this was not clear to all Parliamentarians of the day; there was at least as much of violence and selfishness and lawlessness on the side of the Parliament, as on that of the King. Conflict always stirs up bad passions, and we have still to see the Revolution in which good and evil shall be entirely arrayed on one side or on the other: and yet here as elsewhere God uses the powers of evil to

---

* *Table Talk* (ed. Arber), p. 38.

bring forth His own good purposes. It is true, moreover, that the great upheaval was largely an attempt of the powerful Puritan nobles to regain a privilege which was even more a thing of the past than that of the King himself. And when all is said, the House of Commons was rather the representative of the substantial yeoman and the comfortable burgesses than of the great mass of the people ; whilst then, as at other times, elections could be " managed " in particular interests. All this is true ; but however little the Commons themselves may have seen it, the fact remains that, as Mr. Gardiner says,* the true character of the epoch is a time of struggle, during which the idea of law was gradually evolving itself in the midst of a conflict of opposing wills.

All this, I say, is clear to us, or most of us, at the present day. Even if we have not seen it willingly, facts are too strong for us : we can only say—

> Lead, and I follow ; if against my will
> A baffled rebel I must follow still.

But it was not nearly so clear two and a half centuries ago. It was no wonder that many great and good men could see nothing but lawlessness and rebellion in the attitude of parliament. And Laud was one of them. It is true that he declared in his trial that he was " ever a friend to parliaments," and that on the scaffold he said " I understand them, and the benefit that comes by them, too well to be " an enemy to them. He was ever desirous that the King should

---

* *Hist. of England*, ii. 77.

govern by them : and it was he who, with **Strafford**,
advised the summoning of Parliament at the end of the
eleven years' tyranny, and doubtless often before. But
I fail to see that he ever meant more than that parliaments were the natural and the most proper means for the
administration of government, and that if it was impossible
to govern by them, the King could use some other. To
him the King was all-sufficient, Heaven's High Steward ;
the necessity for under-stewards depended upon him,
and was of such an altogether different magnitude as to
be comparatively immaterial. The King was to him
the agent, Parliament merely the instrument of government. To him the words spoken in the Parliament
of 1628, " It is better to be brought low by foreign
enemies than to be obliged to suffer oppression at
home," must have sounded ridiculous. There is in the
Record Office a speech of Sir Benjamin Rudyerd made
in 1628, in which he declares that it is the destiny of
Parliament by degrees to regulate and restrict the
exercise of the royal prerogative. Laud has appended
observations upon this speech, in which it receives his
unsparing criticism.* The idea of any change in the
relative importance of the factors of government is
absurd to him ; and naturally enough, the England of
the Tudors is his archetype of the Constitution.
" He appealed," says Mr. Gardiner,† " to the law and
the law alone. It was nothing to him that the law had
been drawn up half a century or a century before, at a

---

* State Papers (Domestic) Vol. cii. No. 43. (*Calendar* 1628-9, p. 92).
† *Op. cit.* vii. 113.

time when the temper of men's minds was very different from what it had become in his own day."

We must of course remember that a practical statesman has to deal with the facts of the present. It is for to-day that he must act : whatever may be coming, the obligations and duties of the moment are clear and decisive. And we must remember that, in any time of conflict, there are sure to be elements of good lacking as well on one side as on the other. It would have been well nigh impossible for William Laud to have done that great work for the English Church for which we return thanks to Almighty God, without being what many of us think greatly in the wrong in other ways;— without at any rate holding views and constitutional theories which are now things of the past. Whether at the Reformation or at any other crisis, many, perhaps most, of the noblest and holiest and truest men will always be found to support the old order of things. This they have tried ; they know by experience that "hitherto hath the Lord helped them ;" all their dearest memories and most sacred associations are bound up with it ; and whatever other ways God may have for other men, this at least he has had for them. They do well to hold on fast to that which has been ; for continuity is essential to true life. And yet they who are wise will see that

> The old order changeth, yielding place to new,
> And God fulfils Himself in many ways.

They will strive to discern the signs of the times : they will be glad if need be that in the words of Savonarola, the car of Christ should roll on through the world, even though it should crush them in its course.   And

Prophet eyes may catch a glory slowly gaining on the shade

in spite of all the storm-clouds and all the din of conflict.

In days when reverence for the King formed such
an exaggerated part of the ideal of religion—when the
very existence of the Church of Christ in England was
held to be almost dependent upon the form of government, it were little to be wondered at if few Churchmen
caught the real meaning of the political struggle.   But
we may not forget that there were some.   When in
1628, as Rushworth* tells us, " one Sibthorp, who not
being so much as a Batchelor of Arts, had the Title of
Doctor conferred upon him," had preached an Assize
Sermon in which he taught the plenary legislative
authority of the King and inculcated passive obedience,†
Archbishop Abbot stoutly refused to license its publication, as being contrary to the constitution.   Again and
again the King endeavoured to move him, but in vain ;
and at length he angrily commanded the brave Archbishop, then lying ill in bed, to leave London at once :
whilst directly afterwards the order followed him " that
he meddle no more with the High Commission."   And
if it be thought that Abbot is no fair instance, a greater
and holier than he, our own Bishop Andrewes, may be
quoted to much the same effect.   According to the well-
known story told by Waller, on one occasion, as Andrewes
and Bishop Neile, of Durham, stood behind the King's

---

* *Hist. Collections* i. 281 (8vo Edition).

† Quoted in Prothero, *Const. Documents*, p. 437.

chair, James I. asked them, " My Lord, cannot I take my
subjects' money when I want it, without all this form-
ality in Parliament ? " The Bishop of Durham readily
answered, " God forbid, Sir, but you should ; you are
the very breath of our nostrils." Whereupon the King
turned and said to Bishop Andrewes, " Well, my Lord,
what say you ? " " Sir," replied the Bishop, " I have
no skill to judge of Parliamentary cases." The King
answered, " No put offs, my Lord, answer me presently."
" Then, Sir," said he, " I think it lawful for you to take
my brother Neile's money, for he offers it."

Laud's matter-of-fact mind, devout and reverent as
it was, had no place for this prophetic insight. With
matchless devotion to duty and a love for his country
which carried him far, he allowed himself to become the
minister of the King's tyranny. That the period of non-
parliamentary government *was* a tyranny there can be
no question. That on the whole the country was well
governed, that the royal impositions of taxation caused
no great hardships, that commerce and manufactures
flourished, that England became respected abroad by a
foreign policy which was the prototype of Cromwell's,
that there was no armed force to back the government
of the King, or to protect even his own person—all
these things are true, but they are nothing to the point.
It was a return to arbitrary government all the more
dangerous because a velvet glove covered the iron claw ;
and Laud must bear his share—and no small one—of
the responsibility. But in common fairness, if nothing
else, we are bound to remember that his fault was only

in continuing to do what others had done before him, and in failing to discern the signs of the times. After the Restoration Laud's plans for the Church prevailed at once, for his plans, whatever we may think of his methods, embodied the highest and truest spiritual ideal of the English race, excepting indeed that a real toleration was still wanting. The Savoy Conference vindicated Laud's ecclesiastical policy and ratified his work; and in the splendid position taken up by the English Bishops there, as shown by their own weighty words, is laid the coping-stone of the English Reformation. But his political aims failed, after the Restoration, in spite of every possible advantage of time and circumstance, simply because they did *not* embody the true ideal of the English constitution. Laud, like every other man, could "do nothing against the truth, but for the truth."

The same fundamental fault which marred Laud's secular statesmanship is to be found likewise in his administration of the Church, though here, fortunately, it is possible to separate his aims from his methods more clearly. He was as ready in the Church as in the State to bring in the royal authority, and to do by its means what should have been done, and could have been done, in proper canonical ways. Laud has been called an Erastian: the charge is in no sense justified, for the Church was never to him a mere department of the State. The two were indeed mutually dependent; "the Commonwealth," said he, "could not flourish without the Church;" but he never for a moment derives the authority of the Church from the State. It is not accurate, then, to say

that he completely identified Church and State; for
although in common with most men of his age he held
that the Church had a jurisdiction in secular things, he
never acted in the Church by his authority as the chief
minister of state, or *vice versa*. The great fault is, as
before, that he does everything by the royal authority :
but it must be remembered that the King was to him
a sacred personality, with a real authority in spiritual
things. And it was the King in this spiritual capacity
whose authority Laud made use of on every possible
occasion. Here, too, Laud had the whole weight of the
law on his side. According to the law, as Mr. Hutton
points out, Convocation looked only to the King, and was
in no way responsible to Parliament. " Elizabeth preserved the power of the legislative assembly of the Church
unfettered by Parliamentary control, and subsequent
legislation left Convocation legally subject to royal
authority alone."[*] According to the law, power was
vested in the King to " assign, name and authorise . . .
" such person or persons . . . as your Majesty shall think
" meet, to exercise, use, occupy and execute . . . all
" manner of jurisdictions, privileges, and pre-eminences, in
" any wise touching or concerning any spiritual or ecclesi-
" astical jurisdiction . . . and to visit, reform, redress,
" order, correct and amend all such heresies, errors,
" schisms, abuses, offences, contempts and enormities
" whatsoever, which by any manner of spiritual or eccle-
" siastical power, authority, or jurisdiction can or may
" lawfully be reformed, ordered, redressed, corrected,

---

[*] Hutton, *William Laud*, p. 90.

"restrained or amended, to the pleasure of Almighty God,
" the increase of virtue, and the conservation of the peace
" and unity of this realm."*   In short, the King, not the
King and Parliament, was the legal *defensor* of the
Church.   Not that he was the head of the Church;
the Act of Supremacy pointedly rejected any such idea,
and the distinction is clearly drawn by Selden at this
very time : " There's a great deal of difference between
Head of the Church and Supream Governour, as our
Canons call the King.   Conceive it thus, there is in the
Kingdom of *England* a Colledge of Phisicians, the King
is Supream Governour of those, but not Head of them,
nor President of the Colledge, nor the best Phisician." †
Cosin was no less clear.‡   In his conversation with Dr.
Pleasance, which subjected him to a trial, he declared
that the title "Supreme Head" had been dropped
because it was capable of abuse, and that the meaning
of "Supreme Governor" was that he might "by his
power of supreme dominion command Churchmen at
any time to do their office, or punish them for the neglect
of it. . . .   External co-action . . . whereby men were
forced to obey the jurisdiction of the Church, was only
from the King; but the power of spiritual jurisdiction
itself was from Christ, who had given it to His apostles,
and they to their successors by ordination." §   But

---

* 1 Elizabeth, cap. i. § 8.
† *Table Talk* (ed. Arber), p. 61.
‡ Quoted in Gardiner vii. 47.
§ Laud's Statement in the Speech against Prynne, Bastwick,
and Burton (Gardiner viii. 230), is worthy of careful comparison.
"Though our office be from God and Christ immediately, yet may

this distinction King and Archbishop alike seem incapable of preserving, at any rate in practice. In the "Declaration prefixed to the Articles" composed by Laud himself in November, 1628, and still prefixed to them, the function of the Supreme Governor is stated clearly enough: "We hold it most agreeable to this our kingly office . . . to conserve and maintain the Church committed to our charge in the unity of true religion and the bond of peace." Elsewhere, however, things are very different. From the time that Laud became Archbishop, he was required to furnish to the King every year an account of the state of his province, based upon the accounts of their several dioceses furnished by the Bishops to himself. These "Accounts of his Province" were returned to the Archbishop with marginal notes in the King's own hand; and Laud, methodical to the smallest detail, carefully endorsed and preserved them all. They are not pleasant reading: they read for all the world like the accounts of a steward to his master, with that master's directions upon them. The Bishop of Rochester complains, says Laud, that the Cathedral Church suffers from want of glass in the windows, and that the churchyard lies very indecently, and the gates down: "This must be remedied," writes the King in the margin, "one way or other; concerning wch I expect a particular account of you." "I conceive,

we not exercise that power, either of order or jurisdiction, but as God hath appointed us; that is, not in His Majesty's or any Christian King's Kingdoms, but by and under the power of the King given us so to do." King Charles was so much pleased with this definition that he caused it to be published throughout the Kingdom.

under favour," writes Laud, "that the Dutch Churches in Canterbury and Sandwich are great nurses of inconformity in these parts." "Put mee in mynd of this at some convenient 'tyme, when I am at councell, and I shall redress it." "In Norwich diocese, one Mr. Bridge, rather than he would conform, hath left his lecture and two cures, and is gone into Holland." "Let him goe," says the King : "wee ar well ridd of him." "From the Bishops of Lichfield and Gloucester, I have not received any certificates." "Call for them," says King Charles.*

And this is but an illustration, though a striking one, of what was going on constantly. Recourse was had to the royal authority on every occasion. The Court of High Commission had of course been in operation long before, but its work was multiplied by constant cases which should have been settled by the ordinary ecclesiastical jurisdiction. Strange that one who vindicated the right of a Metropolitan to visit his Province, and the right of the Primate of all England to visit both Universities, should have so acted that men could not but think that all his action tended to confuse Church and State ! It is only too true that what he built up with one hand he pulled down with the other ; that by obscuring the conception of the paternal jurisdiction inherent in his office "he did more to confuse men's minds about the nature of the Church than any of his

---

* "I cannot condemn Cranmer wholesale for his Erastian subserviency to the Sovereign, when I see Laud rendering his yearly 'accounts to King Charles, pretty much as a Roman Primate might to the Pope."—R. Owen, *Institutes of Canon Law*, p. xxviii. cf p. xv.

measures did to make it clear." If his motives were misunderstood, if he was hated and dreaded as a foe to liberty and a troublesome bigot, he himself was largely the cause of it : and the retribution which overtook him ultimately was to some extent of his own making.

But it is time to consider his administration, both civil and ecclesiastical, in greater detail. If he must bear his share of responsibility for what followed, at least he compares very favourably with any other man of his day. The late Professor Thorold Rogers, in his Essay on Laud, strangely says " Williams would have been an incomparably wiser councillor than Laud." The statement cannot be accepted for a moment. It may be that he " would never have advised these violent and repressive measures, which only pent up the forces under which King, aristocracy, Church and Liturgy were overwhelmed at last." But all Hacket's attractive special pleading and all Stanley's magnificent word-painting leave the impression of Williams's baseness as fixed as ever. " He had," says Mr. Gardiner, "nothing of the clergyman but the name." His self seeking—a common enough fault in his age and every age—is too apparent for any disguise to be attempted. The clearest evidence convicts him of actual crime. His is the unenviable honour of having suggested to the King, who accepted it basely enough, the base expedient for consenting to Strafford's death by distinguishing between his public and his private conscience. All men distrusted him, and the Puritan Lord Say and Sele could find nobody to compare him with but Judas who betrayed his Lord. It is abso-

lutely inconceivable that he could have succeeded in
making unity where Laud failed. Nor could any other
have taken his place. The good and gentle Bishop
Juxon, the Treasurer who would never make a joke or
take a bribe, showed admirable diligence and a wonderful
aptitude for careful economy, but he was wholly unfitted
to be the King's chief adviser. Strafford, the brave and
chivalrous friend of Laud, with whom he corresponded
constantly, was already doing his utmost, while the
Cottingtons and the Windebankes and other courtiers
could do little but amass fortunes and titles and quarrel
among themselves, thus doing almost as much to impede
the great champions of " Thorough " as Pym and
Hampden did. " I am alone," Laud writes sadly to
Strafford, "in those things which draw not private profit
after them."* If Laud did not succeed, the King had
nobody else, nor had the Parliament, who was likely to
succeed.

From the first Laud was never really happy as a
minister. At Oxford he had been almost an ideal
head ; his rule had been strict yet conciliatory, mild
yet searching. He was to be almost an ideal Chancellor,
doing for his university what no other single man did or
could ever have done. It might have been expected that
he would succeed equally well in state affairs. That he
did not is perhaps in some measure to be attributed
to the very qualities which had stood him in such good
stead at the university. To the end of his life Laud
was very much of a college don. He has been compared to a fussy but well-meaning college dean, with a

---

* *Works*, vii. 171.

real zeal for reformation; and the comparison is in some
ways a very apt one. He failed simply because a
kingdom is a larger thing than a college. In the comparatively narrow circle of the one, a strong personality
is able to impress itself upon the whole body and stereotype itself by the sheer force of its own individuality.
But in the larger unity the will of the whole body has
freer play, and the single personality cannot diffuse itself
universally. It is still possible, no doubt, to stamp out
individuality; but the attempt if made is far more likely
to result in provoking a reaction of the most destructive
type; and so it did here. The Archbishop grappled
manfully with the vast mass of public business, keeping
all that he could in his own hands, because he could not
trust others to do thoroughly what had to be done.
Most things had to receive the King's express sanction;
and this was none too easy to obtain, seeing that Charles
was very suspicious, and the Queen and the courtiers
and intriguers were for ever besieging his ear. It is not
to be wondered at that the Archbishop, whose mind
naturally embraced a vast number of details rather than
general principles, displeased people by his fussy manner,
or that the old man's temper gave way at times. The
diary begins to tell of late nights of work and exceeding
weariness, as is only natural. It is piteous to notice the
increasing forebodings of disaster; but they never caused
him to flinch from his task. And certainly, in spite of
failures, there is much that is very fine in his administration of affairs, when we overlook the fundamental blot
upon it, that it was an organised tyranny.

Laud has had to endure an unreasoning obloquy for

profaning Sunday by the publication of the Declaration
of Sports, and this from persons who in the same breath
denounce his narrow bigotry.   It is well to recall the
circumstances.   A Puritan confusion of the Christian
Sunday with the Jewish Sabbath had caused the cessa-
tion in some parts of the country, by the arbitrary
direction of the judges, of those comely and regulated
sports which English people had made use of time out
of mind after the close of the Sunday services.   It was
no question of labour on the Sunday : the Church had
been from the earliest times the means of preventing
Sunday labour—and in fact by obtaining from Cnut
the law* that no work was to be done between
None on Saturday and Prime on Monday, it was the
Church which in the first instance provided for all
who labour the Saturday half-holiday.   It was simply
a question of recreation—of getting rid of that mischievous period of idle loafing after service, the
occasion of so much evil, which most country parsons
have to deplore to this day.   It put compulsion on
nobody, but vindicated for the poor an immemorial right.
" Our dear father of blessed memory," says the Declaration, . . . "found that his subjects were debarred from
" lawful recreations upon Sunday after evening prayers
" ended, and upon Holy Days ; and he prudently con-
" sidered that, if these times were taken from them, the
" meaner sort who labour all the week should have no
" recreation at all to refresh their spirits."   And it goes on
to say that, in order to vindicate the freedom of all

---

* Laws of Cnut No. 15 (Schmidt, *Gesetze* 262).

worshippers after Evening Service, "no lawful recreation
"shall be barred to our good people, which shall not tend
"to the breach of our aforesaid laws and canons of our
"Church." So far from interfering with worship, a
special provision bars from this benefit and liberty "all
"such known Recusants, either men or women, as will
"abstain from coming to Church or Divine Service, being
"therefore unworthy of any lawful recreation after the
"said service, that will not come to the Church and serve
"God; prohibiting in like sort the said recreations to any
"that, though they conform in religion, are not present in
"the Church at the Service of God, before their going to
"the said recreations."* At his Trial, the publication of
the Declaration formed one of the charges against Laud;
and the answer is notable.† He himself had ever kept
the day carefully, while vindicating liberty for others—
"For the day, I ever laboured that it might be kept holy,
but yet free from a superstitious holiness." He defended
himself by adducing the practice of Geneva itself,
where "after evening prayer, the elder men bowl, and
the younger train." And, he adds, "What time of the
day fit, if not after evening prayer? And what rest is
there for able young men, if they may use no recreation?"
As he says later on, "Well I pray God keep us in the
mean, in this business of the Sabbath, that we run not
into a Jewish superstition while we seek to shun profaneness."‡ Laud's view of the meaning of the Fourth

* Declaration of Sports (Gardiner *Const. Documents*, p. 31 f).
† *Hist. of Troubles* (*Works IV*. 252).
‡ *Ib.* 255.

Commandment for Christian men was vindicated by the Fathers at the Savoy Conference, when they insisted that it was paraphrased in the Catechism by "and serve Him truly (not one day in seven but) *all* the days of my life."* The Puritan Sabbath, however, was very strong, and survived for two hundred years more; and it is only too much to be feared lest the reaction against it may be now leading to an almost irreligious keeping of the Day of the Lord.

The Archbishop's action in the matter of the Declaration (for he never denied that it was really his work) is on a line with his well-known care and thoughtfulness for the poor at all times. His successful interference in the Lord Mayor's Court on behalf of a poor apple-woman accused of selling apples on Sunday is famous. "As I went to my barge" [on the way to the Tower] writes the Archbishop in his Diary, "hundreds of my poor neighbours stood there, and prayed for my safety, and return to my house. For which I bless God and them." The long list in his *Will* of benefactions to the poor of the "places to which I have, or formerly had, reference," speaks no less clearly; and perhaps most touching of all is an entry in the Churchwardens' Accounts of Allhallows Barking, on January 12, 1644-5 (two days only after Laud's death) "Rec^d of the late Archbpp. of Canterberry's Gent^n for ye poore, 2*l*. 10*s*."

But Mr. Simpkinson has been able to show that

---

* "The Answer of the Bishops to the Exceptions of the Ministers." Of the Catechism § 4 [*Documents relating to the Settlement of the Church of England by the Act of Uniformity*, p. 169].

Laud's care for the poor was of a wider and more statesmanlike character. There is a sudden accession of carefulness on behalf of the people at large during the period of Tyranny which can be traced to none other than the good Archbishop who had learned their needs in his country parishes, and whose Diary is so eloquent a testimony to his thoughtfulness for the people from whose ranks he had sprung. Care is taken to prevent the spreading of the plague, and provision made for the relief of those who were impoverished by it.* Attempts were made to meet the evils of overcrowding,† and proclamations were issued which call to mind the Building Acts of the present day, forbidding the building of houses with overhanging stories, or with rooms below a certain height. Measures are taken to frustrate what we may call a *corner* in wheat; here is Rushworth's account of it :—" Several merchants and others having hoarded up corn to enhance the price thereof, and get false rumours spread of great Transportation of corn licensed by authority, the King by his Proclamation dated Sept. 30 declar'd the said Rumours to be false and scandalous, and prohibited for one year the Transportation of any corn or grain."‡ And at the same time measures were taken to prevent the raising of the price of corn in the London Markets, and to enforce the eating of fish in Lent as a means of encouraging the fisheries. A striking instance of the same kind is the re-issuing of a proclamation of James I. forbidding the sale

---

* Gardiner VII. 160 f.　　† Simpkinson's *Laud*, p. 106 f.
‡ Vol. II. (Octavo Edition) 119.

of weapons to savages in New England.* Care was
taken for the improvement of criminals, the training of
children, the apprenticing of boys whose parents could
not give them a proper start in life: regulations were
made for the proper payment of workmen in the employ
of the State, and of seamen pressed into the navy.†
A commission was issued for the relief of poor debtors,
who were very badly treated for long after this period;
and another to see that the laws for the relief of the poor
were duly carried out.‡

Now, no doubt these social plans of Laud were not
all of the wisest kind. Economics can hardly be considered to have existed till the days of Sir William
Petty; and it is likely enough that many of these plans
only resulted in increasing the evils against which they
were aimed. If so, all that need be said is that the same
thing is true of many similar schemes, right down to
our own day. But the fact remains that the large-
hearted primate had views and ideas much in advance
of his time; the good of the people at large occupied
a place in his thoughts immeasurably greater than in
those of any contemporary statesman. And least of all
can his political opponents compare with him in this
respect. Laud deserves to be commemorated, as,
among other things, a true fore-runner of social leaders
of our own day. To him, at any rate, a man is a man,
and no man can be more: the great, the rich, the educated, had no hope of favour from him; rather he

---

* Rushworth II. 59.   † Simpkinson's *Laud*, p. 108.
‡ Gardiner, *Hist. of England*, VII. 163 f.

reserved his mercy for the poor, the ignorant, and the lowly. Mr. Gardiner tells us that "the best side of Laud's character is his grand sense of the equality of men before the law."*

To turn now to the side of Laud's work which has called down upon him the worst obloquy—his policy of coercion in Church and State. This, of course, centres round his use of the two great courts of Star Chamber and High Commission. The function of these two courts was to supply the failure of ordinary jurisdiction in the State and the Church respectively. Each of them was thus an extension, so to speak, of the King's prerogative. Each of them was entirely in accordance with the law, but, as will be seen from what has already been said, each of them was based upon that worn-out Tudor theory that prerogative was an unlimited thing, which supplied the place of law where that failed, and might, under circumstances of great necessity, over-ride it. Laud, therefore, was in no sense responsible for the existence of the courts : he accepted them just as he did the whole body of the constitution, and made use of them because they were obviously the most natural weapon and the readiest to his hand. He constantly claimed that what was done by them was done in the ordinary course of justice ; that he was but a member, and that the whole court was conjointly responsible. And, subject to the preliminary objection that Laud's share in the entire home administration is greater than that of his fellows, the claim must of course be allowed.

* *Hist. of England*, VIII. 106.

Now the records of the Star Chamber are, I believe, almost entirely lost : but from note-books of proceedings there, and the like, it is possible to get a pretty clear idea of the way in which its work was done at different times.   And the opinion of all those who have studied the facts, including Mr. Gardiner and Mr. Paley Baildon, its latest student, the editor of John Haywarde's Star Chamber Notes, is that it really fulfilled a very necessary place in the State.   "It brought," says Mr. Gardiner,* "the highest legal and the highest political capacity to bear upon cases in which the offenders were too powerful to be reached by the ordinary courts, or in which the evidence was too complicated to be un-ravelled by the skill of an ordinary jury. . . . . In such investigations it showed itself diligent and impartial."   No less a judge than Sir Matthew Hale declared that the suppression of the court left a place unprovided in our judicature.   But a court composed almost entirely of Privy Councillors was the worst pos-sible court in which to try political offenders against the Privy Council ; so used it became a grievous means of tyranny.   Thus it incurred a double unpopularity ; it was unpopular with those who objected to its political decisions, and also with the lawyers and the great people who came under its scourge.

The position of the High Commission Court was not dissimilar.   It was a court to meet ecclesiastical irregularities which could not otherwise be met ; com-posed, as Selden informs us, of a larger number of

---

* *Hist. of England*, VII. 84.

laymen than clergy, although, as he adds, "if the laymen will not come, whose fault is that?" * But such a court was an obvious means of silencing ecclesiastical offenders by a short cut, instead of making use of the bishops' courts; and so Laud used it. He felt it necessary to bring the Puritans into line with the plain mind of the English Church; and he would do it by the shortest method. He failed to see that compulsion could not really succeed: that the passions which he roused were worse than anything that was there before; and that in the long run there might have been found "a more excellent way." And yet Laud had been—as might have been expected from the fact that he was the friend and patron of Hales and Chillingworth and Jeremy Taylor —one of the first to grasp the principles of toleration. "I have always" he wrote to Vossius in 1629, "I have always counselled moderation, lest everything should be thrown into confusion by fervid minds to which the care of religion is not the first object. This, perhaps, has not given satisfaction; but I bear in mind how seriously the Saviour inculcated charity to His disciples, and how cautiously and patiently the Apostles commanded us to treat the weak. . . . For my own part, I will labour with the grace of God that truth and peace may kiss each other. If for our sins God refuses to grant this, I will hope for eternal peace for myself as soon as possible, leaving to God those who break that kiss asunder, that He may either convert them, as I heartily desire, or may visit them with punishment."

---

* *Table Talk* (ed. Arber), p. 37.

This is great indeed; and if in later days Laud departed from this ideal of toleration so far as ceremony was concerned, the great aim of a noble and united Church, which seemed to make it necessary, must at least be borne in mind. And we must remember, too, that he himself conscientiously and instinctively believed in authority and compulsion by authority; as Shelley makes him say in his fragmentary drama,

" I
Could suffer what I would inflict."

But in truth there are few subjects upon which more ignorant nonsense has recently been written than Laud's so-called " persecutions " for civil and religious liberty. " The great Whig legend " is already breaking down; but it has left its traces far and wide. From the language which has been used one might think that Laud was the worst of persecutors. The facts, as shown by contemporary authorities, are very different. And although it is true that a man cannot be entirely acquitted because he has done no wrong according to the standard of his own age, yet it is equally true that no judgment can be fair which fails to take account of that standard. Judged by that, there is little which can be called undue severity in his action. The fines imposed afterwards by the Parliament are beyond all comparison larger than those imposed by the Courts during the Tyranny. His suspensions and deprivations cannot compare for a moment with those carried out by the Parliament in 1643. His punishments by the pillory and ·the executioner's knife are nothing by the side, say, of the punishment of the

Romanists in the reign of Elizabeth, or the executions under the Parliament, or the imprisonings and butcheries and transportations into slavery in Ireland and England under the Commonwealth. No single person was ever put to death by Laud's authority; and in this respect his administration stands alone in the period. Of course, mutilation always sounds far more barbarous than beheading; but it may be questioned whether those who are sentenced to the latter would not willingly commute it for the former. It must be borne in mind too, that such punishments for such things sink into insignificance beside the punishments for witchcraft, felony, and high treason prevalent at that day.

Of course, these considerations are not put forward as being, in any sense, a justification of Laud's method of securing conformity. But, as a matter of common honesty, it is only fair to recognise that Laud used no method that outraged the moral standard of the time. His methods were mild in comparison with those of his enemies when they came into power, and the extent of his punishments has been exaggerated vastly and unscrupulously. The number of clergy suspended because they would not obey the laws of their Church cannot have been more than two or three score at the most. In the tenth volume of his History,* Mr. Gardiner has given a list of all the ministers deprived or suspended by the High Commission during two years and three months from Feb. 1634, just the time when the action of the Court was most vigorous. Two were sentenced

to be deposed, one for crime, and the other for heresy ;
and in the latter case the punishment was remitted.
Four were deprived, for nonconformity, or reviling their
parishioners ; and in two cases the sentence was
lightened ; and eight were suspended, in three cases
for crime, and in the remainder for nonconformity ; in
one case punishment was entirely remitted, and in
another partially. The total is remarkably small,
fourteen cases of condemnation in all, out of which five
or six are for crime, while the penalty was remitted
wholly or in part in five out of the other cases.

Nor is the state of things very different if we turn
to the lay Court or Star Chamber. The fines imposed
certainly sound alarmingly high, but in many cases they
were never inflicted, whilst it is a known fact that a
regular system of "taxing" was in force, so that, in many
instances, a fine only cost the person upon whom it was
imposed a tenth part of its nominal amount—although
there are also cases in which the proportion was much
higher. And with regard to the revolting mutilations,
here too, the number for political offences was far
smaller than is usually supposed. The country was
flooded with vile and seditious and blasphemous libels—
a form of literature which would seem, judging by our
own experience, to be by no means obsolete at the
present day, where the name of Laud is concerned.
These were peculiarly obnoxious, and peculiarly
dangerous to a government which was based on tyranny,
and was well aware that it was losing ground daily in the
popular esteem. And they were especially irritating to

the worn, touchy, over-worked Archbishop, who was
spending and being spent, day by day, with the most
single-hearted and loving desire for the public weal.
Then followed a series of barbarous mutilations, the
most typical being those of Prynne, Bastwick, and
Burton, for which, by the way, the Church got all the
blame. "The people think," says Selden, "the Bishops
only censured Prin, Burton and Bastwick, when
there were but two there, and one spake not in his own
cause."* They did no possible good. and satisfied
nobody. Let old Fuller† say why :—"This censure fell
out scarce adequate to any judgment, as conceiving it
either too low, or too high, for their offence. High
conformists counted it too low, and that it had been
better if the pillory had been changed into a gallows.
They esteemed it improvident (but by their leave, more
of Machiavel than of Christ in such counsel) to kindle
revenge, and not to quench life, in such turbulent spirits.
. . . Most moderate men thought the censure too
sharp, too base, and ignominious, for gentlemen of their
ingenuous vocation. Besides, though it be easy in the
notion, it is hard in the action, to fix shame on the pro-
fessors and sever it from the professions of Divinity, Law,
and Physic. . . . Let canvas be rough and ragged,
lawn ought to be soft and smooth ; meekness, mildness,
and mercy being more proper for men of the episcopal
function." On the whole, Fuller's statement fairly
represents the popular feeling. It is clear that nobody

---

* *Table Talk* (ed. Arber), p. 37.
† *Ch. Hist.* III. 433.

was shocked at the acts as being cruel; the general feeling of the people was, that here were men who were fighting their battles, and suffering on their behalf, and that such low punishments ought not to be inflicted on gentlemen.

But gradually, as time went on, the nation was aroused; and at length the Tyranny came to an end. Of course, it could only be put down by means which were themselves unlawful; that was unavoidable. From time to time the necessity arises for getting rid of some abuse that is no longer tolerable. There may be differences of opinion as to the existence of such an abuse, but, granted the fact, all men must surely agree that the absence of legal forms by which it may be removed cannot be allowed for an instant to stand in the way of the removal. It had to go, and if, for a time, the kingship suffered too, it was but a fitting Nemesis upon all that had gone before. The main instrument of the tyranny, the main-spring of the ecclesiastical and social ameliorations of the day, was lodged in the Tower. For what followed—the dreary imprisonment with its scoffings and revilings, the protracted mockery of a trial whose single aim was to provide an excuse for a death sentence—for these there was no justification. No true justice could find him guilty for upholding laws written, and doing what had been done before by others. But to his enemies he was, as one of themselves said, like Naaman the Syrian, a great man and a mighty, but—a leper. There was that against him which they could neither forget nor

forgive. And so at length came the ordinance of death
—voted in desperation by some, in vengeance by others
—which the judges themselves were forced to declare
should not become a precedent, so monstrous was it.
Still, it was the act of men who looked upon him, and not
without some reason, as dangerous to civil and religious
liberty ; and I, for one, do not altogether dissent from
the words of a writer in the *Times* of January 14th : " It
was cruel and illegal to kill him, but he was a powerful
agent in making the Revolution which did so."

We who are met together to commemorate William
Laud are not mere partisans. We have no common
programme which we swallow whole and wish to force
upon others. Indiscriminate eulogy may say what it
pleases, we desire soberly to consider all the facts of
the case, and to hold fast that which is good. We
have no wish to defend Laud's action through thick and
thin, but we have joined together to commemorate, and
to learn from, and to thank God for, all the noble gifts
that he gave to this His servant, and the great things
which He did through him. We thank God for
his noble care for the poor, and his large and generous
aims for the English race ; for his splendid example
of diligent service in Church and State; for his work
as the great promoter of learning of his age. And,
above all, for his work as one of the Fathers of the
English Reformation, with Cranmer and Parker and
Jewell and Hooker ; one of those to whom, under God,
we owe all that we hold most dear. We reverence him
as a typical Englishman, who faithfully preserved the

principles which he believed in to the bitter end; one
who was loyal and disinterested and courageous in all
his dealings. It is easy to see why Laud was the best
hated man in Great Britain, and yet why everybody who
knew him well loved him tenderly. Human infirmity
occurs readily to one's mind in connection with William
Laud; not so readily human sin. His irritability, his haste,
his absorption in details, is in everybody's mouth. But
where, among statesmen, can we find so much of purity,
of piety, of penitence as here ? There are few records of
a man's life which reveal so single-minded and reverent
a character. And there are few records of a man's death
which can show so beautiful or so Christian an end.

III.

LAUD'S EDUCATIONAL WORK.

D. S. Margoliouth, Esq., M.A., Laudian Professor of Arabic in the University of Oxford.

LAUD'S EDUCATIONAL WORK.

THE subject that has been assigned me is in many ways a fortunate one for an occasion in which encomium rather than criticism is in place. Laud's work as a statesman and as a Churchman, however high may have been his guiding principles, was not in any case absolutely successful, and the lecturers on these subjects must necessarily have endeavoured in some way to account for the unfavourable as well as the favourable judgments that have been passed on him in these capacities. Where such very different opinions have been held, it is likely that the truth lies somewhere between the two sides. But of his work as a patron of literature and a leader of education, there is only one opinion ; or rather those who have spoken on this subject find themselves literally lost in admiration. The long career of Laud at the university had given him the fullest practical insight into its needs and defects. He was afterwards given as Chancellor absolute power to deal with the university as he chose. For those defects which money could supply he had a liberal hand, and where his own means were insufficient he pressed others into service ; where the remedies required were rather new ideas, his mind was not wanting in expedients, and still less in energy and perseverance to carry his reforms out. All the factors which go to make a great educational founder and reformer would seem to have been for once united ; the power, the

will, the knowledge, and the means; sufficient tenacity
of purpose, and sufficient length of tenure of office.
Hence it is that in Oxford the same may be said of
Laud as is written of Christopher Wren in St. Paul's,—
if you seek a monument, look round ; of the great catalogue of benefactors whose names are recorded in the
Bidding Prayer every Commemoration Sunday, there is
certainly no one whose services will bear comparison
with his.

Laud was appointed Chancellor of the University
in the year 1630, on the death of the Earl of Pembroke.
The Chancellor had originally been the resident head of
the university, who held office for one or two years.
In time it had become customary to appoint to the
office bishops or powerful noblemen, who could defend
the interests of the university at court, and the office
had come to be held for life. The autocratic power
that we find exercised by Laud is said to have been
first assumed by the notorious favourite of Queen
Elizabeth, Robert, Earl of Leicester, who held the
Chancellorship for many years of her reign, and seems
to have been incompetent and unfaithful in this as well
as in other trusts. That power was maintained by the
more conscientious noblemen who succeeded him, of
whom the Earl of Pembroke, Laud's immediate predecessor, was both a benefactor to the university, and
also a reformer—in both matters following Laud's
direction. The election of his successor was carried
with unbecoming haste, and possibly with some ille-
gality, for at Oxford as elsewhere there was an anti-

Laudian party with an antipathy to the Prelate. The choice, however, was a wise one, among other grounds because, as has been remarked by many, the great man never forgot any place or person who had had any share in his promotion. We find him late in life bestowing the most munificent charities on the corporation of his birthplace Reading, charities which to this day make his name gratefully remembered there; among them being the endowment of the grammar-school, where he apparently enjoyed indifferent instruction. But the Corporation of Reading had given him his scholarship at St. John's College, the first step in his brilliant career, and he would not leave the obligation unpaid. To St. John's College in the days of his power he gave a fresh quadrangle and valuable presents of books; for from the presidency of St. John's College he had risen to his grander preferments. His benefactions to the university itself were acts of gratitude to that place as well as due to a profound policy and a genuine love of learning.

Of his Chancellorship he has left a history, or rather the materials for a history; it consists mainly of a series of letters illustrative of the academical annals, interspersed with comments. This collection was made by him according to his custom while in office, and first published in the year 1700. Many of the documents it contains certainly refer to matters not now ordinarily supposed to concern education; such as the censure of sermons of an unorthodox tendency or on forbidden subjects, the conduct of the students in chapel. In those days the university was mainly regarded as a nursery of ministers of religion. Had the Chancellor's mind grasped the happy idea of religious toleration more than it seems to have done, it would still have been his duty as Primate of the Church to see that the training-school for the Church bred up ministers in Church opinions. And in Laud's case his careful inquiries into such matters are more easily intelligible, inasmuch as the university was certainly intended to be an instrument in his Church policy—the policy of making the Church of England a rival of the Church of Rome, inferior to it neither in dignity nor pretensions.

The most remarkable monument of his chancellorship is probably the codification of the statutes, a work which had been frequently commenced previously to Laud's time, but which it required his energy and power of making others work to bring to a successful issue. It was characteristic of his methodical mind to regard this task as a necessary preliminary of that course of academical reform which he purposed, and to some extent carried out. Opportunities must be given to people to learn their duties before anyone could insist on their performance of them. That reform was needed may be learned from the fact that the universities more than any other places in the kingdom had suffered from the frequent changes of religion under the Tudors, whose alternations had rendered all places unsettled, and at times reduced the numbers of the students to ridiculous figures. When the statutes had been collected and arranged in titles by delegates appointed for that purpose, convo-

cation voted the Chancellor full power to deal with them
as he liked. After making his own alterations, Laud
had them printed, and sent copies on vellum to each of
the Colleges ; the statutes, like newly-elected fellows,
were to be put on trial for one year, after which a written
volume containing their final form was sent to the convocation-house, bearing on it the royal seal as well as the
seals of the Archbishop and Chancellor. This volume
was symbolically embraced by the vice-chancellor of
the time, and sworn to by the proctors and other
authoritative officials. It still remains the statute-book
of the university, though the work of commission after
commission, as well as the internal legislation, have left
few of its enactments unaltered ; excerpts from it for the
guidance of students were from time to time printed, but
the original code itself seems to have remained in MS.
till a few years ago, when it was issued as a relic of
antiquity by the Clarendon Press. Laud appointed a
new official, called the keeper of the archives, to take
care of this as well as other important documents.

Of the changes introduced by the Laudian legislation possibly the most important was one which was
not inserted in the statute-book till two years after its
completion—the ordinance by which examination for
degrees was made part of the university system. It
does not seem that the author of this plan foresaw how
it would revolutionize the university, though in more
than one of his letters he has occasion to speak of its
excellent effects. Of the forty-eight pages of the
statute-book which are concerned with the exercises

necessary for the acquisition of a degree the few that deal with this ordinance are the only ones that yet contain a spark of vitality ; the rest are occupied with arrangements for public disputations in the mediæval style. A degree was on the old system to be obtained by listening for two years to Latin debates, and for two years more taking part in them; by reading aloud theses and declamations; and by obtaining testimonials. The examinations were *viva voce*, of course, for it was not till this century that paper work formed any important part of the system. The performance was in public, and was a test no less for the examiners than the examined. One of Laud's correspondents thus describes the scene :

"I ever entertained a very fair opinion of this course for examinations as apparently conducible unto the advancement of learning among the younger, and the preserving the same in masters. But I confess the course did not make so deep impression while I barely apprehended the same as did the solemn executions thereof while it was let in at my eyes and ears, being the last week present with Mr. Vicechancellor and other heads at that exercise. The eminency of the places for the vicechancellor and proctors at the upper end, and the like on each side for the examiners and the examined, make the exercise passing solemn, and cannot but beget an extraordinary care in the actors on both sides, to fit themselves unto that awful trial. For my own part upon fuller consideration, I take it to be the most absolute course that was ever devised for the honouring of the university ; this single course giving life to the private pains of tutors, and the public pains of readers, making the auditors diligent if they come, which is for their advantage."

And in several other places in the history of the Chancellorship we read of the bracing effect that this new institution produced. The present elaboration of the system was not even suggested till late in the last century, and has all been introduced in this; but the commencement, so to speak, was Laud's. For the acquisition of certain mental habits, such as readiness, perspicacity, and the power of stating a case, these exercises were not wholly fruitless, especially in the case of younger students, for whom the university was much more adapted than would suit modern ideas and standards; but they had the great disadvantage of tending to become mere forms, over the due discharge of which it was considered bad taste to take much trouble.

The Chancellor's ideas of reform are classified by the Proctors of the year 1630 as consisting in the " taking notice of formalities, laying hands on the liberty and reins of dispensations, and looking to the performance of other duties." To the first and third of these belongs the perpetuation of those institutions which are peculiar to the English as opposed to the foreign universities—the college system with its moral and religious discipline, and the academical dress. The students are all to be subjected to the strict discipline necessary at a school. The code prescribes the way they are to live, how they are to dress, and how they are to spend their time. In part these arrangements are to be explained by the age of the students, many of whom came to the university far earlier than any now matriculate; provision is indeed made for youths of quite tender years. In part they are to be regarded as representing the discipline of a religious seminary, and hence the sons of the nobility are exempted from some of the regulations. And in part they seem to have been consonant with and to have satisfied the demands of the national character, and hence are still to a great extent maintained.

As far as the constitution of the university is concerned, Laud endeavoured to do for Oxford what he did for Dublin. The royal seal was affixed to the Statute-Book as a sign that the Crown only had the right of legislating for the university; and a very considerable literature exists dealing with the question whether it has the right of altering anything in the Laudian Statutes; on which till comparatively recent times competent authorities held different opinions. The historian of the English Universities praises the Laudian Statutes for placing no further restriction on the democratic element of the university, the Convocation-House, which was allowed to retain the right to appoint to office, while the initiative of legislation was left to the standing committee of Heads of Houses, whence the Hebdomadal Council has sprung. The sole innovation was that the disturbances which had previously accompanied the election of the proctors were put an end to by the construction of a cycle whereby the appointment was given to the Colleges in order in frequency proportioned to their numbers; this had been suggested by Laud to his predecessor in the Chancellor-ship, and the arrangement still exists.

In our time, and indeed ever since the Class-lists were introduced, there has been no difference between the attainments required for the degree of Bachelor and Master of Arts; the higher degree is taken in due course after the lapse of a certain number of years by payment of fixed sums of money. The Statutes, however, contemplated a difference; the courses prescribed for Bachelors reading for the higher degree represented the higher education as then understood. For this some-thing had already been done by other benefactors; for the love of learning displayed by the Tudor princes and James I. had not been ineffectual: by a proceeding without example indeed an English army shortly after the foundation of Trinity College, Dublin, had contributed a sum of money to supply its library with books. At Oxford Savile had recently founded the Professorships of Astronomy and Geometry; Thomas White the Chair of Moral Philosophy; Richard Tomlin a lecture in Anatomy. Laud would not be behind any of these.

Of his benefactions connected with the teaching work of the university, two especially call for notice. Although he does not himself seem to have been a linguist, his philological interests were exceedingly keen. It may be noticed that in the statute introducing examinations he lays stress on the testing the candidates for a degree in Arts in philology and not only in

philosophy, as had been the case in the former age.
Through his influence the Turkish traders received
orders to bring home with each vessel at least one Arabic
book, which was not to be a copy of the Koran, "for
we have choice of these." The study of the Semitic
languages in Europe was then in its infancy, the Hebrew
professorship, which alone represented the subject at
Oxford, poorly paid. To this Laud caused a Canonry
of Christchurch to be annexed. But the foundation
which is more closely connected with his name than any
other, is the Laudian Professorship of Arabic, founded
by him first 'for the benefit of Edward Pococke, and then
endowed by him in perpetuity. What was it that
attracted Laud to a study of which he does not seem to
have tasted the sweets ?

The fashion of studying Arabic had been set by
Joseph Scaliger, who had been imitated by his friend
and admirer Casaubon. In two letters dated 1607 and
1608 addressed to one Stephanius Ubertus, Scaliger
gives an account of his progress in Arabic, in which having
been unable to find a teacher, he had been compelled to
instruct himself ; and the second of these letters contains
a rather interesting list of the books out of which he
had compiled his never published lexicon ; the only
dictionary at his disposal having the interpretation in
Turkish, of which he knew far less than Arabic.
Though it cannot be said that Scaliger himself made
much way in spite of his efforts, it was owing to his
encouragement that Thomas Erpenius set about a
study of the language which resulted in a grammar

which for a long time remained the standard work on the subject, and the scholarly editing of several texts.

The arch-critic had perceived that the lamp of culture had been held by the Arabs during the dark ages, and in his monumental work on chronology makes not unfrequent use of Arabic documents. In these pre-critical times it was thought that the Arabic versions of the Old and New Testament which were known to be in existence might be of some importance for the sacred text; and portions of such versions had been issued at Rome in the sixteenth century, and at Leyden in the early seventeenth, at the press of the indefatigable Erpenius. Moreover Jewish scholars had long before these times observed that the dead language of the Old Testament could constantly be elucidated from the living and inexhaustible language of the Arabs; and among Laud's contemporaries in Holland there were scholars like de Dieu who were pursuing the study of all the Semitic languages as branches of one stock in a manner almost worthy of a far later age. It is indeed remarkable that this source of illustration of the Old Testament, though drawn upon unremittingly for centuries, seems not yet to have dried up. Then it must be observed that Professorships of Arabic had long existed in catholic universities, owing to the fact that the philosophy of Aristotle was to a great extent first known to mediæval Europe in translations from the Arabic; and though the Oriental translators failed egregiously when they attempted to handle subjects such as poetry and rhetoric, for which a specific acquaintance with Greek literature was required, they succeeded excellently in interpreting the logic, and according to high and impartial authorities even in such subjects as the analysis of the soul.   Then it is worthy of note that about the time of Laud's birth direct diplomatic relations had first commenced between this country and the Porte, English traders having previously gone to Constantinople under French protection; and Queen Elizabeth in her despatches certainly endeavours to identify the cause of Protestantism in its war against idolatry with that of Islam : she calls herself *veræ religionis contra idolatras invictissima propugnatrix.* And as those that are enemies of the same are friends of each other, it would really appear that the Porte assigned better treatment to the Lutherans, as all the Protestants were indiscriminately called, than to those who acknowledged the authority of the Pope or of the King of Spain.   All these facts gave the classical language of Islam a prominent place in the eyes of the learned ; and indeed for the two subjects of astronomy and medicine some knowledge of Arabic was regarded as necessary till late in the seventeenth century.

In the British Isles the study had not been altogether neglected.   Matthias Pasor, celebrated once as a mathematician, theologian, and orientalist, had during his exile at Oxford found a sufficient number of students ready to give fees for a lecture in Arabic ; and Thomas Bedwell, whose name figures often in the correspondence of Scaliger, the incumbent of Tottenham High Cross, had endeavoured to compile an Arabic Lexicon, for which he had gone to Holland to secure the materials collected by Scaliger. Another lexicon likewise never destined to see the light was composed by the brother of Archbishop Ussher, himself an accomplished orientalist. Edward Pococke, for whom the Arabic chair was founded, had studied under Pasor and Bedwell, and after taking Priest's orders had been appointed a chaplain to the British factory at Aleppo, where he had good opportunities of procuring native instruction, of which he did not fail to take advantage. It is not certain that Pococke's appointment was in any way due to Laud, whose first letters to him bore date after his arrival at Aleppo, where the Prelate employed Pococke's services in purchasing MSS. in the ancient languages to be afterwards presented to the Bodleian library. However Pococke's second journey to the East, in which he spent considerable time at Constantinople, was undertaken with Laud's aid, which was also bestowed on his companion, the famous astronomer and orientalist, John Greaves, whose brother Thomas supplied Pococke's place during his absence. The desirability of securing Pococke for Oxford was probably the reason that determined Laud to found the chair, which he did in 1637. The high opinion of him held by Laud was fully justified by the fame he acquired and the services which he rendered to the study of Arabic, though all his works in this department appeared after his patron's execution. His notes on the Specimen of the History of the Arabs taught Europeans the first rudiments of the Mohammedan sciences, but also contained the quintessence of what Mohammedan writers had collected on the origin of their leading institutions and the early history of their race. He gave Europe its first scholarly edition of an Arabic poem, and through one of his pupils introduced a knowledge of Arabic metre ; through his son, who under his guidance edited the Self-taught Philosopher of Ibn Tufail, he showed to what heights Arabic philosophy could soar, and that the Orientals could in this department produce work not inferior to that of the Greeks in hardihood of speculation and continuity of thought. He was regarded as the oracle of his time on all oriental subjects on the continent as well as in England.

The following letter was sent to Laud by the University on the occasion of his making the endowment perpetual in 1640 : "You have greatly enriched the Bodleia-Laudian treasury, by importing Araby into Oxford, but when this store of literature reached us, being confined to books it remained mute, being restrained by its unknown characters ; but when a stipend was attached as a key, with a lecturer to unlock the learning of Barbary, the tongue was unloosed. Even so it was not made immortal, as it hung on the single thread of your existence, which we hope indeed may be immortal. Then this difficulty was remedied by your untiring munificence, an annual rent from your ancestral lands being conferred upon it. Your patronage of the Arabic language far surpasses the wealth of Araby ; being Arabized by you we must necessarily be either Happy Arabians or Rocky Arabians : happy if we yield due obedience to your mandates, but otherwise stony and arid."

A third university office of which he augmented the emoluments, was that of Public Orator, to which he caused a canonry to be attached which has since been withdrawn. This was doubtless in order to encourage the employment of correct and elegant Latin, on which in his Examination Statute he lays great stress. No candidate was to be recommended for a degree unless he had shown that he could express his thoughts on ordinary subjects with ease and correctness in that language. Similarly in the statutes he compiled for Merton College the habitual use of Latin by the members of that society is enjoined. In his letters written as Chancellor he likewise often insists on the necessity of making the students practise themselves in it. In the year 1636 he complains that, to the no small dishonour of the university, at the service held at the beginning of term the prayer was said in English while the sermon was in Latin ; and insists on the service being read in the ancient language also. He had intended to put this important regulation into the statutes, but after consultation with the king thought it might disgrace the university in future times if it ever became known that such a regulation had been necessary. All this seems to us now very retrograde and archaic, but must be judged from the standpoint of a time in which even so ruthless an innovator as Bacon wrote his most important works in the ancient language of Rome, as any other dress would have rendered them un-intelligible to the greater part of the audience for whom they were intended. Moreover Laud, who in his corres-

pondence with foreign scholars apologizes sometimes
not wholly without ground for his own awkwardness in
handling the language, may have had personal reasons
for insisting on this matter.

Laud's correspondence reminds us of what he did for
continental scholars.   The learned sovereigns Elizabeth
and James I. had done something to attract learned
men from abroad ; and it is at least likely that the
patronage of the latter prevented the Roman Catholics
from securing so distinguished a proselyte as Isaac
Casaubon.   Casaubon's son Meric, the only one of his
large family who shared the father's tastes, got through
Laud's influence a living ; and through that of
Buckingham Laud obtained a prebend at Canterbury
for Vossius.   Between this scholar and the Prelate a
correspondence lasting a score of years has been preserved and frequently printed; and the latter's judgment
in selecting him as a fit recipient of the national patronage
must be approved by all those who recognise the place
he filled at that time in the minds of the learned world.
Gerhard Vossius was one of the last of those renaissance
scholars who, living before the division of intellectual
labour, embraced the whole field of literature.   He held
at different times professorships of Theology, Philosophy,
History and Rhetoric ; and was offered a chair of
political science.   The six folios in which his works are
collected contain treatises at one time very famous on
all these subjects.   Laud was attracted by his elaborate
work on the Pelagian heresy, and in letter after letter
urges him to complete his answer to the annals of

Baronius, that great bulwark of Roman Catholic theology. Archbishop Ussher had endeavoured to attract him to Ireland; another invitation had come from Cambridge, which he also refused; and the canonry which Laud procured for him did not necessitate residence. For one of his sons the Archbishop through King Charles I obtained a fellowship at Jesus College, Cambridge; but the correspondence referred to seems to show that the young man was unworthy of the favour. Complimentary messages are often sent in these letters to the illustrious Grotius, whose religious opinions bore so close a resemblance to Laud's; and at the historic interview between Grotius and Pococke in Paris, at the latter's return from Constantinople, the Professor of Arabic was charged with a message to the Archbishop then in prison, bidding him escape to the Continent, to which of course Laud did not listen. Another foreign scholar who enjoyed Laud's patronage was the orientalist Ravius, who received recommendations from him at Constantinople; but whose subsequent conduct did not justify them.

If Laud's interest extended itself to learned men abroad, it did not neglect native desert; and the list of men whom he helped to promote, including such names as Jeremy Taylor, Selden, one of the first of English epigraphists, Lindsell, editor of Theophylact, Bedell, who endeavoured to provide the Irish with a translation of the Bible in their native language, and a host of others, is testimony to the Archbishop's keen eye for desert of all kinds and readiness to encourage it.

The Oxford University Press, which has without doubt done very much during the last three centuries to maintain the reputation of this country for learning, and which can rarely have rejected any work calculated to increase that reputation, is not indeed called after Laud, but was nevertheless founded by him. It would appear that when Henry VIII. gave the Universities their charters the Cambridge authorities secured for themselves the right of printing, being in that matter and in others in the opinion of Laud, more careful about their rights than their brethren at Oxford. The university would appear however to have maintained, or rather subsidized a printer; and it would also appear that books were issued with the authorization of the university; the usurpation of right not having been noticed. The omission of any such privilege from the university charter was, Laud tells us, noticed by him accidentally. Early in the year 1633, therefore, he procured a royal patent for Oxford, similar to that granted to Cambridge, giving the university not only the right of printing, but besides securing for the works printed at the press a certain number of years' copyright. The newly established press contracted with the Stationers' Hall Company not to print Bibles and certain other remunerative literature for the space of three years, on condition of receiving the sum of two hundred pounds a year, to be devoted to the purchase of stock. Trouble was taken to get a skilled compositor from Leyden for the Oriental languages, for at Leyden the Arabic works of Erpenius had appeared. Great encouragement was given to those who would undertake the publication of Bodleian MSS. And indeed, when the King's printers in London had published a Bible marred by the omission of the negative in the Seventh Commandment, and had thereby incurred a fine, Laud got them excused the fine on condition of their purchasing matrices of Greek type, and publishing at their own expense one Greek text a year; an achievement to which he attaches so much importance that he mentions it at the end of his diary among the main projects of his life which he had succeeded in accomplishing. In the chapter of the statutes containing regulations for the newly-founded press the university is instructed to see that the paper, types, and other appliances employed should be the best of their kind ; a regulation which the press has to this day most faithfully observed. A chief typographer was to be appointed to see after this ; and to make him more faithful he was to have the reversion of a fairly lucrative post. The three printers whom Laud provided for the university then have swollen in the two hundred and fifty years into one of the largest and most important establishments in the world.

Another honourable monument of Laud's care for the university is to be found in his benefactions to the Bodleian Library, to which he added an extra wing to contain his gifts. The Bodleian Library, which has since acquired a world-wide fame, was then a recent foundation. The old university library founded by Humphrey Duke of Gloucester, had fallen into a ruinous condition, when in 1597 Sir Thomas Bodley

undertook to repair and furnish it at his own cost, and
also to endow it with a sum of money for the purchase of books.   Laud's gifts of MSS. and coins were
made repeatedly during his Chancellorship, and each
time he received the thanks of the university in most
effusive terms.   This language was not unmerited;
for the MSS. were over 1,300 in number, and in a score
of languages.   By his influence with his predecessor he
had previously procured for the library the important
Baroccian collection of Greek MSS., and he also
procured a collection from Sir Kenelm Digby, which till
the time of the present librarian was not separated from
the Laudian collection.   The conditions of gift forbade
the lending out of these MSS. for any other purpose than
publishing, and the rule which now holds is stricter still.
Had the Oxford scholars been more energetic and taken
advantage of Laud's conditions, some at least of the
great light that has been thrown on the East in this
century by the publication of so much of its literature at
Oriental and continental presses might have been antici-
pated here.   In the collections of photographs intended to
serve as specimens of the Laudian benefactions there is a
page of Ghazzali's " Revival of the Religious Sciences,"
a work of so much authority among the Mohammedans
that it has been thought that, if the rest of their literature were to perish, this book would suffice to give the
world a true account of Islam.   The book, though not
unknown to Pococke, remained unprinted till the
middle of the present century; had it been published
with a translation it might have served better perhaps

than any other work to enlighten the world on the strength and weakness of Mohammedanism. The copy of the Samaritan Pentateuch was presented to Laud by Archbishop Ussher. Ussher had been one of the first to introduce this document into Europe, and had indeed purposed publishing it, but had been unable to find a bookseller willing to undertake the risk. It was printed shortly after Laud's time in Bishop Walton's Polyglot. The Græco-Latin MS. of the Acts is thought to have been the identical copy used by the Venerable Bede. One of the Persian MSS. photographed represents one of several copies in Laud's possession of the famous Rose-garden of Sa'di, the publication of which might have fitly inaugurated the study of Persian in England ; but this language was then known to very few in Europe, and but a few years before Laud's time Casaubon complained that he could get no grammar of it. Many other of the languages in the collection were in the same case. Laud obtained these MSS. partly by sending agents as we know ; but we are also told that owing to his fame as an antiquarian everyone who had any curiosity to dispose of naturally brought it to Laud.

But not only did he enrich the university with which he was more particularly connected, with monuments of his beneficence; his watchful eye surveyed the whole educational field to notice what was amiss or wanting. As Archbishop he had the right of visiting the colleges of Eton and Winchester, and his dealings with the former institution show both vigilance and justice. The relations

he had with Winchester were purely ecclesiastical; but
a curious letter exists from him to the Visitor of New
College, Oxford, pointing out how few distinguished men
were produced by William of Wykeham's joint foundation
and suggesting a curious reason for the phenomenon;
this was the too early training of the New College
scholars in Calvin's Institutes, a book of which he speaks
with respect, but regards as fitted for advanced students
rather than beginners. It was in order to prevent the
students from the Channel Islands going to Geneva to
study theology, and there drinking too deeply of the
waters of Calvinism that he obtained money to found
fellowships for their benefit at Exeter, Jesus and Pembroke Colleges. At an early period of his career he
dissuaded Buckingham from sequestrating the funds of
the Charterhouse. He provided statutes for the Cathedral
School of Canterbury. We have already seen what he
did for Reading.

He was made Chancellor of the newly-founded
University of Dublin against his will, as he thought
Archbishop Ussher, being on the spot, could have done
more for the place; but Ussher, though perhaps more
profoundly learned than his colleague, was wanting in
firmness and power of organization, and was conscious
of these defects. This office was with Laud no
sinecure, as his correspondence with Strafford sufficiently
proves; and by the Charter and Code which he provided,
he left a permanent mark on Trinity College. The
arrangement by which the Fellowships, which had
originally been of seven years' duration, were made

tenable for life, was the most important innovation in his code.

These then are the chief facts which have been collected about Laud's work as an educational reformer and benefactor ; the catalogue is not complete, but the whole of it, or half of it, would be more than enough for an ordinary lifetime ; and when we reflect that the educational work of Laud was a parergon or subordinate employment of one who was Archbishop of Canterbury and chief adviser to the king, the amount of work done appears yet more marvellous.

Viewed merely as a means of perpetuating the name,—a desire common to the majority of mankind, though pursued in a variety of ways,—educational and literary endowments are probably the most practical ; the love of knowledge is common to all well-regulated minds, and institutions intended for its benefit command the widest and most intelligent sympathy. But in Laud's case this was not the only motive, nor has it been the chief result.

When Laud says in one of his farewell letters to the university that no Chancellor had ever loved it as he, his words are probably nearer the truth than those of most people who describe their sentiments. The peculiar character of the English universities inspires a kind of attachment to them to which it is improbable that the Continent offers any parallel. Continental scholars study at several universities, whence their attachments are for particular teachers rather than any particular place. An English university claims sole and

undivided allegiance, and by endeavouring to do far
more for a man than merely instruct him, claims a large
share of his affection.   Laud loved his university as
only an Englishman can.

His love of learning was besides very genuine, and
raised him above many of the petty prejudices of his
time.   The apology which he makes to the university
for presenting it with a specimen of an Indian idol shows
that in his time such a gift might be misinterpreted ;
" though most averse to idolatry himself, he would, by
this gift, better enable the University to deride the superstition of the Gentiles."   And indeed one of the accusations brought against him at his trial was that he had
in his possession several copies of the Koran, to which
he very properly returns a scornful answer.   He found
time among his varied duties to classify and catalogue
the large collection of ancient coins which he presented
(it must be confessed, under somewhat stringent regulations) to the Bodleian Library.   His correspondence with
Vossius shows that he followed with interest that
scholar's efforts in the fields of ancient history, philology,
archæology, and rhetoric.

Thirdly, his scheme of a great national Church was
was ever present to his mind.   In his educational policy
these three motives are mixed, and cannot easily be
severed.

The immediate result of his university policy was,
as Mr. Simpkinson has shown, a great advance in the
numbers of the students, and in the efficiency of the
teaching.   That he did not abolish the whole of the

cumbrous and pedantic system of exercises, which long after his time continued to stifle practical study, is scarcely to be wondered at; his mind was averse from radical reforms, and aimed, like that of many an English reformer, at the restoration of an ideal antiquity. He was not so much an original constructor, as a skilful administrator, bent on rendering existing machinery more and more effective. For more than a century " the Oxford of Laud " remained much as he had left it; in succeeding expansions his work was included, but not effaced.

IV.

LAUD IN CONTROVERSY.

The Rev. W. H. Hutton, B.D., Fellow and Tutor of S. John's College, Oxford.

LAUD IN CONTROVERSY.*

It has fallen to my lot to treat of a subject which I would willingly avoid.

That controversy should ever touch the intimate mysteries of religion, that man should ever contend over the deep realities which lie between his soul and God, is a very piteous feature of the world as we know it. It gives the readiest handle to opponents, to men of bad life and men of illreasoned belief. And it is a reproach which Christians must bear, even when they do not deserve it. No scoff is more ready than that against the *odium theologicum*, and we cannot easily cure the sting of Gibbon's contemptuous references to the disputes of "theological insects."

And indeed for ourselves, if we claim to judge justly and dispassionately, and as men to whom the religion of Christ is the one thing which brightens and glorifies life, there cannot but be a constant clear and unhesitating condemnation of controversy as we too often have read of its use in the past and as we have too often seen its expression to-day. No sphere of human action more clearly needs to be brought under the rule of Christ than the sphere of controversy.

So long as men believe any truth to be vital : so long as men recognise that a firm and carefully reasoned belief, based upon settled foundations, is a necessity for

---

* This lecture is printed as delivered. Thus references are added only in a few cases.

any man who is called upon to think as well as to pray :
so long in fact as men recognise that there is any truth
or any science at all, and that these must be matters of
constant enquiry—so long there will be controversy.
Our Divine Master Himself could not avoid it, and He
left us, as always, principles, perfect and permanent, to
guide us when we too must establish our teaching and
our belief by argument. Absolutely fearless assertion of
the truth as we know it : a stern denunciation of anything
like unreality in argument, or sham, or subterfuge, and of
those who "hold the truth in unrighteousness:" a readiness to take the ground, and use the materials, of the
adversary—to argue with him, that is, on his own principles, from the truths which appeal to his own mind :
these I suppose are some of the lessons which we take
from the controversies of Christ. We learn too, I venture
to think, that homely illustration and irony are not
incompatible with dignity or gentleness or an instinctive
reverence for the holiness and beauty of Divine Truth.
If we must controvert, let us controvert in the spirit of
Christ.

We are commemorating the life of a great English
Archbishop, a man who lived in the thick of great
fightings, in days when men could as readily battle for
their convictions with the sword as with the pen. It is
impossible for us to avoid considering the attitude of
William Laud towards controversy in general and
towards the controversies of his day.

Laud was not a controversialist. There are men
whose work in the world it clearly is to " contend

earnestly for the Faith," as well as men whose is the
more obviously beautiful calling to "minister to individual souls." Upon Laud was laid something of the
insistence of both these great demands. But he was not
absolutely given up to either of them. He does not stand
with either Hooker or George Herbert. We do not know
much of his work as a parish priest. In controversy—
properly so called—that is, literary controversy—we
know that he mingled only as it were by accident. He
did not sit down as a scholar in his study to write a
great book to demolish his opponent: he was called
suddenly, on pressing and almost unexpected occasions,
to make public assertion of the views which he held, and
that as champion of the Church to which he belonged.
And his controversial works are but three :

(1) A relation of the Conference between William
Laud, then Lrd. Bishop of S. David's, and
Mr. Fisher the Jesuite.

(2) The answer to the speech of Lord Saye and
Sele touching the Liturgy.

(3) The answer to the speech of Lord Saye and
Sele upon the bill about the Bishops' power in
Civil affairs.

There is other controversial matter, of course, in his
works. The speech upon Prynne, Burton and Bastwick,
for instance, contains some brief answers to their attacks
upon Church order—but these three publications are all
that can be called strictly controversial. And these are
"occasional" writings. Laud's work was that of an

H

administrator : he was called suddenly to answer some opponents : he made his reply and went back to his proper work.

I think it is fair to say that he was not a controversialist ; but since he could not avoid controversy it is necessary to a complete estimate of his power and of his work that we should discuss the positions he assumed and the methods by which he argued them.

It will be best, I think, that I should speak first, briefly, of his two answers to Puritan attacks.

Lord Saye and Sele was an obstinate and eccentric nobleman with that curious and unwarranted confidence in his own judgment, and that ignorant contempt for the opinions and the birth of other people, which sit so characteristically upon some reforming peers. Both the speeches of his to which Laud thought fit to write answers were made after the Archbishop was imprisoned, and when he was unable to answer for himself in debate in the House of Lords—and there was a special meanness in such an attack as Lord Saye's, when the object of it was standing trial for his life.

The first speech "touching the Liturgy"* was divided into three parts, (1) a contemptuous account of Laud's origin and career ; (2) a plea for extemporary rather than written forms of public worship ; (3) a vindication of himself and his friends from the charge of separatism. To the first point the Archbishop had a very dignified reply : and indeed the matter does not concern us. The birth of an archbishop neither justifies nor

---

* Laud's reply is in his *Works* (1857) Vol. VI. pp. 83 sqq.

condemns his theology. To the two other points there
was more need to reply, and it is not without interest
to-day, when we have been told that there could have
been no dissent but for Laud, to observe the form the
reply took.

A vindication of the right of the Church to ordain
set forms of prayer. The apostles certainly had power,
and exercised it, to enjoin doctrine, and used a form of
ordination by imposition of hands, and a "form of whole-
some words." And, indeed, "no question can be made
but that the Church of Christ had and hath still as much
power to ordain a set form of prayer as any of these
things." Lord Saye and Sele said that the use of fixed
forms of prayer made men preach but poorly. There
have been at different times many reasons given for bad
sermons. This of Lord Saye's was a strange reason in a
church of great preachers and of fixed forms, and Laud
had no difficulty in showing its absurdity. Again, would
not learned bishops be better employed in making prayers
of their own than in repeating those of other people?
Laud answers this too, and sums up by saying, "The
question is not whether a negligent set form of prayer,
or a good form of set prayer negligently and without
devotion offered up to God (as too often they are, God
help us), be better than other prayers, carefully composed
and devoutly uttered; but simply whether a good set
form of prayer (such as the Liturgy of the Church of
England is) be made so evil, only by the enjoining of it,
as that therefore the service itself ought to be refused."
It was, indeed, a strange contention to which Lord Saye

had brought himself—that because forms, lawful in themselves, had been enjoined by public authority, they must be rejected by the individual conscience.

The question of separatism brings us still more clearly into the controversies of the present day. Lord Saye and Sele assumed the position with which we are now familiar—that by adherence to the Universal or Catholic Church was meant nothing more than the holding of the chief articles of the Christian faith, that there was no schism but in rejecting these, and that every particular church and congregation might do as it pleased in the matter of order, of liturgy, of worship. Two lines of argument may be taken up in answer to this : (1) The lawful demand of authority upon the individual conscience ; (2) The practical impossibility of differing in order and worship from the Church without also departing from the faith. Both these Laud emphasises. It is absurd to deny that you separate when history and the evidences of men's eyes and ears are against you. " I humbly conceive that it is certain that he, whoever he be that will not communicate in public prayer with a National church which serves God as she ought, is a separatist. But the Church of England, as it stands established by law, serves God as she ought ; therefore, my lord, by his general absenting himself from her commands in prayer, is a separatist."

This is a logical and complete answer. You must allow those who have adhered to a continuous historic religious body to define what they mean by separation from it. And Churchmen considered Lord Saye and his school to be separatists.

It was as easy to show that Brownists and Independents had in many cases departed from the Faith—and indeed, that all Anabaptists and Brownists " agree that the Church of England is unchristian : " and it was a good occasion for a stern condemnation of Calvinism. " Almost all of them say that God from all eternity reprobates by far the greater part of mankind to eternal fire, without any eye at all to their sin. Which opinion my very soul abominates. For it makes God, the God of all mercies, to be the most fierce and unreasonable tyrant in the world. For the question is not here, what God may do by an absolute act of power, would He so use it upon the creature which He made of nothing ; but what He hath done, and what stands with His wisdom, justice and goodness to do."

Laud knew at least how to go to the root of the matter, and in this answer he puts it very clearly that the Puritan position was nothing but this—that the Church government of the day was unchristian and the Church wrong in fundamentals.

The second speech of Lord Saye's which Laud answered was his oration against the Bishops on the Bill for taking away their votes in the House of Lords. The Archbishop's answer * was a defence of the historic Ministry. (1) He sketched the history of the priesthood in the Old Testament, showing its Divine sanction and its continuous succession, and the place of the priesthood

---

* *Works* Vol. VI. pp. 147 sqq.

in temporal affairs. " Nothing of like antiquity can well be more clear than that four thousand years before, and under, the Law, the priests, especially the chief priests, did meddle in and help manage the greatest temporal affairs." (2) He discussed the bearing of the Old Testament on Christian usage. (3) He defended the historic order of Episcopacy—" It is the constant and universal tradition of the whole Church of Christ, which is of greatest authority next to Scripture itself, that Bishops are successors of the Apostles and presbyters made in resemblance of the seventy disciples." (4) He explained, and justified by history and the advantage of the nation, the right of Bishops to sit in the House of Lords. Some shrewd sayings must have gone home. " The Bishops of England have been accounted, and truly been, grave and experienced men, and far fitter to have votes in Parliaments for the making of laws than many young youths that are in either House. . . . . If they spend their younger studies, before they meddle with divinity, as they may and ought, sure there is some great defect in them, if they be not as knowing men in the rules of government as most noblemen. Others there are who spend all their younger time in hawking and hunting, and somewhat else." From this he passes to a general justification of clergymen's mingling in civil affairs— a sensible and temperate assertion of the wisdom of admitting their share in the common life. In history, indeed, Laud was more than a match for his opponents. The Constitution recognises, for a longer time that it recognises any other power but that of the Crown, the

right of the Bishops to sit in the chief council of the
nation.

All this is very tedious—we may think, naturally,
to-day—and yet it has a certain significance for our own
time. But the important point to observe is that,—with
all the tedious emphasis on detail which makes the
seventeenth century controversies so intolerable to
modern taste—Laud always contrives (1) to seize the
true point at issue, and (2) to raise the discussion to the
highest level. Lord Saye's two speeches against the
Liturgy and against the possession by the clergy of any
political power afford the Archbishop the occasion of
showing in clear but temperate language that a fixed
form of worship is more reasonable, more historical and
more reverent than extemporary effusions, and that
reason, history and common sense allow to the clergy
(who owe their spiritual power nevertheless to God
alone) the right to act as their brethren, justly, honourably,
and not as partisans, in the politics of their country.

The controversy in which Laud was engaged with
the Puritans was doubtless keenest in practical life; but
his printed works show as clearly what the real point of
contention was. Should the English Church depart from
her history and undergo a new reformation after the
model of the foreign Protestants? To this Laud by his
writings, as by his deeds, has helped her to answer decisively No.

These two pamphlets, in which his reply to the
Puritan attack is summarised, have a pathetic interest.
They were written by the old man in the Tower, weak

and ailing, and standing in deadly peril of his life.   They
were his protest for what he believed to be the right,
uttered when others were silent who might with much
less danger to themselves have spoken.   They showed,
if nothing else, the indomitable courage of the man and
his deep sincerity.   The Church system was to him no
accretion upon a primitive faith but its true and
eloquent expression ; and what he held for truth, that no
terrors could induce him to suppress.

Interesting though these pamphlets are, Laud's
fame as a champion of the English Church in controversial writing rests indubitably on his contribution
to the conflict with Rome.   No writer of his age was so
famous on this ground.   The English Church welcomed
his book as the clearest expression of her principles that
had ever been produced.   Clergy and laity alike read
and re-read it.   Contemporary literature is full of
references to it.   The King, as we know, analysed it
himself : and in that last pathetic interview with his
children gave it to them, with Hooker's Ecclesiastical
Polity and Andrewes's Sermons.   I love those passages
in the memoirs of Herbert and of Warwick, which
speak of the King's last gift, and of Laud's own
position.*

---

* The evidence which he gave against Popery is manifested by
as learned and as judicious a book (and so acknowledged even by
his adversaries) as ever was written on the subject by any man since
the Reformation, and is so esteemed by all abroad as well as at
home.   Which book was so well digested by his Master's Royal
heart and hand (for Bishop Andrewes, Laud, and Hooker were this
Prince's three great authors) that if that epitome which His Majesty

They are—the three books—indeed a choice expression of the best side of English Theology, patient, honest, learned, clear, devout.

Laud's conference with Fisher * was like many of the controversies of the time, caused by a pressing personal case of conscience. The Countess of Buckingham, mother of the brilliant George Villiers, had probably already been converted to Romanism, by one Percy, or Fisher, a very notable Jesuit : she had been followed by her son's wife, and the Duke himself seemed very likely to be lost to the English Church. Conferences at first took place, by Buckingham's wish or the King's command, between Dr. Francis White, Rector of S. Peter's, Cornhill, and Fisher. After two meetings had been held, the King desired Laud, then Bishop of S. David's, to take part in the discussion. Fisher printed his account of the conference—and White also : and Laud at last was compelled to do the same. Reply and retort followed, and eventually in 1639—seventeen years after the conference had taken place—Laud found it necessary to publish a complete record of the pro-

---

made thereof, and I have seen under his own hand, might be communicated, it might be lookt on as another ἔικων βασιλικη. And this good Bishop, like his Master, maintained it as well with his blood as his ink ; for when he was murdered and martyred upon the scaffold (no time for dissimulation) he died with this profession. —WARWICK'S MEMOIRS, p. 82.

He gave to the Princess Elizabeth, Andrewes's Sermons, Archbishop Laud against Fisher (which book, the King said, would ground her against Popery), and also Hooker's Ecclesiastical Polity. —HERBERT'S MEMOIRS, p. 130.

* Printed in his *Works*, Vol. ii.

ceedings. The form of the book makes it irksome reading to moderns. Sentence by sentence Fisher's book is taken, and dissected, and answered. Such a method has the advantage of completeness, but it can hardly fail to be extremely tedious. It is difficult to collect and marshal the arguments : it is hard to see the wood for the trees.

I must, however, give some account of the contents of this famous book before I enquire as to the principles upon which Laud conducted this, his most important controversy.

The points round which the battle was fought were chiefly :

(1) The Apostolic succession as the guarantee of the infallibility of the Faith in the Church : the Jesuit claimed that this could be found only in Rome.

(2) The Roman claim that "the Roman Church only, and such others as agree with it in faith, hath true Divine, infallible faith, necessary to salvation."

(3) The Roman statement that the faith had never been changed by the Roman Church.

The chief point was what was meant by the infallibility of the Church. The ground was very different from that of the Puritan contention. It was admitted by both sides that there is a continual and visible Church : but the meaning of its infallibility was in question.

And first there was the familiar Roman claim that

the Fathers recognised the Roman Church as infallible.
Here it is little more than a question of translation.
S. Cyprian and S. Jerome and S. Gregory Nazianzen,
S. Cyril and Rufinus—what did they mean in some
passages quoted? Laud had no difficulty, we should
say, in showing that none of them thought of any
permanent infallibility in the Roman Church or Bishops.
And to that point he returns when the arguments are
summed up at the end of the controversy. There is no
Scriptural or primitive warrant for an infallible Pope.
A Jesuit attacking Laud's book some years later appears
to have conceded this point, for he says, " Catholic
faith (in this particular) only obliges us to maintain that
the Pope is infallible when he defines with a general
council."*

From a general denial of the Pope's infallibility
Laud passes to a particular assertion of the errors of the
Roman Church and Bishops in special points—in the
" worship of images, and in altering Christ's institution
in the Blessed Sacrament, by taking away the cup from
the people, and divers other particulars." But first he
examines the position of the Greek Church as a permanent witness against the exclusive claim of Rome.
" They continue a true Church in the main substance
to and at this day." The Filioque controversy is discussed with a clearness and accuracy that is none too
common. " That divers learned men were of opinion
that *a Filio et per Filium*, in the sense of the Greek Church,
was but a question *in modo loquendi* "in manner of

---

* *Laud's Labyrinth*, p. 143.

speech, and therefore not fundamental, is evident."*
" You," he says, turning to his Jesuit antagonist, " You
may make them no Church (as Bellarmine doth), and
so deny them salvation, which cannot be had out of the
true Church ; but I for my part dare not do so.   And
Rome in this particular should be more moderate, if it
be but because this article, *Filioque*, was added to the
Creed by herself.   And it is hard to add and anathema-
tise too.   It ought to be no easy thing to condemn a
man in foundation of faith ; much less a church ; least
of all so ample and large a Church as the Greek,
especially so as to make them no Church.   Heaven's
gates were not so easily shut against multitudes, when
S. Peter wore the keys at his own girdle."†   Here again
Laud showed his keen insight into really vital points :
the permanence of the Orthodox Greek Church is a
standing refutation of the exclusive claim of Rome.

From this arose a discussion as to what were
fundamentals of the Faith : Laud said ·" the Articles of
the Creed."   Here occurs the curious passage in which
Laud appears to maintain the actual descent of our
Blessed Lord into the lowest pit of hell and place of the
damned," and not merely into the *limbus patrum*, or into
Hades—appears only, for it cannot be said that he clearly
states the opinion, for he declares that "the Church of
England takes the words as they are in the Creed, and
believes them without further dispute, and in that sense
which the ancient primitive fathers of the Church agreed
in."   And this leads naturally to the discussion of the

---

* Laud's *Works* Vol. ii. p. 27.   † *Ib.* p. 29.

liberty which the Church allows. Here England, says
Laud, stands boldly free and tolerant, where Rome is
rigid and bitter.

"She comes far short of the Church of Rome's
severity, whose anathemas are not only for Thirty-nine
Articles but for very many more—above one hundred in
matter of doctrine—and that in many points as far
remote from the foundation; though to the far greater
rack of men's consciences, they must all be made fundamental, if that Church have once determined them:
whereas the Church of England never declared that
every one of her Articles are fundamental in the faith,
for it is one thing to say No one of them is superstitious
or erroneous; and quite another to say Every one of
them is fundamental, and that in every part of it, to all
men's belief. Besides, the Church of England prescribes
only to her own children, and by those Articles provides
but for her own peaceable consent in those doctrines of
truth. But the Church of Rome severely imposes her
doctrine upon the whole world, under pain of damnation."*

The positive Articles of the English Church claim
all to be founded on Holy Scripture—the negative to
be refutation of doctrines not so founded. But how,
says the Jesuit, do you know Scripture to be Scripture?
Laud will not answer "solely by the tradition of the
Church," but rather—(1) the unanimous and constant
witness of the Church; (2) the internal light and testimony which Scripture gives to itself; (3) the testimony
of the Holy Ghost in the souls of men; (4) natural

---

* *Ib.* p. 60.

reason considering the books. These together give
evidence which may commend itself to any thoughtful
and earnest enquirer. Reason, indeed, is the bulwark
not the slave of religion. " For though I set the mysteries of faith above reason, which is their proper place,
yet I would have no man think they contradict reason
or the principles thereof. No, sure : for reason by her
own light can discover how firmly the principles of religion are true ; but all the light she hath will never be
able to find them false."*

This question of evidence for the Scripture is argued
at great length : and Hooker is cited and defended : and
tradition is weighed, and the Roman claims for it all
examined : yet Laud maintains his position, that the
supremacy of the Bible rests upon cumulative not particular proof. " The key that lets men into the Scriptures,
even to this knowledge of them, that they are the Word
of God, is the tradition of the Church : but when they
are in, they hear Christ Himself immediately speaking
in Scripture to the faithful ; and ' His sheep ' do not
only ' hear' but know ' His voice.' "† Perhaps in few
parts of his treatise is Laud more clear and trenchant
and rational than he is here, or more strictly theological.
Faith and reason have never perhaps more clearly had
their claims vindicated and their limits admitted. The
terseness of the language is the fit symbol of the accuracy
and condensation of the thought.

" Though the evidence of these supernatural truths,
which Divinity teaches, appears not so manifest as that

---

* *Ib.* p. 89.   † *Ib.* p. 115.

of the natural; yet they are in themselves much more
sure and infallible than they. For they proceed immediately from God Himself, that Heavenly Wisdom,
which being the foundation of ours, must needs infinitely
precede ours, both in nature and excellence. ' He that
teacheth man knowledge shall not He know ?' And
therefore, though we reach not the order of their deduc-
tions, nor can in this life come to the vision of them, yet
we yield as full and firm assent, not only to the articles,
but to all the things rightly deduced from them, as we
do to the most evident principles of natural reason.
This assent is called Faith ; and ' faith being of things
not seen,' would quite lose its honour, nay itself, if it
met with sufficient grounds in natural reason whereon to
stay itself. For faith is a mixed act of the will and the
understanding ; and the will inclines the understanding
to yield full approbation to that whereof it sees not full
proof. Not but that there is most full proof of them,
but because the main grounds which prove them are
concealed from our view and folded up in the unrevealed
counsel of God ; God in Christ resolving to bring
mankind to their last happiness by faith and not by
knowledge, that so the weakest among men may have
their way to blessedness open."*

Miracles, he very clearly asserts, even our Lord's
and the Apostles' miracles, are not in themselves and by
themselves " evident and convincing proofs."

And so the argument went on, till the Countess of
Buckingham herself broached the question upon which

* *Ib.* pp. 118-120.

all depended—Would the Bishop grant the Roman Church to be the right Church ?

On this his answer developes the chief points on which his own position as an English Churchman was based, and which he repeated in his history written in the Tower, as the only grounds on which the English Church can justify her separation from Rome.

There were errors in faith into which Rome had fallen which made it necessary for the Church of England to reform itself. This she did without departing from the Catholic Faith once for all delivered to the Saints. And she did not depart from the essential unity of which that faith is the bond, or from the Apostolic discipline and ministry which preserve it. Thus Rome is a true Church, though erring—yet not *the* true Church. England also is a true Church. Errors there were in the Reformers, as there were in the Popes: and the work of Reformation is admittedly a most difficult one. And yet through it all the essence has been preserved, and the English protest against nothing but the errors of the Roman Communion.

The Jesuit on the other side repeats the claim of the infallibility based on the Rock of Peter : and Laud denies that the rock was Peter's person, and asserts that it was his faith.* So the English separation is not from the " General Church," but from the Church of Rome—and " even here the Protestants have not left the Church of Rome in her essence but in her errors ; not in the things that constitute a Church, but only in

---

* *Ib.* p. 257.

such abuses and corruptions as work toward the
dissolution of a Church."

And who is to be the judge ? A general council :
it is Laud's appeal, and that of the whole English
Church since the Reformation. And where that cannot
be had we fall back on the Holy Scriptures : for the
Council of Trent had no general assent of the Catholic
Church, and the claim of the Pope to continuous
supremacy is contrary to historical fact. The Church
in general cannot err in a fundamental point, having the
perpetual presence of Christ. A particular Church can
err and particular Churches have erred. General councils
may err, as that of Constance* erred when it ordered that
the Holy Eucharist should be received by laymen only
under one kind, and made this rule "a law which may
not be refused :" and such judgments, being contrary to
the command of Christ, may be reversed. So again
the debate turns back upon the Pope's infallibility : and
Laud declares that the doctrine of intention alone as
defined by the Council of Trent refutes the claim. For
he cannot be infallible unless he be Pope, and the
intention of conferring the Sacraments by which he has
received his spiritual powers and privileges cannot be
proved. We have been recalled to this argument
lately : "let us not forget," says the Abbé Duchesne,
"that part of the French clergy derive their orders from
M. de Talleyrand."

From this he comes to the errors that he saw in
the practice of the Roman Church of his own day in

---

* *Ib.* p. 288.

the common teaching of Transubstantiation, of communion in one kind, of invocation of saints, of adoration
of images—errors all of them practical, but not all to be
found in the avowed teaching of the Roman Church.

As the debate narrows, the Jesuit turns from
particulars, which are hard to defend, to a general
assertion which appeals powerfully to the timid. " You
admit," he says, in effect, " that we may be saved : are
you not safer therefore with us, as we deny there is
salvation in your Church?" "This will not hold," replies
Laud : " on this ground, indeed, you should accept the
Anglican doctrine of the Eucharist, for you only add the
' manner ' of that Presence which we admit to be Real.
For we admit the salvation of Romanists as individuals
not as members of the Roman Communion—that is, as
they believe the Creed and hold the foundation Christ
Himself, not as they associate themselves willingly and
knowingly to the gross superstitions of the Romish
Church." Thus obstinate teachers of false doctrine are
without excuse, though their sincere and simple followers
may be in a state of salvation.

And so finally we return to the confidence which
may be reposed in the English Church.

" To believe the Scripture and the Creeds, to
believe these in the sense of the ancient primitive
Church, to receive the four great General Councils, to
believe all points of doctrine generally received as
fundamental in the Church of Christ, is a faith in which
to live and die cannot but give salvation."*

* *Ib.* p. 361.

More there is to be said—an assertion that the English Church truly holds the Catholic doctrines of Baptism, of the Real Presence and the Sacrifice in the Eucharist—(of this I have spoken in my book upon Laud :* and I do not wish to repeat here what I have said before)—but all returns to the same climax. Rome is not infallible, and England holds to the firm faith of Christ.

It is a remarkable and courageous assertion—not I believe to be ranked above that of the detailed contro-versialists of the English Church—but extraordinarily bold, clear, uncompromising and vital, in its treatment of the real questions at issue between England and Rome. Laud, whatever may be said about details of his book—and those, to my mind, are on the whole marvellously accurate and appropriate—did unquestion-ably go to the root of the matter : and it is upon the lines on which he treated it that the controversy, so long as it continues, and until God in His own good time gives us union, must be pursued.

Remarkable as is the evidence which this book affords to the clearness and the prescience of Laud's mind, there is in it, perhaps, a still greater claim on the respect and gratitude of Christians. It contains a plea, large and liberal indeed for the times, for toleration and mercy and an avoidance of that " cursing spirit " which Hammond, Laud's true disciple, so strongly condemned. " The Church of England never declared that every one of her Articles are fundamental," and " I will never take

---

* *William Laud* (Methuen & Co.), pp. 150–151, 237–238.

it upon me to express that tenet or opinion, the denial of the foundation only excepted, which may shut any Christian, even the meanest, out of heaven."*   Laud in this, as in his Catholicism, expressed, I have no doubt, the true mind of the English Church.

This, strictly speaking, is all we can say of Laud in controversy.   In these speeches and in these argu- ments alone was he concerned.   He entered into controversy swiftly and decisively, but rarely.   He was not a controversialist, though he left memorials of his work in that field of which any controversialist might be proud.

Such was his public work in controversy.   In private, so far as we can judge, we find him patient yet eager in personal efforts to deal with individual cases. Chillingworth was largely his convert from Romanism. Hales he won to a ready concurrence with his views. They spoke long and sharply in the Lambeth garden, walking up and down in argument, Heylin tells us, till they were ruddy of countenance and short of breath, but coming at length to a perfect agreement.   The State Papers contain many records of personal interviews. Dr. Yonge for instance, writing to Laud in 1631, says he himself is witness of the Bishop's patient forbearance with those who objected to conform, " giving them time to consult conformable ministers and vouchsafing to confer with them himself."   Much of his time, already greatly trespassed on by busybodies, was given, I think there can be little doubt, to conference with clergy in

---

* *Ib.* p. 402.

that fatherly counsel which belongs to the episcopal office.

Such instances of his general action as we have, show him, in controversy, in a kindly light. Hasty no doubt he was when he was busy and hurried; but he had a genuine readiness to minister to the consciences and to resolve the doubts of all those who came to him in their troubles.

Laud, I have said, was not strictly speaking a controversialist himself: but it might be said that he had an army of controversialists under him. Cosin, Jeremy Taylor, Widdowes, Heylin, Hall, Mountague;—there are many more names—indeed his own chaplains and the leading ecclesiastics of the day were chivalrous in their readiness to defend the Archbishop's policy and principles. Jeremy Taylor's " Episcopacy Asserted " is a famous defence of the Divine order of Bishops. Giles Widdowes's " The Lawless, Kneeless, Schismatical Puritan," is a sharp popular defence of Church reverence, of such practices (strange that they should need defence) as taking off the hat in Church. Prynne answered it, we remember, in " Lame Giles his haltings," a poor bit of railing. Mountague brought popular writing on Church principles to perfection, and was unremitting in his attacks on the " Romish Rangers " who tried to steal the hearts of his flock, and in his assertion of the firm hold of the English Church on Catholic doctrine. His anti-Roman theses might have been of Laud's own making—certainly they had Laud's warmest approval. He asserted " that the present Roman Church is neither the Catholic Church nor a sound branch of the Catholic Church : that the present English Church *is* a sound member of the Catholic Church : and that none of the points which the former maintains against the latter was the perpetual doctrine of the Catholic Church . . . . or the dogmatical resolution of any one father for 500 years after Christ." And his " New Gag for an Old Goose " was just the kind of writing, on his own side, to which Laud had been accustomed in his youth. Buckingham and Laud stood firmly by the side of Mountague when he was attacked, and it was Laud who consecrated him Bishop of Chichester, on the very day when the news came of Buckingham's assassination. Till Mountague's death, in 1641, Laud and he were closely associated—and Mountague's English pamphlets, witty and popular, must have greatly assisted in making clear to the people the anti-Papist and anti-Puritan position which the next generation so cordially accepted.

Another man whom Laud influenced was the gentle, tolerant, learned Hammond, who did so much for the Church during the period of its suppression. Hammond was scarcely a controversalist, but from him proceeded one of the best and noblest statements of the Church's tolerance, as opposed to Puritan fanaticism, that these troubled times brought forth.

Such names as Andrewes, his forerunner in controversy, from whom, there can be no question, he derived something of the force of his own position—as Jeremy Taylor, and Hammond —in their close connection with the great Archbishop, show the sympathy between his character and all that was best in the English theology of his day.

His known opinion, his sturdy belief in the English Church, in its prayer book and its historic order, his knowledge of the fathers and councils, reacted upon the Church of which he was so prominent a member. Thus, whatever his direct influence in controversy, his indirect influence on thought profoundly affected the English Church. He saw clearly that there was before the men of his day the momentous choice between a new reformation and an adherence to the historic past. The Puritans, we must never forget, would not be content to stand in the old paths: they were determined to advance, and bring the English Church to the Genevan model. It was this that Laud, in controversy and in the influence of his opinions and of his life, prevented: and it is for this that we honour him. He was, says Mr. Gladstone, the most tolerant Archbishop of Canterbury for many generations: more than this, he was the man who prevented the English Church from being bound in the fetters of an iron system of compulsory and Calvinistic belief.

His work in controversy was a protest for the true "undenominationalism," the Catholic simplicity of the Creed. He saw and asserted, as the English Church asserts, that the Catholic Faith is faith in God, and centres in a Person, and that the significance of all things lies in their nearness to or remoteness from that centre. The Catholic Faith gives us a dogmatic theology which is concerned primarily with God, not

with invocation of saints, or purgatory, or justification,
or inspiration : it does not give us, Laud says,
a centralised authority with power to elevate any
doctrine outside the Creed to a primary position.

If you grant the Roman position, faith becomes
merely belief in the assertions of a spiritual permanent
oracle, through which each proposition becomes of
equal importance and equal certainty. There are no
degrees in faith, says the Romanist, it is all or none
—to deny a detail is to betray the whole position.
Thus it becomes logical and natural for a scholar to
renounce Christianity because he cannot accept the
authorship of Daniel. This absolute want of the sense
of proportion is the real bar to Catholic unity. Rome
will not reunite, except on the condition of the acceptance of so remote and dubious a deduction as the
inherited privilege of S. Peter : the sectarian will not
reunite except on the acceptance of his theories as to
justification or the like. This is not the Catholic
freedom. And the Catholic freedom was what Laud
fought for. The Catholic Faith is this—that we worship
one God in Trinity and Trinity in Unity : and from
that centre there gradually shade off the nearer and the
remoter beliefs which we hold and cherish only in proportion to their nearness to the central Truth. Because
he saw this and fought for it it is that I venture to
say that we reverence Laud because he preserved to
the English Church both her Catholicity and her
freedom.

V.

LAUD'S PERSONAL RELIGION.

THE REV. C. H. SIMPKINSON, M.A., RECTOR OF
FARNHAM, AND EXAMINING CHAPLAIN TO THE
LORD BISHOP OF WINCHESTER.

LAUD'S PERSONAL RELIGION.

THE subject allotted to me is Laud's personal religion; and the only measuring rods I can find of personal religion are a consciousness of the presence of God, a self-consecration to the service of God, and a constant delight in intercourse with God. Such a condition may be indicated by what a man says; it can be proved only by what he does. Therefore, we must examine how far this man's actions were governed by an appreciation of the guiding presence of God.

Was Laud sincere? Had he high aims? Was he devout?

Such an examination it appears, from the common talk about him, is by no means unnecessary. The personal religious character of the Archbishop has not escaped from that recklessly thrown mass of dirt with which the literary Street Arabs of to-day delight to besmirch any character, dead or living, whom they think to be unpopular with their readers: and the influential group of writers, who dislike religion and do not wish to admit the conspicuous parts which religious leaders have played in the progress of their country, have not scrupled to sneer and smile sardonically over a personal holiness which ought to be the treasured possession of every Christian and every Englishman. The political agencies and alliances which Laud employed for his religious work have been proved by experience to have been

unwise.   None the less, he remains the Reformer
par excellence of his own day, the Chief Advocate of
the Working Classes, the Defender of the Poor, the
Leader of the Educational Movement, an Administrator
who endeavoured to exterminate the corruptions in
the Civil Service, and an Ecclesiastic who proposed
to widen the boundaries of the English Church.
Why then is he savagely maligned as a reactionary
and an enemy to pure Christianity by the people who
profess themselves (and I think honestly believe themselves) to be advocating the very same cause for which
he died on the scaffold; the cause of the Poor and the
Weak, the cause of Jesus Christ ?   Well, it is the penalty
and the proof of greatness to be hated for centuries.   No
one troubles to find fault with Judas of Galilee or
Theudas, but to discover an error in St. Paul or St.
Peter is still worth the while of the slanderer who
burrows to undermine faith.

It is my impression that the force of the angry wave
is spent.   The sober classes of Englishmen begin to do
justice to a great Religious Statesman, without shutting
their eyes to his very serious mistakes.   Therefore
to-day I ask you to allow my omission of eulogistic
preferences of Laud above other notable ecclesiastics
and saintly teachers of other generations; such as invite
revolt by their claim to an impossible knowledge.   The
muse of history shows a man in his own time, and
teaches us that human ignorance can never picture him
justly in the seat of other men.   I find no measure
by which I can pronounce him wiser than his

predecessors, greater than his successors, noblest of martyrs and holiest of saints; great and good though he was. But we will try Laud's personal religion by three tests. We will consider first what was the inspiration of his life. We will next examine how far his character remained Christian amid the soft flatteries and silken luxuries of success. Finally, we will enquire how well he faced the uses of adversity, which convert the noble nature into a saint, or degrade the mean and base into a slave. Never was man more thoroughly tested, for never did stranger vicissitudes of fortune fall to human lot.

And first, the sense of a great purpose in this man's life appears to have been common to friends and foes. As a young Tutor of St. John's, preachers in the Oxford Pulpit, writers from Cambridge Colleges, thought him important enough to be personally assailed. Archbishop Abbot and Lord Keeper Williams declared him the most dangerous leader in England. While still only a junior Bishop he was attacked by name in the speeches of the Leaders of the House of Commons.

On the other side the shrewd Bishop Neile marked him for promotion at the lowest point of his fortunes; Nicholas Ferrar turned naturally to him for ordination and counsel before beginning his work at Little Gidding; his was the chosen influence to con-strain George Herbert to go to Bemerton. Rome, Germany, the East, canvassed his character and imagined his intentions.

All the onlookers in that age of heroes admitted that it was, no mere accidental upcast of the whirlpool of society which placed William Laud swiftly upon the crest of the wave and gave him the highest place in the nation. They might have been, they were puzzled as to what the aim of his life was; they might form false guesses; they might (many serious minds hold the same opinion to this day quite honestly), they might consider that his purpose was a bad one. But even Hamilton, the timeserver, his most bitter rival, believed him ready enough to die for what he considered God's will; and no one who knew him questioned his resolve; and certainly he believed in himself, since for years his own letters show him to us expecting death at every moment of dejection as the reward of his diligence, and yet setting his face like a flint to that work which he was convinced had somehow to be done before he might rest and be with Christ.

And this purpose of his life was the shaping of a great religious system which should train souls for heaven, by securing for them the best environment, social and spiritual. An eminently practical man was William Laud. Not the victory of any dearly favoured dogma: certainly not the predominance of any special set of theological opinions was his object. If he had been alive to-day he would probably be the special leader of no particular party, but the head and champion of all. And the enquirer who studies his works to discover " his views " goes away grievously dissatisfied. What he wanted, what he was convinced his countrymen wanted, was a system of spiritual training, varied for varying characters, and moulded to changing circumstances, which should make them more like Christ on earth and ready to be with Christ in heaven. God had brought him back for this from the almost fatal peril of an early sickness. God had formed him for this by the remarkable influences which He had placed round him through his days of childhood and youth : God would use him for this so long as he was wanted ; and when he had ceased to be the necessary instrument, others doubtless would be found to take up the task.

I omit to-day his wide-reaching social efforts ; but I venture to think that it is not foreign to the subject of Laud's personal religion, to bring before you very concisely the methods which he, as the chief religious Teacher of the day, adopted to give personal religion to others. A man's religion is always best judged by his actions, and the teacher teaches what he himself loves. These methods we will summarise from the Instructions sent out in 1629, adding detail from other arrangements of the Archbishop. First, he insisted on securing for the people Instruction in the elements of the moral and spiritual life. Laud's religion, as I have pointed out, was essentially practical, and he saw that the old Romanism with all its superstition and its deliberate encouragement of ignorance, had yet brought before the people many of the simple facts of our salvation, with a clearness and distinctness which was missing from the involved elaborate Puritan Sermons. Jesus Christ must be set forth, the facts of His life and death and Resurrection, what He told His followers to do, what He taught them was wrong, and what He taught them was right, how to pray, what to ask for, and what to tell to God. The Clergy must train their flocks to religious habits, they must talk to them about every-day matters. Nothing was so insignificant as not to need the hallowing of Religion. " Whether ye eat or drink or whatsoever ye do, do all to the glory of God."

We are informed in the sermons of Bishop Andrewes how careless professing Christians had become about prayer and worship in those days. They listened to sermons. They wanted to hear the last new thing. They loved doctrinal discussion. But to Laud a regular system of public and private prayer seemed as necessary for the soul as regular meals for the body. Congregations were to be instructed that if they did not worship, they could not come to the Sermons. Preachers were first to be " bedesmen for the flock" before they became their teachers. Worship was to be made as bright and as congregational as possible. For this he encouraged the frequent publication of new hymns and tunes.

And obviously all these devotional exercises culminated in the Holy Communion. Then worshippers came into the very awful presence of God Himself. Laud did not wish to be very rigid in his own definitions, he certainly did not desire to make his own feelings about the Eucharist the only standard in the English Church. But to treat the Holy Communion as a vague Commemoration was to him to misunderstand the teaching of the Saviour Himself. Then Christ imparted to the believer His own Body and Blood. The doctrinal Puritan, who sat or stood as if he were eating a meal in his own house, shocked him as irreverent, as ignorant of that mysterious presence of God for which he had come. And because Laud's religion was so personal, so conscious of the nearness of God, so intensely full of the Divine intimacy, this standing he dared not, as the Chief Pastor of the Diocese, allow for a moment, lest the recalcitrants should imperil their own soul's health. If they would not kneel, they should not receive. They might stay in their seats, and there kneel to receive; this he disliked, but permitted. But at kneeling his toleration (mark the word) drew the line.

One of the Archbishop's numerous Communion Prayers expresses this position so exactly that I will venture to quote it. It is unlike the others in being doctrinal :

"O Lord God, hear my prayers, I come to Thee in a steadfast faith, yet for the clearness of my faith, Lord, enlighten it : for the strength of my faith, Lord, increase it. And behold I quarrel not the words of Thy Son my Saviour's blessed Institution. I know His words are no gross unnatural conceit, but they are spirit and life and supernatural. While the world disputes, I believe. He hath promised me if I come worthily, that I shall receive His most blessed Body and Blood, with all the benefits of His passion. If I can receive it and retain it (Lord, make me able, make me worthy) I know I can no more die eternally, than that Body and Blood can die and be shed again."

And after reception he was wont to pray :

" Lord, I have received this Sacrament of the Body and Blood of my dear Saviour. His mercy hath given it and my faith received it into my soul. I humbly beseech Thee speak mercy and peace to my conscience, and enrich me with all those graces which come from that precious Body and Blood, even till I be possessed of eternal life in Christ. Amen."

A MAN WITH A MISSION. So the great ecclesiastic stood before himself. " O Lord, I beseech thee," so he was wont to pray, "make me remember how much more than other men I have need to call upon Thee. My charge is great and my strength little." And to have a conscious mission is the first consecration of every life. Now and then to the poor erring judgment of humanity the mission may look small or narrow, the care of some single hard-tried life, the charge of a handful of children, the conversion of a little street or dark alley ; then again it appears magnificent when a great statesman builds up a nation or shapes an empire, or a prophet proclaims some new doctrine, or a priest models a Church. But small or great, the man or woman with a mission is the interesting figure in history or society; there is a halo round each, wherever you meet them, which marks them off from the ordinary flotsam and jetsam of mankind ; God has touched their souls, there is in them a spark of the Divine fire. They may frighten us. They may even repel us. But we must admire. This it is which, not to go beyond those same times, keeps our eyes fixed upon Oliver Cromwell, with all his eccentricities and his inconsistencies, combining projects of personal ambition and domestic tyranny and foreign conquest with the passionate desire to make his country great. This it is which compels us to pause and look after Harry Vane, so stiff and rigid, so unlovable with all his accomplishments, dipping his hands with so perverted a conscience conscientiously into the blood of the noblest of his fellow-countrymen, but intent on the creation of a religious monarchy and dying so beautifully for its sake. This it is which makes even the gloomy Harrison interesting, and poor cowardly Argyle conspicuous. And this it is which marks off William Laud above all the famous ecclesiastics of that grand age, the saintly Andrewes, the politic Williams, the industrious Harsnet, the devout Cosin, the eloquent Calamy, the affectionate Baxter, as the one greatest man among them all, who had something to do and who did it, and who sealed it gladly with his blood, leaving a work behind him (which has lasted already 250 years)—our beloved Church of England, Apostolic and liberal, devout and full of missionary zeal, national in organisation, and œcumenical in sympathy; so cautious to preserve all the ornaments which the long struggles of history have won, yet boldly stripping off the chains of that strange Roman slavery which, for a time, seemed even to great and good minds the necessary condition for success.

This consciousness of a great mission is then the first religious characteristic of William Laud. You

see it in his letters and in his Diary. You see it
in his speeches. You see it in ᶦthat dream which he
chronicles for Sept. 1625, which reminded him that he
belonged to God, and not to the World, yet had a work
to do at the Court. You see it most curiously distinct
of all in the record he has left of his own defence of
himself, with its clever arguments about legality, and
its playful touches of sarcasm as he looks round upon a
world turned so strangely upside down where a man has
come to be treated as a saint because he is a slanderer,
and it is considered a proof of devotion to have been
disgustingly irreverent in God's House, and Judges no
longer think it worth while to listen to the defence of
of a prisoner condemned before he has been heard, and
Members of Parliament go away to dinner till they are
wanted to vote off a fellow-creature's head. Amid all
this confused bustle now and again the mighty purpose
breaks out in an indignant vindication of some act of
mercy, or of some plan to increase the honour of God's
name.

The mission was too great to make him proud. It
drove him to his knees. The mission was not an idea
of his own. It was God Who set him to it. "Gracious
Father," he prayed, "the life of a man is a burden upon
earth, and the dangers which assault us are diversely
pointed against us." The mission did not depend on
him, he had but to do his utmost, then God if it
pleased Him would give the increase. But he might
not take back his hand. Lonely, without family
and with few relations ; compelled by his separation for

the great purpose to be simple and ascetic; obliged to
work every hour of the day; with no amusement and no
relaxation, having no time to hunt like Abbot, or to study
like Andrewes, the man with the mission must roll his
Sisyphus-like stone to the hilltop, doubtful whether it
will become the foundation of a magnificent structure,
or totter back and crush and mangle him in its swift
descent into the valley of desolation. Very weary, very
painful, were those years at Lambeth, yet always cheered
and always rendered happy by the intimate communion
with our Saviour which is given to the men with missions;
each day marked off into short spaces by the delightful
milestones of constant prayers, by the few minutes given
seven times a day at least to the society of God, and
now and again gladdened by some splendid vision such as
that set down in his diary for no human eye, "My dream
of my blessed Lord and Saviour Jesus Christ, one of the
most comfortable passages that ever I had in my life."
"O come hither and hearken all ye that fear God and I
will tell what He hath done for my soul," is the opening sentence of his Devotions.

But the man with a religious mission carries with
him a load additional to the burdens set upon the backs
of ordinary mortals. Being brought into close and
constant contact with God Himself, and at the same
time compelled to mingle intimately with the world, he
feels a peculiar consciousness of sin. Some people call
that horror of sin, that dejection which would despair
if God were not so near, morbid and even unchristian.
It marks Augustine, it marks Francis of Assisi, it is

conspicuous in Loyola and in Luther, in Bunyan and Teresa of Spain, it is characteristic of St. Paul and of St. John. Some hasty fault, some ill-considered act of impulse which men of less enlightened conscience quickly and comfortably forgive themselves, becomes to these men with missions the sorrow of a lifetime. Need I remind you that two such sins lay upon Laud always, never forgotten, unutterably irksome. A secret penitent this for some forty years, not omitting to keep the feast of St. Stephen and the 28th of July as days to be passed in an agony of repentance for long-distant sins. None knew the horror of that sad self-reproach till the little Diary with its few bare notes of things great and small, which for some reason the Archbishop wished to recollect, together with his Book of Devotions, was torn away from him by his enemies. Then there was published to the world his unsatisfied contrition for the two or three blots on his holiness of life, which all but himself ought by then to have forgotten, a foolish cause of momentary triumph to his enemies, in reality a proof of the man's genuine sincerity. His own words for St. Stephen's day will best set the penitence before you :—

"Behold I have brought scandal upon Thy name, helping my own ambition and other people's sins." "How much better would it have been if I had remembered the name of this day and rather suffered martyrdom with Thy proto-martyr by refusing what my friends persuaded, either from treachery or from wickedness." "O Lord, how heavy still is the recollection of this sin after so many prayers have been so often repeated and

poured out before Thee by my sad and wretched soul."
" Spare me, Lord, and forgive my sins." And constantly
he repeated, " I have gone astray like a sheep that is
lost ; O seek Thy servant ·that I may not forget Thy
commandments, but return unto Thee."

Such then was the purpose of this man's life ; such
the means by which he kept always before his eyes the
greatness of his vocation and his personal unworthiness
to be the choice of God. Still we must not for a
moment leave out of sight that four men, each in his
own degree, influenced and modified his idea of the
vocation wherewith he was called. We find Elisha as
well as Elijah among the men with a mission, St. John
as well as St. Paul. Buckeridge, Tutor of St. John's
and afterwards Bishop of Rochester, took him to the old
Fathers of the Church, gave him Ambrose and Basil,
Cyprian and Athanasius to be the models of his life.
Launcelot Andrewes fired his ecclesiastical enthusiasm
and guided his devotional piety. You have in this
Exhibition the treasured copy of his Devotions which the
elder man gave to the younger. George Villiers, Duke
of Buckingham, dazzled him with the vision of great
schemes which that magnificent favourite's brilliant
imagination could picture, but his fickle impatience
could not achieve. Thomas Wentworth laboured with
him at the effort to make England as well as Ireland
happy and prosperous, educated and devout. But none
of these gave him his ideals, for the grand model of his
mission came direct to him in his prayers and his
meditations. Buckeridge could show him how the dream

had been turned into a reality; Andrewes could guide him by intimacy with one of the most beautiful lives ever lived on earth. Laud never ceased to be Laud, learning but not following, assimilating but never imitating, from his first public appearance at Oxford, as a young Bachelor of Divinity, to that last glorious day when he walked briskly through the crowds from Tower Gate to Tower Hill to teach men how to die cheerfully and humbly for a great cause.

But if the first principal effect of religion has been shown and has been accepted as truly present in the character of William Laud, and you (ladies and gentlemen) admit him, as I think you must, to have been a man of a great purpose, and deliberately consecrated to the Divine Service, an important question straightway confronts us. Men with a mission, conscious of a claim to have a special vocation from God, are unhappily often induced by power and opportunity to commit atrocious crimes in the name of religion. Paul IV. and Pius V., greatest among the 16th century Popes, intensely earnest, devoutly religious, convinced that God had given them the highest duty upon earth, were both merciless persecutors. They thought human life of no value if it thwarted their mission. Cromwell and Harrison did many terrible acts; of which the massacre after the surrender of Drogheda is but a specimen. Vane began his career in England with a deliberate deed of treacherous cruelty, which turns most of us away sick and sad at the very threshold from any sympathetic study of a truly noble character. Religion was positively hated in England at the Restoration because of the evils sanctioned by its name. And Laud, shall we say, was like the rest of them, intolerant, bigoted, a persecutor? He died bravely, it is true, so did others; but he only took the lot which he had destined for his enemies. It was the chance of the throw. It was the sad necessity of the case.

If this terrible theory were true—that power makes men with a religious mission invariably persecutors, we might truly tremble for the stability of our faith. But of course there is no sanction for it in the life of our Lord, and He has never been without genuine followers of His merciful teaching.

In this matter Laud was certainly not perfect. Power to some extent blinded his eyes. But I do not think it would be an indefensible position to say that if we wished to produce a thoroughly sifted character who, under the most trying conditions, by constant prayer and humiliation, by the study of Jesus Christ and by stern self-examination, kept himself extraordinarily free from intolerance and bigotry and persecution, only just once and again, under the stress of temptation, pushing his exercise of power over the verge of Evangelical gentleness, we should bring forward William Laud.

The long lists of the State Papers when they are searched, give no impression either of systematic persecution or of general dissatisfaction. They show us a small passionate skilful opposition, they bring before us a few individual cases of hard usage. But they prove a very different condition of government to that of the great despot Elizabeth, or of the parliament - ruled administration of Charles II ; and the contrast of the Laudian mildness and general conciliation with the illegalities and brutalities of the Protectorate, is certainly startling.   And the strange argument about the unpopularity of the Church System as evidenced by the Great Rebellion falls to the ground when you remember that it was to Laud's pupils that the House of Commons willingly confided the re-organisation of the Church in 1660, and kept them in power for 60 years.

The thumbscrews and scourges, the axes and gallows, which so many reckless writers always suggest in the dim background of Lambeth during the archiepiscopate of Laud, existed only in those dark recesses into which he cast them till the House of Commons and the Romanist Reactionaries dragged most of them out again.   The irresistible point, the point still unanswered is this: through the years of his influence no life was destroyed for religion or for politics, and of how many such periods long before and even long after could this statement be sustained; and of what other nation or country in his lifetime could such a fact be truthfully recorded ?   Torture also disappeared during his rule, it is to be hoped for ever, from English legal history.   Thus Laud took the first great stride towards that complete tolerance which, if it ever is to be seen on earth, has certainly not been fully comprehended by this nineteenth century; and wrote in clear letters on the pages of our history that whatever might be allowable in the conflict of opinion. for his opinions no man must suffer death. "Ink rather than blood" was his own playful saying about controversy.

And this degree of tolerance in religion was almost unique in his own time. The so-called champions of liberty, Eliot and Pym, whose names ought not to be mentioned without reverence as honourable workers for progress, yet understood so little of freedom of conscience that they clamoured for the lives of Romish Priests, and persuaded the Commons to pass bloodthirsty resolutions against all who did not say their shibboleths on the impossible questions of Predestination and Election. If people must call names, here were the bigots. Here were the intolerant. Here were the persecutors. Not at Lambeth, but at Westminster was sharpened that two-handed engine which smote its first stroke on the neck of Strafford, the author of the Petition of Right and the Benefactor of Ireland, and did not lie idle till after twenty-one years of constant bloodshed, it had smitten off the head of his destroyer, the high-souled Vane. For twenty years before, axe and stake and gibbet had played no part in the politics, civil and religious, of England. Let Laud's detractors prove this false before they mutter about the Inquisition and compare the Archbishop Primate to Torquemada.

Yet even men, who ought to know and might know better, say " Laud would never convince an opponent if he could suppress him." Twice has this been written by serious men quite recently in Oxford—think, in Oxford— the beautiful learned liberal Oxford which Laud himself helped to create, Oxford from which he stirred England to the revival of free discussion, and of bright and reverent worship. Did Laud burn Arians like Abbot? Did he execute Roman priests like Pym? Did he send Hales to prison for reasoning with him at Lambeth, or shut up Chillingworth in the Lollards' Tower, because he had doubts about the Articles? When we write history let us first seek for truth. A pretty epigram this, but an ugly slander.

For the Archbishop was not intolerant. His religion was a religion of practice. I have already said he did not insist on his own view of any special doctrine disputed in his time. He would include in the Church men of all opinions. He did not believe in conversion by axe and stake. Doctrinally he was satisfied with an adherence to the Creeds which in his day few men openly questioned. But he did maintain there must be limits to the public discussion of doctrines; and he worked to enforce silence on the followers of Gomar and the followers of Arminius alike, when they wrangled over the insoluble problems of Free-will and Fore-knowledge. His position was this. Such hot disputes have caused bloodshed in Holland. They will assuredly (and they did) cause bloodshed if they are publicly maintained in England. Nor are these dogmas helpful, to the spiritual life of the men and women who have to struggle as best they can amid the temptations of this wicked world.

He took one step further in opposition to the preaching of the doctrine of the Divine Decrees through the country. How could simplehearted peasants and

artizans be persuaded to love a God who they were told
had doomed to everlasting destruction and eternal
suffering the huge majority of the mankind of which
He was called the Father? How could men walk
straight when their responsibility was emasculated by a
decree of Election which allotted them Hell or Heaven
as a fixed fate from their birth? If it was intolerance
to argue against these beliefs, Laud was intolerant. If
it be bigotry not to agree with Calvin's more exaggerated
disciples, Laud was a bigot. But no serious person
would so argue. Take down his strongest expressions
against his enemies, penned in the privacy of friendly
correspondence, and often with a caution that they
should be burnt at once; and set them by the side of
his adversaries' deliberately published utterances. Study
Laud and his fellow Bishops in the High Commission
reasoning for hours to convince, if it may be, some violent
opponent of the Church system, at least to persuade him
for the sake of peace to teach about Jesus Christ and
leave the insoluble problems of Election and the vexed
boundary of the rights of Bishop and Presbyter alone;
nor to insist that every man must keep the Sunday just
as he or the presiding Archbishop kept it; and consider
on which side was really the party of the bigots. Was
not Bishop Hall, champion of the Dort Synod, appointed
by Laud's wish to his Bishopric of Exeter, and employed
by Laud to write in defence of the Church? Who
promoted Morton to Durham, Potter to Carlisle, and
Cook to Hereford? Who was the friend and patron of
Prideaux and Fell and Palmer and Taylor and Jackson?

All Calvinists these; all with Puritanic leanings; but all, Laud considered, good and valuable men. As Mr. Gladstone said the other day, when these facts were submitted to him: " Laud's breadth of view and his liberality were very remarkable as is shown, *inter alia*, by his appointments." Certainly the most tolerant and least bigoted this of the Rulers of the 17th century in England; though he was a man with a mission, though he was ready to die for his opinions.

Still, do not suppose that I am trying to persuade you that Laud's principles of tolerance were exactly similar to those of this decade of the 19th century. After all, each generation has its own ideas, and you cannot judge a man harshly because, though in advance of his age, he does not hold 19th century opinions in 1640. And, after all, nobody doubts even now that there is a limit to political and to religious tolerance. In England we do not tolerate Mormons, nor do we tolerate very appalling blasphemy in public, nor do we tolerate the Anarchist casting his dynamite, in his eager propaganda of his religious and political ideas, for the destruction of the sovereign people assembled in the street or coffee house, though all these complain in the name of toleration. Nor are men spared scorn and sarcasm, and even more bitter annoyance in the atheist factory because they believe in Christ. Persecution is not dead yet; sometimes we think it is fast reviving; and any of us who have studied even a little sample of society well know that bigotry and intolerance are not yet uprooted.

But in the 17th century most men thought wrong opinions deserved a prison, if not death. Laud did not agree to this; but he did consider that the State had a right to control the expression of opinion if it were likely to cause bloodshed and tumult. Within the Church he expected the Clergy to comply with the laws to which they had sworn obedience, and to maintain silence on doubtful questions at the command of their Bishops. Without the Church established by law in England he maintained that the State was justified in forbidding public worship. None of us would ask for such a system now; some of us feel it wrong in itself. Others dislike it because they know it must fail. But to call a man intolerant, a bigot and a persecutor, because he was not convinced that it was wrong in the 17th century is to argue a hopeless ignorance of History. For tolerance Laud was a champion beyond his time. That is enough to defend him. And he had learnt tolerance from a direct study of his Bible. Let me quote to you from his godson and favourite pupil, Chillingworth, writing under his immediate direction (Works II., p. 63), " To induce Christians to unity of communion, there are but two ways that may be conceived probable :—The one by taking away the diversity of opinions touching matters of religion; the other by showing that the diversity of opinions which is among the several sects of Christians ought to be no hindrance to their unity of communion." The former is not to be hoped for, he says, " without a miracle "; and therefore he goes on to reason for the latter method. Notice, unity in work and a moderate uniformity in worship is the proposal, not a dead level of opinion.   Is this really impossible for reasonable men ? If it is, the Church of Christ can never be united.

But how about the Pillory and the cutting off of ears ?   These sentences were not ecclesiastical.   They were pronounced by the secular law courts as the regular penalty for libel, ugly it is true, but common enough in those days.   The High Commission might not touch life or limb.   The ear-clipping was decreed by the Judges, not by the Bishops.   In France the Puritan Pamphleteers would have been slowly put to death, with each limb broken in turn upon the wheel. In Spain they would have been burnt in the market place.   In Italy they would have perished in the silent underground dungeons of the Inquisition.   They would have fared badly enough at Geneva or at Stockholm. In England the Bishops did not interfere to save them from the pillory.   I confess it would have been the more perfect Evangelical spirit to have defended these libellers from legal penalties ; and if the Bishops had thanked God that they were allowed to suffer shame from insults which after all were but a repetition of what their Master had borne.   But, alas, the old Adam is not dead in any one of us ; and Laud considered, wrongly perhaps, that while he forgave and helped such men personally, publicly he must defend the character of the Church Rulers.

When you study the almost boundless power of the Archbishop for many years, when you read the ferocious libels which were published against him, you wonder that that power was not used more often in self-defence and that no life was sacrificed in that long weary struggle; till you turn to his daily prayers and see how he kept always before him our Saviour's example, and tried in spite of hot temper and flaming indignation to do as his Master would have done.

No man was more conscious of the danger of power. Among his daily prayers were these:—" Lord, this is the time of fear ; keep Thy servant from presumptuous sins lest they get the dominion over me." And "O Lord, I beseech Thee, forgive mine enemies all their sins against Thee, and give me that measure of Thy grace that for their hatred I may love them, for their cursing I may bless them, for their injury I may do them good, and for their persecution I may pray for them. Lord, I pray for them, forgive them for they know not what they do."

And do not forget that the power which the libellers assailed was being used all these years not only to strengthen the position and influence of the religious teachers in England, but principally to educate the gnorant, to feed the hungry, to protect the orphans, and to defend the weak. "Arise, O Lord God, and lift up Thy hand, forget not the poor," was not only a daily phrase of prayer but a daily principle of action with the Archbishop. Historians neglect too often the details of administration which are of supreme importance to the nation and to individuals.

But let us turn aside to consider for a moment the methods by which the spiritual intercourse with God

L

was maintained by this Prime Minister through the busy period of his power.   Thus only can we account for his general clemency.   It is surprising to discover how ignorant those who claim to speak with authority are of the devotional arrangements of the Laudian period.   A well known newspaper treated the matter the other day as if worshippers of those times were satisfied with its writer's own scanty meal of a Sunday Service with sermon. Twice at least every day was Almighty God humbly worshipped with prayer and praise at Whitehall and at Lambeth, as well as in the Cathedrals and in many a Parish Church.   Regular attendance at the public prayers seemed essential to the Archbishop.   He might, and often did, hurry over with rough impatience some ceremonial visit of a great magnate.   He was never in a hurry in his interviews with God.   The Services at Lambeth were constant and they were ornate.   He wished to give his Creator all the most costly gifts he had to offer.   The Chapel had been decorated with the arts which that magnificent and æsthetic age could lend to the due honour of the Almighty's House.   Melodious music, gorgeous ritual were not forgotten.   Sunday was spent as essentially a day to be passed with God. While the Archbishop thought it dangerous to be very strict in the rules enforced upon the general community for its observance ; he himself let none of its hours be lost from worship and prayer and meditation, so far as he could secure them.   Besides these, were the constant private devotions every day divided into seven divisions for seven short periods of silent self-recollection—confession — thanksgiving — intercession — in the presence of God.

It would be humiliating to Christianity if it could be proved that a man so constant in making up his accounts with his Maker was revengeful. But revenge, as we have seen, he trod resolutely out of his nature. It was a triumph of grace when the all-powerful ruler of the land succeeded in actually and genuinely forgiving his private enemies. From the day when he loaded with benefits his bitter personal opponent among the fellows of St. John's, to the day when he sat on his rough prison bed good-humouredly assisting Prynne while his private luggage was rifled in the Tower, only now and again did any real act of anger break out from Archbishop Laud. He was severe to Leighton, though the story that he took off his cap and thanked God for his condemnation has to be decisively dismissed for want of any evidence; but he had apparently arranged with the king that even that rancorous libeller should have escaped his punishment if he had not broken prison. He was severe to Bishop Williams, to whom he is groundlessly accused of being indebted for his Bishopric, because he considered him, wrongly in all probability, to be a disgrace to his order. He was severe to Burton, Bastwick and Prynne in the ugly and barbarous sentence of the Star Chamber in which he did not concur, but which he did nothing to prevent. But he took care that Prynne should have comforts in the Tower, and he arranged that his nominal imprisonment for life should be no worse than a banishment under gentle restraint.

In the weariness and painfulness of that long laborious ministry, he grew hot sometimes, and spoke unadvisedly with his lips, and regretted it and begged to be forgiven. But it was a constant petition, "Lord, set a watch upon my mouth and a seal of wisdom upon my lips, that I fall not suddenly by them, and that my tongue destroy me not." And on the whole his religion stood the test, and he stands out among public men as one who was no self-seeker and gratified no petty personal spite.

But how would this man's faith face the trials of a prison-house, the crushing disappointment of apparent failure? Here was a test under which even St. John the Baptist winced; and sent doubtingly to his Master. But at last we have reached a point on which there is agreement.

Some of Laud's critics have denied that he possessed any real personal character; they have seen in him a second-rate Oxford tutor thrown into high place for the convenience of greater minds, and played with as a puppet in a show to cover their schemes. Others have ticketed him as an Erastian servant of a powerful king who prostituted the forces of the Church of Christ to secure tyrannical authority for a master upon whom he tremulously depended. Others have pictured him as a superstitious designer of petty ceremonies, with no personal knowledge of God and an absolute indifference to human souls, loving to trick himself out in gaudy finery, and to surround himself with a gorgeous train, that he might strut for a little like a mindless peacock on the world's stage. Others, Romanists themselves, have thought they detected the blind and anxious admirer of Rome hoping to win some little praise and some small reward at last from the Infallible and Omnipotent Viceroy of God upon earth.

All these ideas, it is true, crumble into dust directly they are tested by the actual doings and sayings of the Archbishop who, whatever else he was, knew full well the road he was treading, and deliberately risked his life to make the Church of Christ once more powerful in the nation, and restore her to her place as the leader of education, the guide of opinion, the defender of the poor, and the consoler of sinful souls.

But his worst enemies to-day do not deny that he was calm, and brave, and patient, and resigned in his long imprisonment. He had always expected it. The shadow of the axe had been across his path through the whole period of his power.

As the storm gathered, one of the three ministers on whom the King had depended, forsook him and made terms with his enemies, having first, so he said, gained the King's approval to his desertion. On his two great colleagues the deliberate verdict of this treacherous Marquis of Hamilton, compelled to admire while he prepared to destroy, was spoken just before their fall, " The one, (Strafford,) is too great-hearted to fear, the other, (Laud,) is too bold to fly." It is a grand and a discriminating tribute. The impeached Strafford enters with proud and gloomy look and makes toward his place at the board-head, dauntless and defiant, in the House of Lords, amid the hisses of men who had pro-

fessed themselves his willing servants, confident that
he could cow them into submission to his imperious will,
nor, to the last days, did he believe it possible that he
could be sent to die : Laud on that short December
morning of his accusation took boat across to Lambeth to
make his preparations for prison, with that quiet calmness
which comes to the man who has always expected to be
destroyed by the cunning and hatred of his enemies, yet
knows that he has that one surest security of victory, by
which many a defeated leader of a lost cause has re-
gained the battle against overwhelming odds, offering
joyfully the sacrifice of his own life. And yet he had
always disliked the thought of a violent death, and
played for years to be delivered from the hands of
his enemies. " But," he went on, " if my bones also
must be broken, O Lord, I beseech Thee give me
courage and abundance of patience that no torment
may make my faith fall away from Thee, for Jesus
Christ, His sake."

Certainly it would be difficult to exaggerate the
effect of Laud's imprisonment on the future of the
Church. Everything in its details and its length proved
the reality of his past profession. He was imprisoned so
long that the whole nation had time to contrast the
brightness and the liberty of the Church policy, which
he had set before them, with the bald ignorance and
ugly narrowness of the warring systems which jostled
one another in a vain effort to win a permanent succession to the place of the English Church.

Rome was open to him still, yet he stayed rather to

die with the English Prayer Book in his hand; all could
see by experience that he was more dangerous far to
Rome with his calm resistance to her encroachments
upon Christian liberty, than the noisiest ranter of the
crowd which loaded her with reckless abuse.

Month by month through the four years of his imprisonment came forth stories from the Tower of the
sufferings of the late Prime Minister, his privations from
the want of property confiscated before he had been tried
to the private profit of his enemies; the insults which
preacher and visitor heaped upon him; the savage
threats by which the skeleton of a Parliament at White-
hall attempted to compel him to acquiesce in proceedings which were against his conscience; his courteous
and resolute resistance. Then at last the gates opened,
he was exposed deliberately to public insult; yet he
never lost his quiet patience. Fearlessly he looked out
of his prison coach, with those keen grey enquiring eyes,
on angry mobs instigated to tear him in pieces. They
tried him for his life, but not one shadow of a charge of
treason could they bring home to him. Then they
made a special law to put to death a man who it was
well known always refused to employ the ordinary laws
of the land against his adversaries' lives, and the Tower
gates opened upon him for the last time: his day of
liberty was come. And he hastened cheerfully to the
scaffold, and in his sermon and his prayers, and by his
quiet dignity and submission to the Will of God, he
taught the flock for whom he had so long laboured, how to
die a Christian death, and quitted this life as a shepherd

dying for his sheep, with the light of immortality shining upon his face.

He had tried his best, by such Divine knowledge as was given him, to serve his Master : he had passed the three examinations of Faith, of Work, of Endurance ; he had proved himself to have learnt to say from the heart, " Hallowed be Thy name, Thy kingdom come, Thy will be done;" he was gone to the seat of Divine Judgment : and the onlookers knew they also would have to face that dread tribunal, before which to gratify personal hatred his enemies had hurried him. Fifteen years later, his judges, Say, Northumberland and Manchester, with his accusers Prynne and Maynard, would be doing what they could to rebuild, as the neces-sary bulwark against Rome and unbelief, that Church edifice, for defending which they had doomed Laud to die. One asks oneself; was it after all his enemies and his patience which gained his cause ?

And whatever our liking for the man may be, what part of his character had so permanent an influence on his own and future generations as his personal religion? To have lived strenuously might have been of no avail : to have suffered so long and so bitterly without complaint and with such sweet resignation, argued a fulness of the Divine vision, and proved him a martyr and a saint to those who had witnessed his departure. He had pleaded his cause before God and he had won it by the verdict of his fellow-Englishmen.

Serious and open-minded critics may differ in their estimate of his political plans ; but surely it argues an implacable fanaticism to refuse to see in this man a sincere champion of religion ; and all must agree that in life as well as in death he was a conspicuously sincere follower of our Saviour Jesus Christ. As he prepared in the Tower to die he had prayed constantly in a prayer he has bequeathed to us : "Not for my sake, Lord Jesus, but for Thine own, for Thy name's sake, for the glory of Thy name and for Thy truth, to confirm Thy mercies so numerous, great and marvellous, for the sake of Christ the Mediator and the Holy Ghost the Comforter, receive Thy servant who has come to himself and who returns to Thee. Amen."

ARCHBISHOP LAUD.

From *The Times* of Jan. 11, 1895.

ARCHBISHOP LAUD.

[*The following leading article, from* THE TIMES *of Jan. 11, 1895, is here reprinted by the courteous permission of the Editor.*]

The ceremony which took place in Trinity Square yesterday is a symptom of a curious and perhaps not unimportant change of public opinion. The choirs of St. Nicholas Cole Abbey and Allhallows Barking went in procession to the spot where, two hundred and fifty years ago, William Laud, Archbishop of Canterbury, met his death upon the scaffold. The *Te Deum* was sung and the story of the Archbishop's death read by one of the clergymen who attended. The ceremony appears to have been simple and dignified, though it may, perhaps, be doubted whether Laud himself would have approved of a function not ordained by regular ecclesiastical authority. However this may be, it is certain that nobody would have thought a very few years ago of performing such a rite, while it would have been hard to find an historian of learning and impartiality to speak as the Bishop of Peterborough spoke yesterday of the famous Archbishop. The prejudices of the illustrious writers who built up the great Whig legend in the first half of the century have dominated our histories and our historians until the other day, and against no man

were those prejudices stronger and fiercer than against
Archbishop Laud.   Macaulay, as usual, is the most
rancorous in his abuse.   He entertains for Laud " a
" more unmitigated contempt " than for any other
character in our history.   He is never tired of jeering at
the " ridiculous old bigot " whom he describes as " a
" lower kind of St. Dominic," guilty of acts of oppression
as the luxuries of a mean and irritable disposition, the
" excesses natural to a little mind in a great place."
" The mean forehead, the pinched features, the peering
eyes " of the prelate are pronounced worthy of the brain
which could produce " that incomparable diary which
" we never see without forgetting the vices of his heart
" in the imbecility of his intellect."   Yet this is the man
whose toleration as a theologian is praised by Mr.
Gladstone and the Bishop of Peterborough, whom the
former declares to have set " the impress of his own
" mind " on the Anglican polity and worship as in the
main they still subsist, and to whose large sympathies,
liberal views, and wide conceptions in Church matters
the latter bears testimony.

Perhaps even yet the time has hardly come to pronounce a definite opinion on the character and the acts
of the Archbishop.   Probably the personal views of his
latest eulogists incline them to form too favourable a
judgment on his career, just as the party passions of the
old Whigs biased their minds against him.   Undoubtedly
he was one of the chief instruments of the despotism of
Charles I., and for the severities and the illegalities of
that despotism he must be held largely responsible.

There seems, however, to be good reason to believe that the pictures of the Archbishop's life and character drawn by his admirers are nearer to the truth than those drawn by his political foes. It is inconceivable that the idiot depicted by Macaulay, whose malice is only half excused by his incapacity, could have played the part which Laud played in the civil and religious government of the kingdom throughout a memorable period. It is equally incredible that a petulant bigot should have won for himself the affection and the respect of so large a body of English Churchmen. The truth seems to be that, though Laud's Church government earned for him the undying hatred of certain powerful interests and classes, his ecclesiastical measures, at all events, were not of a kind to provoke the enmity of a large proportion of the population. Laud himself came from the people, and one of his recent biographers argues with a good deal of force that he never forgot his origin, and that the policy which caused Puritans like Mrs. Hutchinson to sneer at his " base birth " was regarded with anything but aversion by the poor. The " masses," however, had no political power in Laud's day, and it is therefore all the more to his credit that he frequently showed a sincere regard for their welfare. He seems to have been a model parish priest himself, and to have been deeply impressed by the miseries, temporal and spiritual, of the peasantry, and by the oppression they endured at the hands of the landowners. There was no " labour vote " under the Stuarts, but when Laud rose to power measures were taken to better the position of the labourers

employed by the State and that of the seamen pressed
for the Royal Navy.   It is probable enough that the
peasantry in most parts of the country were not sorry
for his efforts to revive the old Sunday sports and pas-
times condemned by the Puritans; and Laud's endeavours to restore some stateliness and beauty to the ritual
seem to have been partly caused by the not unreasonable
conviction that solemn rites and ceremonies appeal
more forcibly to very simple and ignorant men than
erudite lectures on the comfortable doctrine of eternal
reprobation.   On the other hand, Laud showed that he
was no respecter of persons in the administration of
ecclesiastical discipline, and his fearlessness in this
respect must have made him many bitter enemies.   "He
" intended the discipline of the Church should be felt as
" well as spoken of," says Clarendon, "and that it
" should be applied to the greatest and most splendid
" transgressors, as well as to the punishment of smaller
" offences and meaner offenders."   The Courts of Star
Chamber and of High Commission have an ill name,
which, doubtless, they did much to deserve; it is, however, only fair to remember that at the same time they
often did good service to both Church and State by
punishing offenders who would have been safe enough
from the ordinary tribunals.

On the great question of his day Laud took up a
position diametrically opposed to that of the Commons.
He ardently defended the Royal supremacy, but it was
the Royal supremacy acting by the advice of Convocation,
and not by the advice of Parliament, which doubtless

meant in practice the Royal supremacy acting by the
advice of William Laud. Convocation, he contended
at the same time, must be the judge of spiritual causes,
and he declared the submission of such causes to
temporal tribunals to be forbidden by Christ. His
views of the true position of the Anglican Church were
of a kind which have always been received by a large
body of Churchmen. He held that she was a branch
of the Catholic Church, but, to the unspeakable horror
of the Puritans, he admitted that the Latin Church was
a branch, though a corrupted branch, of the same body.
He was extremely anxious to promote closer relations
with the Churches of the East, and to the interest
which he took in their history and antiquities we owe
·no small part of the splendid collection of Oriental
manuscripts with which he endowed his much-loved
University of Oxford. On the other hand, Laud himself
seems to have realized the impossibility of a reconciliation with Rome on any terms save terms of complete
surrender. He says, indeed, that he was offered a
Cardinal's hat, though the authenticity of the offer may
perhaps be doubted ; but he rejected it, and he told the
King that if " he wished to go to Rome the Pope would
" not stir a step to meet him." Laud himself did not
allow his own predilections as a theologian to blind him
to the merits of men like Hales and Chillingworth, who
belonged to a totally different school. He was, in his
private life, a pious, sincere, and upright man. His
superstition was not greater than that of others of his
age. He was in some respects narrow-minded and

M

prejudiced, but he seems to have had a clear conception of a popular Church directed and governed by the Bishops under the protection of the Royal supremacy. His ideal did not commend itself to his times ; but it has features which may, perhaps, appeal more strongly to the thinkers of our modern democracy than to the Whigs of half a century ago.

LAUDIAN BIBLIOGRAPHY.

[The books are arranged under the following headings :—

A.—WORKS OF ARCHBISHOP LAUD.

> With an Appendix of books prepared by him, or with his authority.

B.—WORKS RELATING TO ARCHBISHOP LAUD.

> With two Appendices. i. Satirical prints, &c. (other than ordinary portraits). ii. Books dedicated to him.]

A. WORKS OF ARCHBISHOP LAUD.

[Under this head are included Laud's own writings and translations of them. It is not always easy to determine what should be included here. Some books, for example, contain only a few pages by him: in such cases they are classed here unless he is merely quoted for illustrative purposes. In that case the book, if of sufficient importance, is placed in Class B.]

1612.

1. Ivsta Oxoniensivm. [On first page " Lachrymæ Oxonienses Stillantes in Tvmvlvm illustrissimi et desideratissimi Principis Henrici "].

> 4to. Londini, Impensis Johannis Bill. 1612.

ll. 61. With a contribution from "Gvliel. Lavd, Doct. Theol. Col. D. Iohan. Bapt. Præses." [Printed at p. 275 of this volume.]

Brit. Mus. 1213. l. 13.

1613.

2. Ivsta Fvnebria Ptolemæi Oxoniensis, Thomæ Bodleii Eqvitis Avrati, celebrata in Academiâ Oxoniensi, mensis Martij 29. 1613.

> 4to. Oxoniæ . . J. Barnesius . . 1613.

ll. 2 + pp. 134. With a contribution from "Gvil. Lavd. Sac. Theol. Doct. et Coll. Iohan. Præses." [Printed at p. 276 of this volume].

Brit. Mus. 161. b. 45.

1613.

3. Epithalamia. sive, Lvsvs Palatini in nvptias cel-
sissimi Principis Domini Friderici, comitis Palatini
ad Rhenum &c, et serenissimæ Elizabethæ Iacobi
potentissimi Britanniæ Regis, filiæ primogenitæ.

> 4to. Oxoniæ . . J. Barnesius . .
> 1613.

ll. 64. With a contribution from "Gvliel. Lavd Sacræ
Theol. D. Coll. Ioan. Præses." [Printed at p. 277 of this
volume.]
Brit. Mus. 161. b. 43.

1621.

4. A Sermon [on Ps. cxxii 6, 7] Preached Before
His Maiesty, on Tvesday the nineteenth of Iune,
[K. James's Birthday] at Wansted. Anno Dom.
1621. By D. Lavd, Deane of Glocester, one of
his Maiesties Chaplaines in Ordinary. Printed
by commandement.

> 4to. At London, Imprinted by F.K.
> for Matthew Lownes . . . 1621.

One leaf + pp. 44.

1622.

5. A Sermon [on Ps. xxi. 6, 7] Preached at White-
Hall, on the 24. of March, 1621. Beeing the day
of the beginning of his Maiesties most gracious
Reigne. By the Bishop of S. Dauids.

> 4to. London Printed by Bonham
> Norton and Iohn Bill . . . 1622.

One leaf + pp. 49.

1622.

6. Articles to be inquired of in the first visitation of the Right Reuerend Father in God, VVilliam L. Bishop of Saint Dauids in the yeare of our Lord 1622.

> 4to. London, Printed by John Haviland 1622.

A copy in the Bodleian Library [Arch. B. II. 31] has alterations in Laud's own hand fitting it for 1625.

1624.

7. A Replie to Iesuit Fishers Answere to certain questions propoūded by his most gratious Matie King Iames. By Francis White D: of Div. Deane of Carlile . . . Hereunto is annexed a [Third] Conference of the right: R: B: of St Dauids [Laud] wth the same Iesuit . . . .

> Folio. London, Adam Islip, 1624.

ll. 164 pp. 592 + Index ll. 2. Then follows, with a new titlepage and paging, "An Answer to Mr. Fisher's Relation of a Third Conference between a certain B. (as he stiles him) and himselfe, which is here given by R. B[aylie] Chapleine to the B. that was employed in the Conference. London 1624." ll. 2 + pp. 74. This work is really by Laud himself.

Lowndes mentions the "Third Conference" as a separate work ; and it is probable that some copies of it were published alone. Cf. Laud's *Diary*, Ap. 16, 1624, "My conference with Fisher the Jesuit printed, came forth."

On the literature of the Fisher Controversy see Mr. Scott's Preface to Laud's *Works*, Vol. II., pp. [xiv]-[xxiv]. According to Lowndes, a new edition was published in 1637; but this does not appear to be the case.

1816.

8. [Another Edition].

8vo.   Dublin 1816.

pp. 837.

1824.

9. [Another Edition] . . To which is added An
Appendix Describing the Established
and Romish Forms of Divine Worship.
By the Rev. Andrew Staunton . . .
2 Vols.

8vo.   Dublin 1824.

pp. 834.

1625.

10. A Sermon [on Ps. lxxv. 2, 3] preached before His
Majestie On Sunday the xix of Iune, At White-
Hall.   Appointed to be preached at the opening
of the [First] Parliament [of K. Charles].   By the
Bishop of S. Davids. ·

4to.   London.   Bonham Norton
and Iohn Bill 1625.

One leaf + pp. 49.

Bodl. Lib. Tr. 4°. C. 79.   There is no copy in the British
Museum Library.   Laud's other six Sermons are not so scarce.

1626.

11. A Sermon [on Ps. cxxii, 3-5] preached on Munday,
the sixt of February, At Westminster: At the
opening of the [Second] Parliament [of K. Charles].
By the Bishop of S. Davids.

4to.   London, Printed by Bonham
Norton and Iohn Bill . . .
1625 [6].

One leaf + pp. 54.

1626.

12. A Sermon [on Ps. lxxiv. 22] preached before His Maiestie [K. Charles] On Wednesday the fift of Iuly, At White-Hall. At the Solemne Fast then held. By the Bishop of S. Davids.

<blockquote>
4to. London, for Richard Badger
MDC.XXVI.
</blockquote>

One leaf + pp. 53.

1628.

13. A Sermon [on Ephes. iv. 3] preached On Munday, the seauenteenth of March, At Westminster: At the opening of the [third] Parliament [of K. Charles]. By the Bishop of Bath and Welles.

<blockquote>
4to. London, Printed for Richard Badger, and are to be sold by Hugh Perrie . . . 1628.
</blockquote>

One leaf + pp. 35.

14. [Another Edition] . . . By the Bishop of Bathe and Welles.

<blockquote>
4to. London. Printed for Richard Badger 1628.
</blockquote>

One leaf + pp. 35.

15. Articles to be enquired of within the Dioces of London, in the first general Visitation of the Right Reuerend Father in God, William Lord Bishop of London, Holden in the yeare of our Lord God ————.

<blockquote>
4to. London: Printed for Nath: Butter. *s.a.* [1628]
</blockquote>

The year is left blank, to be filled in as might be necessary.

1629.

16. XCVI Sermons by the Right Honourable And
Reverend Father in God Lancelot Andrewes . . .

Folio. London . . . MDCXXIX.

ll. 6 + pp. 1008 + 167. Edited, and dedicated to King
Charles, by Gvil. [Laud] London, and Io. [White] Eliens.

The Sermons were frequently reprinted :—Second Edition,
London 1631 ; Third Edition, London 1635 ; Fourth Edition,
with an alphabetical table &c., London 1641 (all these in
folio) ; New Edition, 5 vols., edited by I. P. Wilson, (Library
of Anglo-Catholic Theology) 8vo. Oxford 1841-1843 ; reprinted
1845.

1631.

17. [Visitation Articles for the Diocese of London].

I have not seen these. They consist of the Articles of 1628,
with two additional ones [Laud, *Works* V. 378].

1633.

18. [Sermon at Edinburgh, June 30. 1633].

It is very doubtful whether this was ever published. See
Works I, viii.

1634.

19. Articles to be enqvired of in the metropoliticall
visitation of . . William . . Lord Archbishop of
Canterbury . . In and for the Deanry of —— In
the yeere of our Lord God 163—, And in the ——
yeere of his Graces Translation.

4to. Printed at London, by Richard
Badger, 163 [4.]

Bodl. Lib. Pamph. 32. Blanks are left for the date and name
of the Deanery. In this copy they are filled up Shoreham, 1634.

1635.

20. Articles to be Inqvired of at the Metropoliticall
Visitation of the Most Reverend Father William,
by God's Providence, Lord Arch-Bishop of Canterbury . . . In and for the Dioces of ———, In the
yeere of our Lord God 163—, And in the ——
yeere of his Grace's translation.

> 4to. Printed at London, by Richard
> Badger 163—[1635?]

ll. 6. Black Letter. The diocese and year are left blank, to
be filled in as necessary.

Brit. Mus. 5155. c. 14.

21. Articles to be inquired of in the metropoliticall visitation of the most Reverend
Father William, Lord Arch-Bishop
of Canterbury, in and for the Dioces
of Worcester in the yeere of our Lord
1635 . . .

> 4to. London. Printed by Richard
> Badger, 1635.

Brit. Mus. T. 1015 (7).

22. [The Same] in and for the Dioces of Winchester.

> 4to. Printed at London, by Richard
> Badger, 1635.

ll. 6.

Bodl. Lib. C. 203 Art.

1635.

23. [The same] in and for the Dioces of
Norvvich.

> 4to. Printed at London, by Richard
> Badger, 1635.

> Bodl. Lib. Arch. B. II. 46.
> [Doubtless other editions were published for the
> other dioceses of the Province of Canterbury.]

1636.

24. Articles to be enquired of by the Churchwardens
and Sidesmen of every Parish within the Arch-
Deaconry of Canterbury.

> 4to.   London R. Badger 1636.

1637.

25. Articles to be enquired of By the Minister, Churchwardens, and Sidesmen of every Parish & Chap-
pelry, within the Deanry of ——— .   In the Yeare
of our Lord 16—, ...

> 4to.   Printed at London by I. B.
> 16— [1637].

> Bodl. Lib. Pamph. 35.   In this copy the blanks are filled up,
> Shoreham, 1637.

26. A   Speech   delivered   in   the   Starr-Chamber,
on   Wednesday,   the   xiv^{th}   of   Iune   MDCXXXVII.

At the Censvre, Of ⎰ Iohn Bastwick
⎱ Henry Burton &   concerning
William Prinn

1637.

pretended Innovations In the Church. By the most Reverend Father in GOD, William, L. Arch Bishop of Canterbury his Grace.

4to. London Richard Badger 1637.

ll. 7 + pp. 77. According to Lowndes, *Bibl. Manual*, 1317, (*ed.* Bohn) only 25 copies of the Dedication to the King were printed. But this must be an error.
Bodl. Lib. 4to. C. 79.

27. [The Same.] Another Edition [Without the Dedication to the King].

4to. London R. Badger 1637.

pp. 77.
Brit. Mus. 883. h. 2 (2).

1730?

28. [The Same.] Another Edition. With the marginal annotations by J. Williams, Archbishop of York.

4to. London 1637 (*sic.*) [1730?]

[Reprinted in Laud's *Remains*, Vol. II [1700], and in the Harl. Misc. IX. 201 (1812)].

1637.

29. Harangue prononcée en la Chambre de l'Estoille a la Censure de Jehan Bastwick, Henri Burton, et Guillaume Prinn. Juin 14, 1637. · · ·

4to. Paris [?] 1637.

1638.

30. [The Same in Dutch.]

4to.   Delff 1638.

Lowndes, *Bibl. Manual* p. 1317.

31. Articles to be enquired of in the triennial Visitation
. . . in and for the diocesse of Lincoln.

4to. Printed at London, by Richard
Badger.   1638.

ll. 7.   The Visitation in the Diocese of Lincoln was delayed
by the resistance of Bishop Williams.   (Laud's *Works*,
Vol. VII.)

Bodl. Lib. Arch. B. II. 50.

1639.

32. A Relation of the Conference Betweene William
Lawd, Then, L^rd Bishop of St Davids ; Now, Lord
Arch-Bishop of Canterbvry : And Mr. Fisher the
Jesuite . . . . With an Answer to such Exceptions
as A. C. takes against it.   By the sayd Most Reverend Father in GOD, William, Lord Arch-Bishop
of Canterbury.

Folio.   London.   Printed by Richard
Badger, Printer to the Prince His
Highnes MDCXXXIX.

ll. 12 + pp. 388.   Some copies of this edition contain the
' Table annexed' mentioned below.   Those without it are not
imperfect, as one such was a presentation copy from the Archbishop.

Mr. Scott, who had not seen the rare Second Edition, considered this to be the Second Edition, and counted the latter
part of No. 7 as the first.   [*Works*, II, p. xxiv. ff.]

For Answers to the Conference, and Rejoinders see Nos. 95,
96, 228, 230, 231f., 239f.

1639.

33. [The Same.] The Second Edition Revised; with a Table annexed.

> Folio. London, Printed by Richard Badger, Printer to the Prince His Highnesse, MDCCCXXXIX.

ll. 12 + pp. 388 + ll. 8.
Bodl. Lib. G. 7. 13. Th.

1673.

34. [The Same.] The Third Edition revised.

> Folio. London: J. C. for Tho. Basset &c. 1673.

ll. 12 + pp. 253 + ll. 7. Probably revised for the press by Dr. Richard Baylie (or Baily), Laud's Chaplain, who died Dean of Salisbury in 1667.

1686.

35. [The Same.] The Fourth Edition . . .

> Folio. London Ralph Holt for Thomas Bassett & others 1686.

ll 7 + pp. 253 + ll 6.

1839.

36. [The Same.] The Fifth Edition [edited by Dr. Cardwell]

> 8vo. Oxford 1839.

pp. xxxii + 336.

1640.

36a. [The Vniform Articles for all visitacions in the seuerall Diocesses in this Kingdome.

> 4to. London, R. Badger. 1640]

No copy recorded: indeed, owing to Laud's arrest, it may

1640.

never have appeared. But it was entered in the Stationers'
Registers by Master Richard Badger in Aug. 1640. [Arber,
Transcript, IV. 492.]

Date uncertain.

37. [A letter on behalf of the sufferers from the fire at
Copenhagen.]

Single sheet, folio, *s.l.* et *a.*

Beginning " Good brother As you cannot but
have heard " and ending " I am, Good Brother,
Your very Loving Friend, W. Cant."

The Bodleian Library Catalogue [4. Δ 260 (8)] attributes
this to Laud ; but it may be by Sancroft, as the paper and
type might well be of his date, and the other papers in the
volume are mostly dated about 1700. A similar incident is
recorded, however, in the *Diary*, Sept. 14, 1626, when Laud
was Bishop elect of Bath and Wells.

I have been unable to trace the calamity referred to.

1641.

38. A Letter sent by William Lavvd Archbishop of
Canterburie [Nov. 6. 1640]. With divers Manuscripts to the Vniversity of Oxford. Which Letter,
in respect it hath Relation to this present Parliament, is here inserted. Together, With the
Answer which the Vniversitie sent him, wherein is
specified their Integrity as he is their Chancellor.
The Tenor whereof ensues.

4to. *s.l.* Printed in the Yeare, 1641,

One leaf + pp. 5. The letters in the original Latin will be
found in *Hist. of his Chancellorship (Works* V. 293 f).

A copy in the Bodleian Library [Wood 514 (1)] has the date
altered to 164⁰⁄₁ in MS, and notes by ' Anth: a Woode, Oxoniensis Antiquarius,' to the effect that the translator has
' mangled it, and abused ye authorities ';—which is true.

1641.

89. The Trve Copie of a Letter sent from the Most
Reverend William, Lord Arch-Bishop of Canterbury, to the Vniversity of Oxford, when he resign'd
his Office of Chancellour. Published By Occasion
of a base Libell and Forgery, that runs under this
title. And also the Answer of the Vniversity to
the said Letter.

> 4to. Oxford, Printed by Leonard
> Lichfield, Printer to the Vni-
> versity Anno Dom. 1641.

One leaf + pp. 8. The letters are given in *Hist. of his Chancellorship* (*Works* V. 300 f). See No. 147 for the forgery which
called forth this publication.

Bodl. Lib. Wood 514, with notes in Wood's handwriting.

40. [The Same.] Another Edition.

> 4to. Oxford . . . . . 1641.
> pp. 12.

[Reprinted in Harl. Misc. V. 570 (1810), and in
Somers Tracts VI. 430-441 (1810)].

1645.

41. The Archbishop of Canterbury's Speech : Or His
Funerall Sermon, Preacht by himself on the Scaffold
on Tower-Hill, on Friday the 10. of Ianuary, 1644.
Upon Hebrews 12. 1, 2. Also, the Prayers which
he used at the same time and place before his
execution. All faithfully Written by John Hinde,
whom the Archbishop beseeched that he would not
let any wrong be done him by any phrase in false
copies.

> 4to. London Peter Cole 1644[5]

pp. 20. With the prayers in Black Letter, and some copies
with portrait.

[Reprinted in Harl. Misc. VIII. 599-607 (1811)]

1645.

42. A Trve Copy of Certain Passages of the
Lord Arch-Bishop of Canterbvry.
His Speech Spoken on the Scaffold
on Tower-Hill immediately before his
his Death Jan. 10. 1644.

> 4to. Oxford Leonard Lichfield
> Printer to the University.
> 1644 [5].

One leaf + pp. 6.
Bodl. Lib. C. 14. 6. Linc.

1660.

43. The Sermon, Last Speech and Prayers of
The Right Reverend Father in God
William, Lord Archbishop of Canter-
bury, Immediately before his Exe-
cution on the Scaffold on Tower-Hill,
January 10, 1644.

> 4to. London, for J. Jones. 1660.

pp. 8.   A new edition of No. 41.

1709.

44. Archbishop Laud's Funeral Sermon,
Preached by Himself, from the Scaffold
on Tower-Hill, on Friday Jan. 10.
1644. Also the Prayers which he
used at the same Time and Place . . .
Published at this time to vindicate the
Memory of that Pious and Learned
Prelate, from the Malicious & Scan-

1709.

dalous Aspersions of those Vile, **Paltry** Scribblers, who write the Review **and** Observator.

8vo. London, Printed for **W.** Hawes & sold by J. Morphew.

pp. 16. A reprint of No. 42.

1645.

45. Des Aerts-bisschops van Cantelbergs oratie oft lyckpredicatie, gedaen by hem selven op't schavot op Tower hill, den 10 Januarii 1645 . . . Alles getrouwelick beschreven door J. Hinde . . uyt het Engelsch . . . in't Neerlandts overgeset.

4to. Amsterdam *s.a.*

ll. 4. A translation of No. 41.
Brit. Mus. 8122. ee. 2 (44).

46. Oratie, ofte Lyck-Predicatie Des Aerts-Bisschops van Canterbury, by hem selfs, op het Scharst, op Tower Hill gepredickt, des Vrydaegs den 20 Januarij 1645 . . . Met de Ghebeben die hy ten selven tijde, ende plaetse voor sijn executie ghedaen heest. Alles ghetrou welijck, gheschreven door John Winde (*sic*), wien den Aerts Bisschop heest versocht, dat by hem niet en sonde eenige Phrase in valoche copyen. Wt het Enghels Exemplaer, tot Londen ghedruckt, by Pieter Cole, ghetrouwe-lijct vertaelt.

4to. *s.l.* et *a.*

ll. 4. Another translation of No. 41.
Bodl. Lib. Godw. Pamph. 1356 (9).

N 2

1645.

47. Lijck-Sermoen van Willem Laud, Aerdtz-Bisschop
van Cantelberg, ende Metropolitaen van Enghelandt :   By hemselven uyt-ghesproocken op't
Schavot, voor alle den Volcke alddaer tegen woor-
dich, als hjs was ghekomen op't Pleyn van den
Tour, in Londen, om syn Hoost te worden aff-
geslaghen, op den xviij^{en} Januarij 1645 [New
Style]. In't achten-tseventichste [*sic* : Laud was
really in his 72nd year] jaerzüns Ouderdoms. . . .
Midtsgaderns Hyn Ghebeden die hy heest ghedaen
op de selfde plaetse.   Effigie van Portrait Willem
Laud.   Door last ende berel eerst gedruckt tot
Londen, by Pieter Cool.

4to. Leyden . . . In't Jaer 1645.

pp. 12.   Another translation of No. 41.
Bodl. Lib. G. Pamph. 2289 (3).

48. Oratie gedaen door den Aerts-Bisschop Van Cantel-
bvrg, Ofte des-selviges Lijck-Predicatie op het
schavot op Tour-hill. . . . .

4to. Rotterdam 1645.

ll. 10.
Brit. Mus. 8122. ee. 2 (45).

49. Sermoen ofte Redenen van den Ertz-Bisschop van
Canterbury, ghedaen op het schavot aen Touwer-
hill . . . .

4to. [Amsterdam] 1645.

ll. 4.
Brit. Mus. 8122. ee. 2 (46).

50. A Commemoration of King Charles His Inaugu-
ration.   Or, A Sermon [on Ps. lxxi. 1] preached

1645.

at Pauls Crosse By William Laud then Bishop
of London, late Arch Bishop of Canterbury,
beheaded on Tower-hill on Fryday the 10. of Jan.
1644. Printed according to Order.

> 4to. London. Printed by M. B.
> 1645.

ll. 2 + pp. 32. With frontispiece of the royal arms.

1650.

51. Officium Quotidianum: Or, A Manval of private
Devotions. By The late R. R. Archbishop of Canterbury. . .

> 12mo. London, Printed for Jo.
> Martin and Jo. Ridley 1650.

ll. 4 + pp. 143.
In a copy in the Brit. Mus. [E. 1411] the date is altered in
MS. to 1649.

52. [The Same. Another Edition.] By the
Most Reverend Father in God, Dr.
William Laud, late Lord Archbishop
of Canterbury.

> 12mo. London . . . 1650.

1663.

53. [The Same.] The Second Edition [*sic*].

> 18mo. London for Richard
> Crofts. 1663.

With portrait.

1667.

54. A Summarie of Devotions, compiled and
used by Dr William Laud, Sometime
Ld Arch-Bishop of Canterbury . . .

8vo. Oxford, Printed by William
Hall. 1667.

pp. 333. As far as p. 140 this corresponds with
the Officium Quotidianum : the rest is new matter.
At the end there is the Abp's speech on the Scaffold,
" according to the original written with his own hand,
and delivered by him upon the scaffold on Tower-
Hill, Jan. 10, 1644, to his chaplain, Dr. Sterne, now
Lord Archbishop of York." With the *imprimatur* of
Abp. Sheldon and Dr. Fell the Vice-Chancellor of
Oxford University.

55. [The Same.]   Another Edition.

12mo. (5$\frac{1}{8}$ × 3$\frac{1}{8}$) London.   1667.

One leaf + pp. 211.   With Sheldon's *imprimatur* only.
Bodl. Lib. 8º Tr. 106 Th.

1683.

56. The Daily Office of a Christian, being the
Devotions of the Most Reverend
Father in God, Dr. William Laud,
late Archbishop of Canterbury.   The
Fourth   Edition,   Wherein   several
Catechetical Paraphrases, and other
very excellent Prayers selected out of
the Primitive Writers, formerly pub-
lisht in Latine, are now made English;

1683.

and the whole reduced to an *exact*
method . . . by J. T.

12mo. London, Printed for Matthew Gilliflower and William
Hensman, 1683.

This is not a new edition of the Officium Quotidianum,
but the whole Devotions abridged and re-arranged.

1687.

57. [The Same.]   Fifth Edition.

12mo. London, reprinted for T. B.
M. G. and W. H., and are to
be sold by Richard Heavisid . . .
1687.

1688.

58. [The Same.   Also termed] The Fifth
Edition.

12mo. London, Printed and are
to be sold by John Walthoe . . .
and Robert Vincent . . . 1688.

ll. 7 + pp 263 + Index ll. 5.   With Portrait.
Brit. Mus. 3455. c. 17.

1705.

59. [The Same.]   The Sixth Edition.

12mo. London : Printed, and are
to be sold, by J. Nutt, near
Stationers'-Hall.   1705.

ll. 7 + pp. 263 + Contents pp. 11.   With Portrait.
The above, with a new titlepage.
Brit. Mus. 3455. c. 32.

1705.

60. [The Same.   Also termed] The Sixth
    Edition.

> 12mo. London, Printed for Samuel
> Keble . . and R. Wellington . .
> and W. & M. Gilliflower . .
> 1705.

ll. 7 + pp. 263 + Contents pp. 11 (not paged).
With Portrait. The same book with a new titlepage.
Bodl. Lib. 138. g. 110.

1838.

61. The Private Devotions of Dr. William
    Laud . . . edited by F. W. Faber.

> 16mo. Oxford, J. H. Parker . . .
> MDCCCXXXVIII.

pp. x + 234. ´A reprint, with notes, of the edition
of 1667. Re-issued, with a new titlepage, MDCCCXXXIX.
[Bodl. Lib. 14010. f. 93].

1855.

62. The Private Devotions of Dr. William
    Laud, Archbishop of Canterbury and
    Martyr.   A New Edition.

> 12mo. Oxford and London, . . .
> Parker. 1855.

pp. xv + 270. A reprint of the edition of 1667,
with the translations of the prayers from the edition
of 1705.

1864.

63. [The Same.]   New Edition.

> 8vo. Oxford & London, . . .
> Parker . . . 1864.

1651.

64. Seven Sermons Preached Upon severall occasions By The Right Reverend and Learned Father in God, William Lavd, Late Arch-Bishop of Canter-bury . . . .

> 12mo. London, for R. Lowndes.
> MDCLI.

ll. 3 + pp. 339. Containing the Seven Sermons already ᴺoticed (Nos. 4, 5, 10, 11, 12, 13 and 50).

1829.

> 65. [The Same.] Reprinted . . . from the last edition in 1651. Edited by the Rev J. W. Hatherell . . .
>
> > 8vo. London, . . Rivington . . . 1829.
>
> pp. xx + 241.

1695.

66. The History of the Troubles and Tryal of The Most Reverend Father in God, and Blessed Martyr, William Laud, Lord Archbishop of Canterbury. Wrote by Himselfe, during his Imprisonment in the Tower. To which is prefixed The Diary of His Owne Life . . . .

> Folio. London, Printed for Ri. Chiswell 1695.

ll. 10 + pp. 616. With Portrait. Containing also the Answer to Lord Say's Speech on the Liturgy, the Archbishop's Will, &c. Edited by Henry Wharton.

1700.

67. The Second Volume of the Remains of the most Reverend Father in GOD, And blessed martyr, William Laud, Lord Arch-Bishop of Canterbury. Written by Himself. Collected by the late Learned Mr. Henry Wharton, And Published according to his request by the Reverend Mr. Edmund Wharton, his Father . . .

> Folio. London, for Sam. Keble . . . Dan. Brown . . . Will. Hensman . . . Matt. Wotton . . . and R. Knaplock . . . 1700.

ll. 2 + pp. 217.

Contents :—Answer to Ld. Say's Speech against the Bishops, Speech at the Censure of Bastwick &c, and History of his Chancellorship.

1737.

68. Concilia Magnæ Britanniæ et Hiberniæ [edited by Bp. Wilkins]. Vol. IV. pp. 480-554. [The Primacy of Archbishop Laud].

> Folio. Londini, MDCCXXXVII.

Containing many writings of Abp. Laud, not previously published : *e.g.* p. 523-524, "A form of penance and reconciliation of a renegade or apostate, from the christian church, to Turcism" : pp. 529-531, "Statuta sive ordinationes per reverendissimum dom. Will. Laud, archiep. Cant. edita et promulgata."

1780 ?

69. A Conference Between Christ and a Doubtful Christian : to which is added, The Good Man's comfortable Companion ; Or, a Daily preparation

1780?

for Heaven . . . Also a Collection of Excellent Prayers for morning and evening, for every day of the week . . . By Archbishop Laud. The Fifth Edition.

8vo. London *s.a.* [1780 ?]

pp. 32, with Frontispiece. Collection of Prayers pp. 22-32. Brit. Mus. 4371. e. 3 (3). I have seen no other edition.

1809.

70. Cobbett's Complete Collection of State Trials.

8vo. London . . . 1809 &c.

Vol. IV. Cols. 315-626. "The Trial of Dr. William Laud, Archbishop of Canterbury, for High Treason: 16-20 Charles I. A.D. 1640-1644. Written by Himself during his Imprisonment in the Tower."
Reprinted from Wharton's edition of 1695, No 66.

1839.

71. The Autobiography of Dr. William Laud, Archbishop of Canterbury, and Martyr. Collected from his Remains. [edited by J. H. Newman].

16mo. Oxford, Parker. MDCCCXXXIX.

pp. xxxix + 448.

1840.

72. Liturgy, Episcopacy, and Church Ritual: Three Speeches by Archbishop Laud.

8vo. Oxford, Parker *s.a.*

pp. 401. Containing the Answer to Lord Say on the Liturgy, the Answer to Lord Say on the Bishops, and the Speech at the Censure of Bastwick, Burton, and Prynne.

1842.

78. Tracts of the Anglican Fathers, with introductions,
notes, &c. 4 vols. Vol. I. On the Book of Common
Prayer.

8vo. London, s.a. [1842].

pp. xvi + 349. Also published in parts. At pp. 195-216
" The great peril of Popery, especially in the matter of the
blessed Eucharist," by Archbishop Laud. Extracted from the
Conference with Fisher.

1844.

74. The Object, Importance and Antiquity of the Rite
of Consecration of Churches . . with . . an Appendix
containing the Consecration Services of Bishop
Andrewes and of Archbishop Laud. By E. C.
Harington . . .

8vo. London . . 1844

At pp. 195 f. "Modus procedendi in negotio consecrationis
ecclesiæ parochialis et cœmeterii " by Abp. Laud.

1847 &c.

75. The Works of the Most Reverend Father in God,
William Laud D.D. Sometime Lord Archbishop of
Canterbury. 7 Vols. [Library of Anglo-Catholic
Theology].

8vo. Oxford : John Henry Parker.
MDCCCXLVII &c.

Vol. I. 1847. pp. xii + 212. Sermons.

Vol. II. 1849. pp. [xxxi] + xl + 440. Conference with
Fisher.

Vol. III. 1853. pp. vii + 463. Devotions, Diary, and History of Troubles part 1.

1847 &c.

Vol. IV. 1854. pp. vii + 504. History of Troubles part 2, and Romes Masterpiece (with the Archbishop's notes).

Vol. V. (In Two Parts) 1853. pp. xv + 635. History of his Chancellorship, Accounts of Province, Form of Penance, Injunctions &c, Canons.

Vol. VI. (In Two Parts) 1857. pp. viii + 708. Miscellaneous Papers, Letters I-CC, Notes on Controversies of Bellarmine.

Vol. VII. 1860. pp. xxiv + 707. Letters CCI-CCCCLII, Appendix, and General Index.

Vols. I and II edited by William Scott ; Vols. III-VII by James Bliss.

In Vol VII. pp. ix-x, there is a list of the sources, printed and MS, from which the Letters were obtained. There are two letters to be added to these ; viz., one printed in the *English Historical Review* for Oct. 1892, and one in this volume (p. 273).

APPENDIX.

Works prepared by Archbishop Laud, or issued with his authority.

1636.

76. [The Book of Common Prayer . . . for the Use of the Church of Scotland].

Folio. Edinburgh, . . 1636.

Prepared by Abp. Laud. An Edition in Black Letter, of which only a few fragments are known to be in existence. See No. 285, and Laudian Exhibition Catalogue, No. 47.

1637.

77. The Booke of Common Prayer and Administration of The Sacraments. And

1837.

other Parts of Divine Service for the
Use of the Church of Scotland.

Folio. Edinburgh, by Robert
Young, Printer to the King's
most Excellent Majestie 1637.

ll. 123. Black Letter.

1844.

78. [The Same.] A fac-simile reproduction of
the edition of 1637, being No. 5 of
Pickering's Reprints.

Folio. London, Pickering. 1844.

ll. 6 + 123.

1847.

79. Reliquiæ Liturgicæ. Documents, connected with the Liturgy of the Church
of England . . . Edited by the Rev.
Peter Hall. Vol. II. The Scottish
Prayer-Book.

16mo. Bath . . . MDCCCXLVII.

ll. 2 + pp. 246. Another reprint of Laud's
Prayer Book.

1636.

80. Canons and Constitvtions Ecclesiasticall. Gathered
and put into forme, for the Government of the
Church of Scotland. . . . Published by Authoritie.

4to. Aberdene, Edward Raban. 1636.

These have been several times reprinted.

1640.

81. Constitutions and Canons Ecclesiasticall ; Treated
upon by the Archbishops of Canterbury and York,

1640.

Presidents of the Convocations . . . and the rest of the Bishops and Clergie of those Provinces ; and agreed upon with the Kings Majesties Licence in their severall Synods begun at London and York 1640 . . .

4to. London, Robert Barker . . .
and the Assignes of John Bill.

These have been many times reprinted.

1888.

82. Statutes of the University of Oxford codified in the year 1636 under the authority of Archbishop Laud . . . . Edited by the late J. Griffiths . . . with an introduction on the history of the Laudian code by C. L. Shadwell. .

4to. Oxford, Clarendon Press. 1888.

pp. xxxii + 339.

A preliminary edition was published in 1634 for use in the University during a year of probation. When the revision was finished, the new matter was inserted in MS. In 1768 an edition was published, but with the addition of matter of much later date: so that the present is the first true edition of the complete Laudian Statutes.—See Mr. Shadwell's Introduction, p. xxix ; and pp. 70, 71 *ante*.

In or about 1840 Mr. Pickering announced " Oxford University Statutes, translated by G. R. M. Ward, Esq., M.A., Vol. I, containing the Caroline Code, or Laudian Statutes promulgated A.D. 1636, 8vo." Apparently it was never published.

83. The Manner of the Coronation of King Charles the First of England at Westminster 2 Feb. 1626. [Prepared by William Laud, then Bishop of St. Davids]. Edited for the Henry Bradshaw Liturgical Text Society [Vol. ii.] by Chr. Wordsworth, M.A.

8vo. London. 1892.

pp. lxviii + 147. See Laudian Exhibition Catalogue No. 10.

B. WORKS RELATING TO ARCHBISHOP LAUD.

[Under this heading are included biographies of the Archbishop, pamphlets, speeches, letters, sermons &c. relating or referring to him, and books in which writings of his or to him are given by way of illustration.]

1637.

84. A Breife Relation Of certain speciall and most materiall passages, and speeches in the Starre-Chamber, occasioned and delivered Iune the 14th 1637. at the censure of those three worthy Gentlemen, Dr. Bastwicke, Mr. Bvrton, and Mr. Prynne, as it hath beene truely and faithfully gathered from theire owne mouths by one present at the said censure. [Ornamental device]

4to.   Printed in the Yeere 1637.

pp. 31.
Brit. Mus. 8122, e.

[Reprinted in the Harl. Misc. Vol. IV. 12 (1809)]

1638.

85. [Another Edition] . . . of Certaine speciall . . . Occasioned And delivered . . . at the Censure of . . . Dr. Bastvvicke, Mr. Burton . . . As it hath beene . . . [Different ornamental device].

4to.   Printed in the yeare 1638.

pp. 31.
Brit. Mus. 4106, a.

[Probably there are other editions of 1638.]

1638.

86. *DIVINE AND POLITIKE | OBSERVATIONS |*
Nevvly translated out of the Dutch language, wherein
they were lately divulged. | UPON | Some Lines
in the speech of the Arch. B. of Canter-
bury, pronoun- | ced in the Starre-Chamber upon
14. June, 1637. | VERY | Expedient for preventing
all prejudice, which as well through igno- | rance, as
through malice and flattery, may be incident to the
| judgement which men make thereby, either of his
Graces | power over the Church, and with the King,
or of | the Equity, Justice, and Wisdome of his
end | in his said speech, and of the reasons used |
by him for attaining to his | said end. | [Prov. 26, 28.
Ovid. l. 2. Eleg.]

> 4to. Printed in the yeare of our Lord |
> MDC,XXXVIII, [Amsterdam ?]

ll. 3 + pp. 62 + one page of errata. Doubtless not a translation, but first written in English. The title page is followed
by *The Translator's* [MS. correction in many copies "Author's"]
Dedicatory Epistle, signed Theopilus. Then follows *The Trans-*
lator to the Reader. Page 1 has, under an ornamental head-piece,
DIVINE AND POLITICALL OBSERVATIONS upon the
Arch-Bishops Epistle Dedicatory to the King, concerning his speech
in the Starre Chamber. On p. 9 the same headpiece is repeated,
with *DIVINE AND POLITICALL OBSERVATIONS upon*
the Arch-Bishops speech in the Starre Chamber.
Bodl. Lib. G. Pamph. 2289 (1).

87. [Another Edition. No titlepage, Dedication, or Preface. Page 1 has, under
the same ornamental head-piece] Divine and Politicall Observations upon
a speech pronounced by the Arch. B.
of Canter. in the Starre Chamber upon
the 14th of June, 1437 [*sic*] newly

1638.

translated out of the Dutch languague
[*sic*].   Wherein They were lately
divulged.

4to.   *s.l.* et *a.*

pp. 62 + one page of errata.   After p. 1 the tract
is the same, page by page, with No. 86, of which it
may not improbably be an *earlier* edition.
Lincoln Cathedral Library *Varia* Rr. 6. 14.

1640.

88. Articles Exhibited In Parliament Against William
Archbishop Of Canterbury [Dec. 18] 1640.

4to.   [London ?]   Printed in the
yeare 1640.

one leaf + pp. 5.
Guildhall Library, London (Catalogue p. 510).

89. Fortune's Tennis-ball . . . or, a Proviso for all
those that are elevated, to take heed of falling . . .

4to.   [London] Anno Dom. 1640.

One leaf + pp. 6.   Woodcut on titlepage.   Verses against
Abp. Laud, &c.

On p. 5. Epitaph " On our Great Bishop
W. L. A. B. C.
If anie stranger shall ask who lies here
Let his new toomb this for inscription beare.
Paint Pope and divell, make the stranger laugh ;
Mix his own shame, and there's his epitaph."

Brit. Mus. E. 160 (5). A copy in the Bodleian Library [Linc.
C. 13. 11] has a note " This is totally distinct from Rob. Baron's
' Fortune's Tennis-ball.' "

1640

90. Ladensium αὐτοκατάκρισις, The Canterbvrians Self-Conviction, Or An evident demonstration of the avowed Arminianisme, Poperie, and tyrannie of that Faction, by their owne Confessions. With a Postscript to the Personate Jesuite Lysimachus Nicanor, a prime Canterburian. [By Robert Baillie].

> 4to. s.l. [Edinburgh ?] Written in March, and printed in April 1640.

ll. 11 + pp. 128 : Postscript pp. 28. On p. 128, " Revised according to the ordinance of the generall Assembly. By Mr. A. Ihonston Clerk thereto : Edinb. 1. of Aprile 1640."

The "Postscript" is in answer to "The Epistle Congratulatorie of Lysimachus Nicanor, Of the Societie of Jesu, To the Covenanters in Scotland . . *s.l.* Anno Domini M.DC.XL [Bodl. Lib. Pamph. 39]

Brit. Mus. 855. b. 2.

91. [Another Edition.] . . the Personat Jesuite . . .

> 4to. s.l. [Amsterdam ?] Written in March, and printed in April, 1640.

ll 11 + pp. 128 + 28. This Edition is printed in entirely different type. With a table of errata, facing p. 128, not in the former edition.

Brit. Mus. 698, g. 9 (5).

1641.

92. Ladensium αὐτοκατάκρισις . . . . The Third Edition, augmented by the Author with a large Supplement. And

o2

1641.

corrected in Typographicke faults, not these onely which in a huge number did escape through negligence and ignorance that Printer at Amsterdam, but these also which in the very first Edition were but too many. Helped also in sundry Materiall Passages, wherein the Author hath received better information.

4to.   [London]   Printed for Nathaniel Bvtter 1641.

ll. 11 + pp. 131. Supplement pp. 70 + one leaf of Errata. Postscript pp. 37. Of the Supplement, which is entitled "A Large Supplement to the Canterburian Self-conviction, opening to the World, yet more of the wicked Mysteries of that Faction from their own Writs . . . Imprinted 1641," many copies appear to have been published separately [*e.g.* Bodl. Lib. 1. d. 139 (4)]

Brit. Mus. E. 168 (13).

1640.

93. A Briefe Examination ; Of a Certain Pamphlet lately Printed in Scotland, and Intituled: Ladensium Autocatacrisis, etc.

4to.   *s.l.* et *a* [1640.]

pp. 56 ; incomplete, and without separate titlepage. After the above heading it begins "There was written in *Scotland*, and directed to the high Court of the Parliament of *England*, at their last sitting, a bitter and malicious Pamphlet, in tituled," &c.

There is a note in contemporary handwriting "This Briefe

1640.

Examoñ : following was found in yᵉ Archbishops Library wher the whole Impression of these seuen sheets was found, but neither beginning nor endinge more than is herein contained. May the 11th 1644."

The British Museum Catalogue dates it 1644 : but it was doubtless being printed in 1640 under the Archbishop's own superintendence ; and owing to his removal to the Tower on Dec. 18th 1640, it was never completed, but seized together with the remainder of his effects at Lambeth.

Brit. Mus. E. 47 (7).

94. A Letter Written By a Learned and Reverent Divine, to William Laud, Now L. Bishop of Canterbury: concerning His Inclination to Popery, perswading him not to halt betweene two Opinions, but to be stedfast to the Protestant Religion.

> 4to. *s.l.* et *a.* Printed in the year of God's great & merciful deliverance from Sundry Romish and Jesuiticall plots against this State and Kingdome [1640 ?].

ll. 4. Printed in Italics. In a copy in the Bodleian Library [Pamph. 39 (12)] the " Reverent Divine " is said (in MS. hand of about 1700) to be Bp. Hall. This is most improbable, as the style does not seem to be his.

The British Museum Catalogue [E. 106 (4)] dates it [London] 1643.

95. Lord Bishops none of the Lords Bishops Or A short Discourse, wherein is proved that Prelaticall Jurisdiction, Is Not Of Divine Institution ; . .

1640.

> wherein also sundry notable passages of the Arch-
> Prelate of Canterbury in his late Booke, Intituled,
> A Relation of a Conference, &c., are by the way
> met withall . . . [By W. Prynne].

> > 4to. [London] Printed in the
> > Month of November, 1640.

ll. 43.
Brit. Mus. 4103. b. 1.

96. A Replie to a Relation, of a Conference Between
William Laude and Mr. Fisher the Jesuite. By a
Witnesse of Jesus Christ.

> > 4to. *s.l.* [Edinburgh] Imprinted,
> > Anno MDCXL.

ll. 24 + pp. 405. The "Replie to a Relation &c." was
almost certainly written by Henry Burton, the companion in
misfortune of Prynne and Bastwick.

[Reprinted in Dr. Cardwell's edition of the Conference, Oxford 1839 (No. 36)].

97.   On Wings of
                Feare Finch Flies away
                Alas Poore Will,
                Hee's forc'd to stay.

> > Broadside, folio. [London (?) 1640.]

Satirical verses on Lord Finch's flight, and Archbishop Laud's
imprisonment. Portraits of Finch and Laud.

Brit. Mus. 835. m. 9 (49).

1641.

98. Artyckelen van't Huys der Geemeente . . . tot verantwoording van hare beschuldinge tegen W. Lavd, Ertz-Bisschop van Canterbury [Dec. 8. 1640.] . . .

4to. *s.l.* et *a.* [1640-1]

ll. 4. A translation of No. 88.

99. The Accusation and Impeachment of William Laud Arch bishop of Canterbury by the House of Commons in Maintenance of the Accusations whereby he standeth charged with High-Treason.

4to. *s.l.* Printed Anno Dom. 1641.
pp. 8.

[Reprinted in Harl. Misc. IV. 574 (1809)].

100. The Charge of the Scottish Commissioners Against Canterbvrie and the Lieutenant of Ireland. Together vvith their Demand concerning the Sixt Article of the Treaty.

4to. *s.l.* [Edinburgh ?] Printed Anno Dom. MDCXLI.

One leaf + pp 38, dated at end 16 Decemb. 1640. + pp 16, dated Ian. 16th.
Bodl. Lib. Pamph. 41.

101. [Another Edition] Whereunto is added the Parliaments Resolution about the Proportion of the Scottish charges,

1641.

and the Scottish Commissioners thank-
full acceptance thereof.

4to. London, Printed for Nath.
Butter 1641.

one leaf + pp. 53.
Bodl. Lib. Linc. C. 13. 11.

[Reprinted in the Somers Tracts IV. 415 (1809).]

102. Articles Exhibited In Parliament Against William
Archbishop Of Canterbury. Feb. 25. 1640[1].
Published by a true and perfect copy.

4to. *s.l.* Printed in the yeare 1640[1].

One leaf + pp. 9. [paged 1-2 and 9-15].
Bodl. Lib. Pamph. 39 (14).

103. A Seasonable Speech by sir Nathaniel Coppinger,
spoken in the high court of Parliament Oct. 24.
1641, for bringing the Archbishop of Canterbury
to his long expected tryall; and concerning the
expulsion of Papists . . .

4to. London . . . 1641.

ll. 3.

104. Fovre. [*sic*] Speeches made by Sr Edward Deering
in the high Court of Parliament. Concerning the
Arch-Bishop and divers other Grievances.

4to. London, Printed for Francis
Coles, 1641.

one leaf + pp. 14.
Brit. Mus. E. 196 (18).

1641.

105. Three Speeches, made by' Sir Iohn VVray, To the House of Commons, assembled in Parliament. 1 Against Thomas Earl of Strafford, and the Bishop of Canterbury. 2 Being a motion for the taking of an oath to maintaine the Religion and vowes established. 3 Against the Oath and Canons made by the Assembly at the last Convocation.

4to. London Printed, 1641.

pp. 8.

Brit. Mus. 100. a. 56.

106. Eight Occasionall Speeches, made in the house of Commons this Parliament, 1641. 1. Concerning Religion . . . 5. Vpon the impeachment of the Lord Strafford, and Canterbury &c. . . . By Sir Iohn Wray Knight and Barronet.

4to. London. Printed for Francis Constable, 1641.

one leaf + pp. 13.

Brit. Mus. E. 196 (10).

107. Mr. Grymston's Speech in Parliament upon The Accusation and Impeachment of William Laud Arch-Bishop of Canterbury, upon high Treason. Declaring his wicked proceedings, and exorbitant power, both in Church and Commonwealth.

4to. *s.l.* Printed in the Yeare 1641.

One leaf + pp. 5. The author was afterwards Sir H. Grimstone Bart.

Bodl. Lib. Linc. C. 13. 11.

1641.

108. The Speech or Declaration of John Pymm, Esq.
To the Lords of the upper House upon the delivery
of the Articles of the Commons assembled in Parliament against W. Lavd Archbishop of Canterbury, in maintenance of their Accusation, whereby
he stands charged with High Treason. Together
With a true Copy of the said Articles.

4to. London. Printed for Ralph
Mabb. 1641.

One leaf + pp. 34.
Bodl. Lib. Ashm. 1003. 15.

109. De Oratie . . . van Iohn Pym Esquire, Ghedaen
. . . op het overleveren van d'Artijckelen vande
[*sic*] Gemeenten . . . teghens William Laud . . .
4to.   Amsterdam 1641

ll. 6.
Brit. Mus. 8122. ee. 1 (7).

110. A Speech of the Right Honourable Lord Viscount
Say and Seele . . . In Answer to the Lord Archbishop of Canterburies last Speech, and concerning
the Liturgie of the Church of England.

4to. *s.l.*   Anno Domini 1641.

One leaf + pp. 8.

111. All to Westminster: Or, Newes from Elizium or
A Packet of Wonders, brought over in Charon's
Ferry-Boat last Spring Tyde . . . . .

4to. [London] 1641.

pp. 6.   Portrait of Laud on frontispiece. A satire on the
Bishops.

1641.

112. Archy's Dream, sometimes Iester to his Maiestie ;
but exiled the Court by Canterburie's malice.
With a relation for whom an odde chaire stood
voide in Hell.

> 4to. *s.l.* Printed in the yeare 1641.

ll. 4. Woodcut on titlepage of Archy in bed.
Bodl Lib. Wood 366 (31).

[Reprinted in Ashbee's occasional Fac-simile
Reprints, No II. (4to. London, 1868). And in
Hindley's Miscellanea Antiqua, Vol. iii. No. 16.]

113. The Organ's Eccho. To the Tune of the Cathedrall Service.

> 4to. Printed in the year 1641.

ll. 2. Twelve satirical verses on Laud. With two small
woodcuts.
Brit. Mus. Rox. III. 573.

114. The Organ's Eccho. To the Tune of the
Cathedrall Service.

> Broadside, folio. *s.l.* Printed in the
> yeere 1641.

In verse, with two woodcuts.
Brit. Mus. 669. f. 4 (32).

115. [Another Edition]

> Broadside, folio. *s.l.* Printed in the
> yeere 1641.

With different woodcuts, and a few verbal
differences.
Brit. Mus. Catalogue of Prints, &c. Div. I.
vol. i. No. 186.

[Reprinted in Wilkins's *Political Ballads* (2 vols.
8vo. 1860)].

1641.

116. A Rot Amongst the Bishops, or, A Terrible Tempest in the Sea of Canterbury, Set forth in lively Emblems to please the judicious Reader. By Tho: Stirry.

4to.   London, R. O. & G. D.
MDCXLI.

ll. 3 + pp. 9.   Rough woodcuts.   A Satire in Verse.

1838.

117. [The Same.]   Reprinted with facsimiles of titlepage and woodcuts, by C. Castle, 82 Fetter Lane.

12mo. London [1838].

pp. 14.

1641.

118. A Discovery of the Notorious Proceedings of William Laud, Archbishop of Canterbury, in bringing Innovations into the Church, & raising up Troubles in the State; his pride in riding in his Coach when the King himselfe went along on foot, and being reproved, would not alight.   With his tyrannicall government both in himselfe and his Agents.   Confessed by John Brown [S. J.] a Prisoner in the Gatehouse, twice examined by a Committee of six from the Honourable House of Commons.   And now brought to view of the world, October 15. 1641.

4to.   London, Henry Walker 1641.

ll. 4.

Brit. Mus. E. 172 (37).

119. A New Discovery of the Prelates Tyranny, in their late Persecutions of Mr William Pryn, an eminent lawyer, Dr John Bastwick, a learned physician,

1641.

and Mr Henry Burton, a reverend divine.   By William Prynne, of Lincoln's Inn, Esquire.

4to.   Printed at London for M. S. 1641.

pp. 48 + 226.   With portraits of Laud, Prynne, Bastwick, and Burton.

Brit. Mus. E. 162 (1).

120. The Archbishops Crueltie, Made knowne in a true Story of one Mr Edward Rood, who was Minister at Saint Helens in Abingdon . . . .   By Giles Gulter, Batchelour of Arts.

4to. *s.l.*   Printed Anno Domini 1641.

ll. 4.

Brit. Mus. E. 166 (4).

121. A Briefe Recitall Of the unreasonable proceedings of Dr. Laud against T. W. Minister of the Word of God; which he conveyed into his hands in a Letter very lately sent to him in the Tower.   To- gether with his absurd answer to the same.   Pub- lished to the World for the honour of his Grace.

4to.   London,   Printed by E. G. for Henry Overton . . 1641.

one leaf + pp. 5.

Brit. Mus. 4103. c.

122. Reader, Here you'l plainly see Judgement per- verted by these three à Priest, a Judge, a Pa- tentee.   Written by Thomas Heywood.

4to. *s.l.*   Printed in the happy yeere of Grace 1641.

With curious woodcut of Abp. Laud, Lord Finch, and Alder- man Abel, which was more than once reprinted in other tracts.

Brit. Mus. E. 171. 2.

1641.

123. England's Rejoycing at the Prelat's Downfall.

> 4to. England, printed in the yeare
> of the Down-falle of the Prelats
> 1641.

ll. 4.
Bodl. Lib. Linc. A. 10. 21.

124. The Lordly Prelate, or Receipts how to recover
a lost Bishop.

> 4to. London 1641.

With portrait.
Lowndes, *Bibl. Manual*, p. 1318.

125. [Another Edition] The Lordly Prelate.
Being, Diverse experimentall receits,
how to recover a Bishop if he were
lost. Written for the satisfaction of
after times, should they desire to recall, what we labour to reject.

> 4to. *s.l.* Printed in the yeare 1641.

ll. 4. With portrait.
Hazlitt, *Bibliographical Collections* iii. 437.

126. The Recantation Of the Prelate of Canterbury:
Being his last Advice to his Brethren the Bishops
of England: To consider his Fall, observe the
Times, forsake their Wayes, and to joyne in this
good work of Reformation . . .

> 4to.   London, Printed 1641.

ll. 2 + pp. 41. Woodcut portrait of Laud falling.
Bodl. Lib. Wood 366 (27).

1641.

127. A True Description, or Rather a Parallel between Cardinall Wolsey, Arch-Bishop of York, And William Laud, Arch-Bishop of Canterbury.

4to. s.l.   Printed in the Yeare 1641.

pp. 8.   See No. 133.

This tract has been attributed to John Milton.   See No. 252. An Edition of Cavendish's Life of Wolsey was published in 1641 [Brit. Mus. E. 166 (14)], with an Advertisement to the Reader that " Who pleaseth to reade this History advisedly may well perceive the immutability of honour, the tottering state of earthly Dignity, the deceit of faltering friends, and the instability of Princes favours."

[Reprinted also in Harl. Misc. IV. 507 (1809), Somers Tracts IV. 431 (1810); and Cavendish's Life of Wolsey II. 231 (Chiswick 1825)].

128. The Bishop's Potion, Or, A Dialogue between the Bishop of Canterbury, and his phisitian, wherein He desireth the Doctor to have a care of his Bodie, and to preserve him from being let blood in the neck, when the signe is in Taurus.

4to. London, Printed 1641.

One leaf + pp. 4.   Woodcut of Laud and Physician. Bodl. Lib. Wood 366. 22.

[Reprinted in the Harl. Misc. VI. 278 (1810)].

129. [Another Edition]. . . . A Dialogue betweene . . . , when the signe is in Paulus. [*sic*]

Broadside, folio. s.l. Printed in the Yeer 1641.

1641.

130. Canterburies Amazement : or The Ghost of the
yong fellow Thomas Bensted, who was Drawne,
Hangd, and Quartered by the meanes of the
Bishop of Canterburie ; who appeared to him in
the Tower, since the Iesuites execution. With
a discourse between the two Heads on London
Bridge, the one being Thomas Bensteeds [*sic*] , the
other the late Iesuites.

4to. [London] Printed for F. Coules
in the Yeare 1641.

pp. 8. Black Letter. Woodcut of Bensted appearing to
Laud on titlepage, and of Bensted's Execution on p. 6.
Brit. Mus. G. 20078.

131. A new Play Called Canterbury His Change of
Diot. Which showeth variety of wit and mirth :
privately acted neare the Palace-yard at Westminster.

In the

1 Act, the Bishop of Canterbury having
variety of dainties, is not satisfied till
he be fed with the tippets of mens
eares.

2 Act, he hath his nose held to the Grinde-
stone.

3 Act, he is put into a bird Cage with the
Confessor.

4 Act, The Jester tells the King the Story.

4to. [London] Printed Anno
Domini 1641.

ll. 4. Three woodcuts (one repeated).
Brit. Mus. E. 177 (8).

[Reprinted in Ashbee's occasional Fac-simile Reprints No. xv.]

1641.

132. Canterburies Conscience convicted : Or, His dangerous projects, and evill intents, tending to the subversion of Religion detected : as also some particulars of those Treasons whereof he is now attained, lying prisoner in the Tower this present. 1641. To the tune of All ye that cry, O hone, O hone ; or The Wandring Souldier.

Broadside folio. *s.l.* 1641.

In verse. With three Woodcuts, one being taken from " Rome for Canterbury " (No. 158.)

133. Canterbvries Dreame : In which the Apparition of Cardinall Wolsey did present himselfe unto him on the fourtenth of May last past : It being The third night after my Lord of Strafford had taken his fare-well to the World.

4to. [London] Printed in the yeare 1641.

ll. 4.
Bodl. Lib. Pamph. 44.

134. England's Glory in her Royall King and Honorable Assembly in the High Court of Parliament, above her former Usurped Lordly Bishop's Synod, with a Discourse betwixt Mr John Calvin and a Prelaticall Bishop, whereunto is added the Bishop of Canterburies Dreame.

4to. *s.l.* Printed in the Yeare 1641.

ll. 10.
Brit. Mus. E. 157 (9).

P

1641.

135. Farewell Myter or, Canterburies Meditations. And Wrenn's Syllogismes. Also, The Divels moane for the discontent of his Servants and Assistants, and his Epitaphs upon each of their Burials. Together with His Chronicles for their hereafter Memories, inserted the 12. day of the moneth Tridemiter, according to the Infernall collateration. peccandi. An. Dom. MDCCCXCV (*sic*) . . . By Richard Newrobe.

> 4to. Printed for William Larnar, in the Yeare, 1641.

one leaf + pp. 6.
Brit. Mus. E. 134 (33).

136. Canterbvries Pilgrimage : In the Testimony of an accused Consjenc [e] For the Bloud of Mr Burton, Mr Prynne, and Doctor Bastwicke. And the just deserved Sufferings he lyes under : Shewing the Glory of Reformation, above Prelaticale Tyranny. Wherein is laid open, the reallity of the Scottish Nation with the Kingdome of England.

> 4to. London, for H. Walker. 1641.

ll. 4. With Woodcut.
Brit. Mus E. 172 (28).

137. A Canterbury Tale, translated out of Chaucer's old English, into our now vsvall language. Whereunto is added the Scots Pedler. Newly enlarged by A.B.

> 4to. London . . . 1641.

pp. 4. Satirical verses against Laud and the Bishops.
Brit. Mus. E. 168 (5). See Laudian Exhibition Catalogue No. 65.

1641.

188. Canterburies Tooles : or, Instruments wherewith he hath effected many rare feats, and egregious exploits, as is very well known, and notoriously manifest to all men. Discovering his projects and policies, and the ends and purposes of the Prelates in effecting their facinorous actions and enterprises.

4to. s.l. et a. [1641 ?]

One leaf + pp. 6. With Woodcut.
Dated 1642 in Bodl. Lib. Catalogue [G. Pamph. 2289 (2).]

139. Canterbury's Will. With A Serious Conference betweene His Scrivener and Him. Also A loving Admonition to his Brethren the Bishops.

4to. [London] Printed in the yeere 1641.

pp. 8. Woodcut portrait of Laud.
Brit. Mus. E. 156 (5).

140. The discontented Conference betwixt the two great Associates, William Archbishop of Canterbury and Thomas late Earle of Strafford.

4to. [London] Printed in the Yeere 1641.

ll. 2. In verse.
Brit. Mus. E. 157 (3).

141. The Discontented Conference betwixt the two great Associates, Thomas late

1641.

Earle of Strafforde and William Archbishop of Canterbury.

Broadside, folio. [London]
Printed in the Yeare, of our
Prelates feare 1641.

With Woodcuts of Laud and Strafford on titlepage.
Brit. Mus. Lutt. II. 47.

[Reprinted in the Somers Tracts Vol. IV. 268
(1810)].

142. A Reasonable Motion In The behalfe of such of the
Clergie, As are now questioned in Parliament for
their places. Together with the Conference
betwixt the two great Associates William] aud
Arch-bishop of Canterbury, and Thomas late Earle
of Strafford.

4to. *s.l.* Printed in the unfortunate
Yeare to Priests 1641.

ll. 4. Woodcuts of Laud and Strafford on titlepage.
Bodl. Lib. Linc. C. 13. 14.

143. The Deputies Ghost; or An Apparition to the
Lord of Canterbury in the Tower. With his
complaint unto the wall after the Ghosts departure.
Being an Acrostick Anagramme of his Name.

Broadside, folio [London] Printed
in the yeare of our Prelates
feare 1641.

Woodcuts of Laud and the Ghost at the head.
Bodl. Lib. Ashm. H. 23 (31)

1641.

144. An exact Copy Of A Letter sent to William Laud, late Arch-bishop of Canterbury, now Prisoner in the Tower, November the 5th 1641, at which his Lordship taking exceptions, the Author Visited him in his owne person, had some private discourse with him, concerning the cruelty in which he formerly raigned in his power, the substance whereof is truly composed by the Author himself, wherein doth appeare a Sign of Complying with thè times and some hopes of his Repentance. [Signed A].

4to. London, Printed for H. W.
and T. B. 1641.

ll 4. Black Letter. Portraits of Laud and the Author on the titlepage.
Brit. Mus. E. 177 (1).

145. A Christian Admonition to Arbp. Laud in the Tower.

4to. London. *s.a.* [1641 ?]

In verse. With Portrait.
Lowndes, *Bibl. Manual* p. 1317.

146. The Copie of a Letter sent From VVilliam Lavd Arch bishop of Canterbury the 28 of June MDCXLI. unto the Universitie of Oxford: Specifying, His Willingnesse to resigne his Chancellor-ship, And withall deploring his sad estate now in the time of his Imprisonment.

4to. [Oxford ?]. Printed in the
yeare, 1641.

One'leaf + pp. 2. With Arms and Ac: Ox: on titlepage.
The letter is printed in *History of his Chancellorship* (*Works* V.

1641.

298 f), in a slightly different text: but it is undoubtedly a
forgery, the work of some person who had seen the real letter
(No. 40.)

Brit. Mus. E. 164. (1).

147. [Another Edition.]

4to.   *s.l.*   1641.

One leaf + pp 2.   With   portrait of Laud
on title page instead of the Arms.   The text of
the letter is slightly different from No. 14*f*, and
from that in the *History of his Chancellorship.*
See Laud's *Works,* V. 289 n.

148. Mercuries Message, or The Coppy of a Letter sent to William Laud late Archbishop of Canterbury, now prisoner in the Tower . . .

4to. [London] Printed in the yeare,
of our Prelates feare 1641.

ll 4.   In verse, with woodcut portrait of Laud on titlepage.
In a note on a Copy of *Mercuries Message Defended* in the
Bodleian Library [Bliss 1. 2614. c], the author is said to be
S. W. H. Ireland Junr.

[Probably there are other editions of this year.]

149. An Answer to the most Envious, Scandalous, and Libellous Pamphlet, Entituled Mercuries Message. Or, The Copy of a Letter sent to William Laud Arch bishop of Canterbury now prisoner in the Tower.

4to. London 1641.

one leaf + pp. 6.   With curious woodcut portrait of Laud
on title.   Signed Tho. Herbert.

Bodl. Lib. Wood 366 (24).   Laudian   Exhibition Catalogue
No. 65.

1641.

150. The Same [Another Edition].

4to. London 1641.

one leaf + pp. 6. With woodcut portrait on back of titlepage, its place on titlepage being taken by a hand holding a knife.

Bodl. Lib. Bliss 1. 2614. b.

151. Mercuries Message Defended, Against the vain, foolish, simple, and absurd cavils of Thomas Herbert a ridiculous Ballad-maker. Wherein his witless answers are clearly confuted, himselfe found guilty of Hypocrisie, catcht broaching of Popery, condemned by his owne words, and here and there for his impudent saucinesse jerkt with the Rod of Correction, to teach him more manners when he writes again. By the Author of the said Mercuries Message.

4to. London, printed 1641.

One leaf + pp. 22. Woodcut of Laud in prison, with Herbert being hanged outside, on titlepage.

Bodl. Lib. Bliss 1. 2614. c.

152. A Second Message to Mr. William Lavd Late Arch bishop of Canterbury, now prisoner in the Tower: In the behalfe of Mercurie. Together With a Postscript to the Author of that foolish and ridiculous Answer to Mercury.

4to. *s.l.* 1641.

ll. 4. Woodcut portrait of Laud on titlepage.

1641.

153. Old Newes Newly Revived: Or, The discovery of all occurrences happened since the beginning of the Parliament: As, the confusion of Patents, the Deputies Death, Canterburies imprisonment. . . .

4to. *s.l.* Printed in the yeare 1641.

ll. 4. Woodcut on titlepage with many figures, including Laud and [Judge] Barkley [in the] Lo[wer] Tower.
Brit. Mus. E. 160 (22).

154. A plot lately discovered for the taking of the Tower, by Negromancie, For the deliverance of the Archbishop, discovered by a Mathematician in Southwarke. Who after some serious debate with himself revealed the Conspiracie to many eminent men. For which thirty Papists most inhumanely beset his house, and pursued him as far as Lambred upon Trent, where they most barberously murdered him; some are taken, & lie in hold, to the mercy of Justice.

4to. London 1641.

One leaf + pp. 5.
Brit. Mus. 8122. c.

155. Read and Wonder: A Warre betweene two entire Friends, The Pope and the Divell.

4to. 1641.

In verse.
Lowndes, *Bibl. Manual* p. 1317.

156. The Pope's Benediction, or His generall pardon onely to be purchased with money without penance,

1641.

sent into England by Ignatius Holy-Water, a
Jesuit, to the Arch-Bishop of Canterbury and to
the rest of his subjects there.

4to.   London 1641.

One leaf + pp. 6.   Two satirical cuts.
Brit. Mus. E. 158, (15)

157. Romes A B C, being a short Perambulation, Or
Rather articular Accusation Of a late tyrannicall
Oppressour.   With A Petition to the Archbishop
of Canterbury, now prisoner in the Tower.

4to. *s.l.* Printed in the yeare 1641.

One leaf + pp. 6.   Woodcut portrait of Laud.
Brit. Mus. E. 156 (15).

158. Rome for Canterbury: Or a true Relation of the
Birth, and Life, of William Laud, Arch-bishop of
Canterbury: Together with the whole manner of
his proceeding, both in the Star-Chamber, High-
commission Court, in his owne House, and some
Observations of him in the Tower.   With his
carriage at the sight of the Deputyes going to the
place of Execution, &c.   Dedicated to all the
Arminian Tribe, or Canterburian Faction, in the
yeare of grace 1641.   Whereunto is added all the
Articles by which he stands charged of High
Treason . . . .

4to. *s.l.* Printed also in the same.
1641.

pp. 8.   The first six pages in Black Letter, the rest (con-

1641.

taining the Articles against Laud) in italics. Woodcut of Laud, on the road from Canterbury to Rome.

According to Hazlitt (*Handbook* p. 328) three editions were published in this year.

Brit. Mus. E. 208 (10).

[Reprinted in Harl. Misc. iv. 377 (1809)]

159. Ruymbaen voor Canterberg, ofte Een waerachtich Verhael van d'afkomste ende 't leben van William Laud, Aerts-Bisschop van Canterberg . . .

4to. *s.l.* Ghedruckt na d'Engelsche Coppe 1641.

ll. 4. A translation of the above.
Brit. Mus. 8122. ee. 1 (14).

160. Lambeth Faire, VVherein you have all the Bishops Trinkets set to sale.

4to. [London] Pr. Anno Dom. 1641.

ll. 6. In verse, with woodcut of the Pope falling from S. Peter's Chair.
Guildhall Library, London (Catalogue p. 504). Brit. Mus. E. 158 (21).

161. [The Same.] Another Edition, with a different frontispiece.

4to. [London] 1641.

Hazlitt *Handbook*, p. 327.

1642.

162. [Another Edition.]   Lambeth Faire :
Wherein the Bishop's Trinkets are
set to sale.

Broadside, folio. [London] 1642.

With woodcuts.
Bodl. Lib. Ashm. H. 23. xxix.

1641.

163. Lambeth Faire's Ended, Or A Description of the
Bishops Holy Ghost lately set to sale at Lambeth
Faire.

4to. [London] Printed in the
yeare 1641.

one leaf + pp. 6. In verse. With woodcut on the titlepage.
Guildhall Library, London. M. 4. 5.

1642.

164. New Lambeth Fayre Newly Consecrated and
Presented by the Pope himselfe, Cardinals, Bishops, Jesvits, &c.   Wherein all Romes Reliques
are set at sale, With the old Fayre corrected and
enlarged, Opening and Vending the Whole Mis-
tery of Iniquity.   By Richard Overton.   With
remarkable Annotations declaring under what
Pope, and in what yeere of our Lord every Relique
and Ceremonie came into the Church.

4to. London Printed by R. O.
and G. D. 1642.

ll. 8.

1642.

165. The Bishops Last Good Night.

> Broadside, folio.   London   Printed
> in the yeer that ended | When the
> Prelates Protestation against the
> Parliament was vended | And they
> were sent to the Tower, as the
> old yeer ended, | By a dozen to-
> gether, | In frosty weather. Anno
> Dom. 1642. |

With two woodcuts, one of Laud, Bishops and citizens, the other of the Pope, and a " Jesuit, Fryer, and Papist." Followed by fourteen verses, the second being

> " *Canterbury* your Armes from the Steeple high,
> The stormes have caused low to lie,
> You know not how soone your selfe may die,
> > Prepare your selfe *Canterbury ;*
> > Down must *Canterbury.*

Brit. Mus. 669. f. 4 (61).

166. A Copie of a Letter VVritten from his Holinesse Court at Rome, to his Grace of Canterburies Palace now in the Tower.   Deploring his Sequestration from his Liberty, but commending him for his late care in performing his Holinesse desires.

> 4to. London, Printed 1642.

One leaf + pp. 4.
Brit. Mus. E. 133 (9).

167. A Letter Sent from the Arch-Bishop of Canterbvry (Now prisoner in the Tower) To the Vice-Chan-cellor, Doctors, and the rest of the Convocation at Oxford, Intimating his humble desires to His

1642.

Majesty, for a speedy reconcilement between Him and His High Court of Parliament. Ordered to be printed,

4to, First at Oxford by Leonard Lichfield, and now reprinted at London for Edward Vere, *s.a.*

pp. 8. This letter is a forgery, written to advance the interests of the Parliament by making it appear that Laud had given up his principles. As the King is said to be at Oxford its date is probably late in 1642; but doubtless no edition of it ever appeared in Oxford.

Dr. Bliss had not seen this edition, but declared against the genuineness of the letter. [Laud's *Works* VI. 596 *note*].

In a volume in the Brit. Museum [E. 8$\frac{3}{3}$] three tracts are bound up together, among many more (Nos. 26-28) : A Declaration of His Maiesties Royall Pleasvre ; A Letter sent from the Arch-Bishop of Canterbvry ; and A Speech Spoken by His Excellence Prince Rupert. They are all forgeries, printed at the same time and place, for political purposes. A note in a nearly contemporary handwriting, at the end of No. 26, says "These are Charged upon Coll. Hurry" ; and they are dated, in the same hand, Decemb. 27, Decemb. 29, and Decemb. 29 respectively.

168. The Organs Funerall or the Quiristers Lamentation for the Abolition of Superstition and Superstitious Ceremonies. In a Dialogicall Discourse between a Quirister and an Organist *An. Dom.* 1642.

4to. London, Printed for George Kirby. *s.a.*

ll. 4. Chiefly in prose, but with 4 four-line stanzas at the end, some referring to the Archbishop.

Hazlitt, *Handbook* p. 328.

1642.

169. Qvatermayns Conqvest over Canterbvries Covrt.·
Or A Briefe Declaration of severall Passages
between him and the Archbishop of Canterbury,
with other Commissioners of the High Commission
Court, at six severall appearances before them,
and by them directed to Doctor Featly; with their
severall Conferences; and the Doctors Reports to
the Court. As also his imprisonment . . . . With
his appearance before the Lords of the Councell
. . . . As also his tryall three severall Sessions
. . . . And lastly, A Prayer, and Thanksgiving,
in an acknowledgement of GOD's mercy in his
Deliverance. By Roger Quartermayne.

> 4to. London, Printed by Thomas
> Paine for Roger Quartermayne
> 1642.

ll. 8 + pp. 39 + 4. Portrait of Laud falling, as in the
Recantation (No. 126).
Bodl. Lib. 110. j. 77.

170. Vox Populi in Plaine English

> Broadside, folio *s.l.* MDCXLII. A
> Present for this New yeare of
> the Prelates feare. Finis.

With verses against Archbishop Laud and others; two
woodcuts, one of a monk and the devil, the other of three
ecclesiastics. Of these, one holds the Bible, the second
the Service Book, the third, who is Archbishop Laud, holds
a book labelled Supersticion. [This woodcut is to be found
also in "Triple Episcopacie" (1642) and "The Apprentices
Advice to the xii Bishops" (1642)].

The title is taken from a tract "Vox Populi, Expressed in
xxxv. Motions to this Present Parliament." *s.l.* 1641.

1643.

171. Een Brief des Aerts-Bisschops van Cantelbergh,
(regenwoordigh gevangen inden Tour van Londen.)
Aen den Vice-Cancelier, ende de rest vande Con-
vocatie tot Oxford . . in onse Nederlandtsche
tale . . overgheset..

> 4to. Ghedruckt t'Amsterdam by
> Joost Broersz . . 1643.

ll. 4. A translation of No. 167.
Bodl. Lib. Arch. B. 2. 200.

172. A Speech concerning the Bishop of Canterburies
Petition deliverd to the High Court of Parliament,
February the 22. 1642 [3].

> 4to. [London] 1642 [3].

173. An Ordinance of the Lords and Commons . . .
Concerning the Arch-Bishop of Canterbury, who
by reason of many great and 'weighty businesses,
cannot as yet be brought to his Tryall.

> 4to. London May 19. Printed
> for Iohn Wright, in the Old
> Bailey 1643.

ll. 2.
Hazlitt, *Bibl. Collections* iii. 137.

174. An Ordinance Of The Lords and Commons
Assembled in Parliament. That all the Temporall
Livings, Dignities, and Ecclesiasticall Promotions
belonging unto William, Lord Arch-bishoppe of .
Canterbury, be forthwith Sequestered by and unto

1643.

the Parliament . . . . Die Sabbathi, 10. Junii,
1643 . . .

4to. Iune 13. Printed for Iohn
Wright in the Old-Bailey. 1643.

ll. 4.
Brit. Mus. E. 105 (29).

175. The Copy of the Petition presented to the Honourable Houses of Parliament, by the Lord Arch-
Bishop of Canterbury. . . . Wherein the said
Arch-Bishop desires that he may not be trans-
ported beyond the Seas into New England with
Master Peters, in regard to his extra-ordinary age
& weaknesse.

4to. London, printed for Io. Smith,
neare the new exchange 1642 (*sic*).

ll. 4. Woodcut portrait of Laud. Signed, From the
Tower of London this 6th of May 1643. Of course it is a
forgery.
Brit. Mus. E. 100 (29).

176. The Copy of a Letter from Alisburg Directed to
Colonell Hampden, Colonell Goodwin, and read
in Both Houses of Parliament, May 18, 1643,
relating how his Majesty hath sent 12 or 1400 of
his Forces, under the Command of Earle of Cleve-
land . . . into those parts, . . . With an Ordinance concerning the Arch-Bishop of Canterbury.
[By John Wittewrong and Thomas Tyrril].

4to. Printed for John Wright in
the Old Bailey 1643.

ll. 4. Black Letter.
Brit. Mus. E. 102 (15)

1643.

177. A new Disputation betweene the two Lordly
Bishops, Yorke and Canterbvry. With a Discourse of many passages which have happened to
them before and since that they were committed
to the Tower. . . . Written in English Prose by
L. P. February the second 1642 [3].

> 12mo. London Printed for J.
> Wright 1642 [3].

ll. 2 + pp. 11. With portraits : that which does duty for
"Yorke" served as "Canterbvry" in the "Answer to Mercuries Message " (No. 149) : it is likewise printed on the titlepage of "A Copy of the Proceedings of some worthy and
learned Divines . . ." London 1641. [Bodl. Lib. Pamph.
41. p. 135.]
Brit. Mus. E. 1113 (2).

178. The Life of William Now Lord Arch-Bishop of
Canterbvry, Examined. Wherein his principall
Actions, or Deviations in matters of Doctrine and
Discipline since he came to the sea of Canterbury
are traced, and set downe, as they were taken
from good hands, by Mr Robert Bayley, a Learned
Pastor of the Kirk of Scotland, and one of the late
Commissioners sent from that nation. Very fitting
for all judicious men to reade, and examine, that
they may be the better able to censure him for
those thing (*sic*) wherein he hath done amisse.
Read & judge.

> 4to. London Printed for N. B.
> in the Yeare of Grace 1643.

ll. 11 + pp. 131.
Brit. Mus. E. 72 (3).

1643.

179. The Pope's Nuntioes: or, the Negotiation of
Seignior Panzani, Seignior Con, &c, resident here
in England with the Queen, and treating about
the alteration of Religion with the Archbishop of
Canterbury in the years 1634, 1635, 1636 . . . .

4to. London 1643.

[Reprinted in Somers Tracts IV. (1810)] .

180. Den Brittannischen Morgen-wecker, ofte Getrouwe
waerschouwinghe van Roomens argh-listigh des-
sein, om Engelandt Paepsch te maken. Blijckende
uyt de onderhandelinge tusschen Seignior Panzani
ende Seignior Cunaeus . . . ende den' Arch-
Bisschop van Cantelberge . . . .

4to. Vrystadt [Amsterdam?] 1643.

ll, 2 + pp. 18.   A translation of the preceding.
Brit. Mus. 8122. ee. 2 (22).

1688.

181. [The Same.]   Op nieuws herdruckt.

4to. Vrystadt [Amsterdam?] 1688.

1643.

182. The English Pope, Or, A Discourse Wherein The
late mysticall Intelligence betwixt the Court of
England and the Court of Rome is in part discovered.
And withall, An Account given of the true Grounds
of this unnatural and more than civill Warre.

1643.

Together With an Epistle to the Reverend Divines now convened by Authority of Parliament . .

4to.   London, Printed for Robert Bostock . . 1643.

ll. 2 + pp. 36.
Bodl. Lib. Th. 4° p. 82.

183. Den Enghelschen Paus, ofte Een Politijck Discours: Waer-in De heymelicke Onderhandelinge, ende't verborghen Verstandt, tusschen het Hof van Enghelandt, ende't Hoff van Roomen, ten deelen ontdeckt is . . .

4to. *s.l.* 20^{en} November 1643.

pp. 40.   A translation of the preceding.   Woodcut portrait of Laud on titlepage.
Brit. Mus. 8122, ee. 2 (21).

184. Rome's Master-Peece.   Or, The Grand Conspiracy of the Pope and his Iesuited Instruments, to extirpate the Protestant Religion, re-establish Popery, subvert Lawes, Liberties, Peace, Parliaments, by kindling Civill War in Scotland, and all his Majesties Realmes, and to poyson the King himselfe in case he comply not with them in these their execrable designes.   Revealed out of Conscience to Andreas ab Habernfeld, by an Agent sent from Rome into England, by Cardinal Barbarino, as an Assistant to Con the Pope's late Nuncio, to prosecute this most Execrable Plot, (in which he persisted a principall Actor for severall yeares) who discovered it to Sir William Boswell his Majesties Agent at the Hague, 6 Septem. 1640.   He under an Oath of Secrecie, to

1643.

the Arch-Bishop of Canterbury (among whose
papers it was casually found by Master Prynne,
May, 31. 1643) who communicated it to the King,
As the greatest businesse that ever was put to
him . . . .

4to.   Printed at London for Michael
Sparke Senior 1643.

One leaf + pp. 36 + 1.

A copy of this tract, with Archbishop Laud's notes, is
printed by Wharton in the *History of the Troubles and Trial*,
pp. 569-606.   [Reprinted in Laud's *Works* IV. 463 ff]

Bodl. Lib. G. Pamph. 1053(7)

185. Roomsch Meester-stuck.   Ofte De Groote Con-
spiratie van den Paus, ende sijne Jesuijtsche In-
strumenten, tot uyt-roeyinge van de Protestantsche
Religie. . . . .

4to. *s.l.* et *a.* 1643.

pp. 38.   A translation of the preceding.

Bodl. Lib. Godw. Pamph. 1355 (5).

1644.

186. Articles of the Commons assembled in Parliament,
In Maintenance of their Accusation, against Wil-
liam Laud Archbishop of Canterbury, whereby he
stands charged with high Treason.   Also, Further
Articles of Impeachment by the Commons in
Parliament, Against the said Arch-bishop of Can-
terbury, of high Treason, and divers high Crimes
& Misdemeanours . . .

4to.   Jan. 19.   Printed for John
Wright in the Old-bailey 1643 [4] .

One leaf + pp. 14.   Black Letter.

Brit. Mus. E. 29. (15).

[Reprinted in Harl. Misc. IV. (1809)] .

1644.

187. Articvlen van't Huys der Gemeente in't Parlement
van Engelandt vergadert, Tot mainteneringe van
haer beschuldinghe tegens William Laud, Aertz-
Bisschop van Canterbury, . . . Item, noch
verdere Articulen van beschuldinge door't selve
Huys der Ghemeente, teghens de voorsz. Aertz-
Bisschop van Canterbury. . . .

> 4to. Amsterdam, Ghedruckt by
> Joost Broerz. na de Copije van
> Londen, by John Wright. Den
> 13 Februarii, 1644 [N.S.]

ll. 5. A translation of the preceding.
Brit. Mus. 8122. ee. 2 (38).

188. [Another Edition.] Artyckelen Van't
Huys der Gemente Vergadert in't Parlement, Tot verantwoording van hare
beschuldinge Tegen Willem Lavd,
Ertz-Bisschop van Canterbury, Waer
in hy aengheklaeght wert van't Huys
ger Gemeente, van hoogh verract,
Crimen ende misdaden, Naer de Copye
van Londen, gedruckt voor John
Wright inde olde Bayley, ende nu
voor Jan van Hilten.

> 4to. *s.l.* et *a.*

ll. 4.
Brit. Mus. 8122. ee. 1 (7).

189. The Bishop of Canterbury His Confession.
Wherein is declared his constant Resolution, his
Plots, and indeavours, to intraduce Popery into
England, and to advance the Roman Catholick
Religion. Being from his owne hand, sent and

1644.

directed to the Popes Holinesse. Expressing to
his Holinesse his sorrow for the unhappy successe,
and failing of all his labours and endeavours, for
the Avancement of Popery.

4to. London, Printed in the Yeare
1644.

One leaf + pp. 6.

In the copy in the British Museum [E. 31 (9)] the date is
altered in a contemporary handwriting to 1643.

190. A Breviate of the Life, Of William Laud Archbishop of Canterbury: Extracted for the most
part Verbatim, out of his owne Diary, and other
Writings, under His owne Hand. Collected and
published at the speciall Instance of sundry Honourable Persons, as a necessary Prologue to the
History of His Tryall; for which the Criminall
part of His Life is specially reserved. By William
Prynne of Lincolnes Inne, Esquier.

folio.   London F. L. for Michael
Sparke Senior, and are to be
sold at the Blew-Bible in Green
Arbour 1644.

ll. iii. + pp. 35 + 9.   Plate of Laud's trial.

A copy of the Breviate, with Laud's notes (not autograph),
is in the Warrington Museum and Library. The notes are
published in Laud's *Works*, III. 261-272.

191. A Prophecie Of the Life, Reigne, and Death of
William Laud, Archbishop of Canterbury: By an
Exposition on part of the 13. and 15. Chapters of
the Revelation of John. Wherein the summe of
all his actions are foretold, his name nominated,
his correspondency with the Pope, his cruelty to
the Church, and the strange wonders declared,

1644.

which in his time should be done by fire from
heaven ; and his Courts, Seals, Marks, yea, the
very Monopolies all clearly foreshewed; Also how
by the supreme Councell he shalbe put to death ;
after which they shall rejoyce, and obtaine a finall
victory over the Papists in Armes against them . . .

4to. [London] Printed for R. A.
1644.

One leaf + pp. 6. With curious woodcut on titlepage,
with the devil, two other figures, and Laud, with horns, and
the number of the Beast on his forehead.

Brit. Mus. E. 18 (8) ; dated in MS. Nouemb. 23.

192. A Spirituall Çordial For my Lord of Canterbury,
Which hath beene long sicke of a Consumption
(evill men and deceevers waxing worse and worse)
made by a Tenant of his in new Prison [*i.e.* New-
gate] . And now presented to him, to see if it may
be a means to recover him, if he be not past cure.

Broadsheet, folio. Printed in
London for W. S. 1644.

Twenty verses of four lines. Signed at the end " Per me,
William Starbuck." With woodcut portrait of Laud.

Bodl. Lib. A. 3. 18. Art.

1645.

193. Hidden Workes of Darknes Brought to Publike
Light, Or A Necessary Introdvction to the History
of the Archbishop of Canterbvrie's Triall. Discovering to the World the severall secret dangerous
Plots, Practises, Proceedings of the Pope and his
Confederates, both at Home and in Forraigne Parts,
to undermine the Protestant Religion, usher the
whole Body of Popery into one Church, and reduce

1645.

all our Realmes to their ancient Vassalage to the
Sea of Rome, by insensible steps and degrees . . .
Together with the true Originals of the late Scot-
tish Troubles, Irish Rebellion and English civill
Wars: Manifested by sundry instructions, Articles,
Letters, Intelligences, Warrants, Bulls of Popes,
. . . and other Papers, found among Secretary
Windebankes [etc.] Writings. . . . By William
Prynne of Lincolns-Inne Esq. . . . . .

> Folio. London: Printed by Thomas
> Brudenell for Michael Sparke
> Senior . . . 1645.

ll. iii. + pp. 256 + ll. 4.   Frontispiece of the Trial.

194. The Life and Death of William Lawd, late Archbishop of Canterburie: Beheaded on Tower-Hill,
Friday the 10. of January 1644.   I. Here is a brief
Narration of his Doings all his life long . . .
II. His Doings & Sayings being compared and
weighed together, his Sayings are found infinitely
too light ; Yet of weight sufficient to presse every
man to make a Threefold use from All, of infinite
concernment to his eternall soul.   By E. W. who
was acquainted with his Proceedings in Oxford ;
was an eye & eare witnesse of his Doings and
Sayings in his Courts here at London ; and other
places under his dominion . . .

> 4to. London, Printed for John
> Hancock ; dwelling in Pope's-
> head Ally.   1645.

ll. 4 + pp. 42.   Portrait of Laud.

In the copy in the British Museum [E. 26 (17)] the date is
altered in MS. to 1644.

1645.

195. A Briefe Relation of the Death and Sufferings of the Most Reverend and Renowned Prelate the L. Archbishop of Canterbvry: VVith, a more perfect Copy of his Speech, and other passages on the Scaffold, than hath been hitherto imprinted.

4to. Oxford, Printed in the yeare 1644[5].

One leaf + pp. 30. By Dr. Peter Heylin. Containing the Speech as in the copy delivered by Laud himself to Dr. Sterne. Nos. 42 and 44 were doubtless printed from the same copy.

[Reprinted with additions in Somers Tracts IV. 441-456 (1810)].

196. Relation de la Mort de l'Archevesque de Cantorberi: 'Auec sa Harangue et Oraison suiuant la coppie imprimee.

4to. A Paris, Au Bureau D'addresse M.DC.XLV.

pp. 15. A translation of the preceding. Brit. Mus. 11405. aaa (2).

197. Relation Memorable de l'Arrest de mort, donné contre l'Archeuesque de Cantorbery, dans la Ville de Londre.

8vo. A Orleans . . . 1645.

ll. 4. Another translation. Hazlitt, *Bibl. Collections* II. 336.

198. An Elegie on the Most Reverend Father in God VVilliam Lord Arch-Bishop of Canterbury: Attatched the 18. of Decemb. 1640. Beheaded the 10. of January 1644.

4to. [Oxford]. Printed 1644 [5].

One leaf + pp. 9. In verse. Reprinted in the *Calendar of State Papers (Domestic)* 1644-5, p. xxiii, from a MS. copy in the

1645.

Record Office. The editor (Mr. W. Douglas Hamilton) suggests that it may be by Waller, but for reasons which are not conclusive.

The copy in the British Museum [E. 271 (8)] is dated in a contemporary hand "Mar. 4 Oxon̄."

199. The Grand Imposter Vnmasked, Or·A Detection of the notorious hypocrasie, and desparate Impiety of the late Arch bishop (so styled) of Canterbury, cunningly couched in that written Copy, which he read on the Scaffold at his execution, Jan, 10, 1644. Alias, called by the publisher, his funerall Sermon. By Henry Burton . . .

> 4to. London, Printed for Giles Calvert at the Black-spread Eagle, at the West end of Pauls, *s.a.*

ll. 2 + pp. 20.
Brit. Mus. E. 26 (4).

200. A Full and Satisfactorie Ansvvere To The Arch-Bishop of Canterbvries Speech, Or, Funerall Sermon Preached by himselfe on the Tower-Hill . . . At which time he was there and then Beheaded. Wherein is a full and plenary Discourse to satisfie all those who have been startled with his Subtle & Jesuiticall Falacies and evasions in the said Speech. And other passages and observations of great consequence, to satisfie the expectation of the Kingdome therein.

> 4to. London Printed by Jane Coe. 1645.

pp. 23.

A MS. note on the copy in the Bodleian Library (Wood 366, xxviii) attributes it to Dr. Burton :—"Henry Burton put out another scandalous answer also."

1645.

201. Een vast ende bondigh Antvvoort of Willem
Lauds Aertsbisschop van Cantelberghs Oratie ofte
Lych-predicatie . . . in't Nederlandts overgeset . .
4to. [Amsterdam] 1645

ll. 7. A translation of the preceding, with the English text
of the Archbishop's Speech.
Brit. Mus. 8122. ee. 2 (47).

202. A Briefe Exposition, Paraphrase, or Interpretation,
upon the Lord of Canterburies Sermon or Speech,
upon the last Pulpit that ever he preached, which
was the scaffold on Tower-hill. Also, upon the
Prayer which he used at the same time and place
before his Execution. Written by William Star-
bucke, Gentleman, to give the people a glimmering
of the Bishops hypocrisie.
4to. London, Printed for William
Starbuck 1645.

ll. 2 + pp. 16. With woodcuts.
The copy in the British Museum [E. 26 (1)] is dated in
MS. Jan. 24 [1644-5]

203. Jehojadah's Iustice against Mattan, Baals Priest:
or The Covenanters Justice Against Idolaters. A
Sermon [on 2 Chron. xxiii. 16, 17] Preacht upon
occasion of a Speech utter'd upon Tower-Hill . . .
By J. H. Minister of the Gospel.
4to. London . . 1645.

ll. 2 + pp. 16.
Bodl. Lib. Linc. C. 7. 15.

204. [Another Edition ?]
4to. s.l. 1645.

1645.

205. Jus Regum: Or, A Vindication of the Regall
Power against all Spiritual Authority exercised
under any Form of Ecclesiastical Government. In
a Brief Discourse occasioned by the Observation
of some Passages in the Archbishop of Canterburies last Speech [by H. Parker].

4to. London . . . R. Bostock 1645.
pp. 38.
Brit. Mus. E. 284 (4).

206. A Charme for Canterburian Spirits, Which, (since
the Death of this Arch-Prelate,) have appeared in
sundry shapes, and haunted divers houses in the
City of London. With his Graces waftage over
the red sea of Cocitus in Charons Ferry-boat;
And his magnificent entertainment into the Dæmoniack Court.

4to. [London] Printed for J. C.
February the 14. 1645 [cor-
rected in MS 1644 (O. S.)]

pp. 8. Curious woodcut representing the " Dæmoniack
Court " on titlepage.
Brit. Mus. E. 269 (18).

207. The Last Advice of William Lavd, late Arch-
Bishop, to his Episcopall Brethren; and especially
to Bishop Wren, who still remains Prisoner in the
Tower. Which was found in the said Arch-
Bishops Studie since his death among his other
Writings, and now set forth to publike view.

4to. London, Printed for J. B. 1645.

pp. 8. Woodcut of the Archbishop in his shroud [which
has evidently done duty for somebody else] on titlepage.
The copy in the British Museum [E. 269 (10)] has the date
altered in contemporary MS. to 1644.

1645.

208. England and Irelands sad Theater or William Laud heretofore Arch-Bishop of Canterbury, his Trance and vision. Wherein is Layd open before us the miserable cruelties & vnheard of Tyrannies Caused by the popish factions. Des Bisschops van Cantelberghs Morgenwecker . . . .

Broadside, folio. s.l. et a. [1645.]

In verse, with title in English and Dutch, and curious woodcut.

Brit. Mus. Catalogue of Prints &c. Div. I. Vol. i. No. 416.

209. A Collection of Ancient and Modern Prophesies Concerning these present Times . . . The Nativities of Thomas Earle of Strafford and W. Lavd Late Archbishop of Canterbury, His Majesties great Favorites . . . And the Speech intended by the Earle of Strafford to have been spoken at his death. By William Lilly Student in Astrologie . . .

4to. London, Printed for John
Partridge and Humphrey Blun-
den . . . 1645.

ll. 4 + pp. 55.
Brit. Mus. 1104 c. 31 (6).

210. A Prognostication Vpon W. Lavd late bishop of Canterbury written Anō: Dom^i: 1641 : which accordingly is come to pass.

Broadside, folio. Sould at the black
bull cornhill neare the Royal Ex-
change. s.a.

In verse, with woodcut of Abp. Laud's Execution. A copy in the British Museum [669. f. 10 (18)] is dated in MS. Feb: 27. 1644-5.

There is a MS. copy in the Record Office [*Calendar (Domestic)* 1644-5, p. 280].

1645.

211. Four Qveries Resolved For The Satisfaction of
all men, who are not willingly ignorant, Touching
the late Archbishop.   I. What his Religion was,
he so coloured-over at his Death ?   II. What His
Church was, he so bemoaned at that time ?
III. What his Confession was ?   IV. And Prayer,
Which his brethren, in iniquity, do so approve-of
at this day.   Concluded, that all those four are so
many abominations before the Lord GOD, and all
good men   Imprimatur James Crauford . . . .

4to.   London, Printed for John
Hancock . . . 1645.

pp. 12.
Brit. Mus. E. 271 (7).   Dated in MS. March 3. 1644.

212. Relation of the Troubles of the three forraign
Churches in Kent [Canterbury, Sandwich, and
Maidstone] caused by the Injunctions of William
Laud, Archb. of Canterbury A.D. 1634 . . .
Written by J. B., Minister of the Word of GOD.
4to. *s.l.* 1645.

213. [Another Edition.]   A Relation of the
Troubles Of the three forraign Churches
in Kent.   Caused by the Injunctions
of William Laud Archbishop of Canterbury.   Anno Dom. 1634 &c.
Written by J. B. Minister of the
Word of God . .

4to.   Imprinted at London for
Sam. Enderbie . . 1645.

ll. 3 + pp. 52.
Bodl. Lib. Th. 4° P. 82.

1645.

214. A Sight of ye Transactions of these latter yeares
Emblemized with engrauen plats which men may
read with out spectacles . . . . [Including the
Death and Last Speech of Archbishop Laud &c.].

4to. *s.l.* et *a.* [1645].

pp. 29. Emblematic titlepage, with figures of Time, Truth
and Envy. With many woodcuts, including " The rising of
Prentices and Sea-men on Southwark Side to assault the
Arch-bishop of Canterburys House at Lambeth " and " Execution of Archbishop Laud."

In the Collection of C. H. Firth, Esq., Balliol College,
Oxford.

1646.

214a. [An Almanac ' wherein the Archbishop is entered
in the Calendar for a martyr,' by Captain George
Wharton student in Astronomy.]

See Hutton's *William Laud,* p. 226.

215. Canterburies Doome, Or the First Part of a
Compleat History Of The Commitment, Charge,
Tryall, Condemnation, Execution of William Lavd
Late Arch-Bishop of Canterbury. Containing the
Severall Orders, Articles, Proceedings in Parlia-
ment against him, from his first Accusation
therein, till his Tryall : Together with the Various
Evidences & Proofs produced against him at the
Lords Bar, in justification of the first branch of
the Commons Charge against him ; to wit, His

1646.

Trayterous Endeavours to Alter & Subvert GOD's True Religion, by Law Established among us, to introduce & Set up Popish Superstition and Idolatry in liew thereof, by insensible degrees; and to Reconcile the Church of England to the Church of Rome, by Sundry Jesuiticall Pollices, Practises: with his Severall Answers to those Evidences, Proofs, & the Commons Reply thereunto. Wherein this Arch-Prelates manifold Trayterous Artifices to Usher in Popery by Degrees, are clearly detected . . . . By William Prynne, of Lincoln's Inne, Esquire ; Specially deputed to this publike Service, by the House of Commons Order ; Dated 4 Martii 1644.

> Folio. London, John Macock, for Michael Spark Senior 1646.

ll. 9 + pp. 565 + ll. 7. Woodcut of the Trial, and portraits of Laud and Prynne.

1648.

216. The Old Malignant in New Apparrell, Discovered by the Marks of Malignancy given in the Declararations, Remonstrances, Orders, Ordinances, Votes, &c. Of one or both of the honorable Houses of Parliament, and in their Articles against Thomas Earl of Strafford, &c., and against William Laud Archbishop of Canterbury whom they put to Death for Malignancy.

> 4to. London. Printed for L. F. 1648.

pp. 8.

Brit. Mus. E. 449. 17.

1649.

217. Engelandts Memoriael tot Eeuwighe gedachtenis. Verhalende de Proceduren Declaratien, Beschuldigingen, Defencien, Vonnissen, Laetste Woorden, en Executien van [Strafford], De Bisschop van Cantelbury, [King Charles] . . . .

4to. Amsterdam . . . 1649.

ll. 46. At l. 9, " Articulen van't Huys der Ghemeente in't Parlement . . . tot mainteneringevan haer beschuldinge tegens W. Laud . . ."
Brit. Mus. 8122. c. (1).

218. [Another Edition] With Portraits.

4to. Amsterdam. By Joost Hartgers . . . 1649.

pp. 88.
Brit. Mus. 8122. aa. 5.

219. [Another Edition] Vermeerdert Engelandts Memoriael Tot Eeuwige gedachtenis, Verhalende de Proceduren . . Defencien . . . Laetste woorden en Executien, van De Vice-Roy van Yrlandt . . . De Bisschop van Cantelbury . . . Den Koningh van Engelandt . . . . .

4to. Amsterdam. By Joost Hartgers . . . 1649.

pp. 8. With excellent portraits of Laud &c.
Brit. Mus. T. 2425 (48).

R

1649.

220. Vollständiges Englishes Memorial . . . Erzehlende
die Processen, Declarationen, Beschuldigungen,
Defensionen, . . . Von [Strafford] . . . , Dem
Ertzbischoff Von Cantelberg . . . , [Charles I,
Marquis of Hamilton, E. of Holland, Lord
Capel] . . . .

4to. *s.l.* MDCXLVIIII.

pp. 100. With Portraits &c. A German version of No. 217.
At p. 17, "Articulen Der Gemeinde in dem Parlament, zu
vertheidigen die Beschuldigung, gegen William Laud . . . "
Brit. Mus. 597, d. 22 (1).

221. [Another Edition.] Sesquiseculum Anglicanum . . . Dabey . . . mit
angehenget das Engländische Memorial . . . . [Strafford, Laud, Charles I]

4to. Leipzig . . . Anno MDCXLIX.

ll. 2 + pp. 90. With Portraits.
Brit. Mus 597. d. 25.

222. Tragicum Theatrum Actorum, & Casuum Tragi-
corum Londini Publice celebratorum, Quibus
Hiberniæ Proregi, Egiscopo Cantuariensi, ac tandem
Regi ipsi, Aliisque vita adempta, & ad Anglicanum
Metamorphosin via est aperta.

12mo. Amstelodami, apud Jodo-
cum Jansonium 1649.

pp. 320. At pp. 42-84, "Acta Cantuariensem Episcopum
attinentia, quibus comprehenduntur i. Capita eorum, quo-
rum accusando reus est factus. ii. Responsio ejusdem . . .
iii. Auctuarium prioribus . . . iv. Orationem Funebrem."
Portrait of Laud facing p. 42.
Brit. Mus. 599. a. 20.

1654.

228. Former Ages never heard of
> and

After Ages will admire.

Or, Politicall Transactions . . .

4to. London . . . 1654.

An enlarged edition of No. 214, continued down to the present year, with most of the same plates (including both of those referring to Abp. Laud) and some others.
In the Collection of Lord Northbourne.

1657 ?

224. Questions propounded for resolution of unlearned Pretenders in matters of Religion, to the doctors of the prelatical pretended Reformed Church of England. . . . [By John Spenser *alias* Vincent Hatclife S. J.]

Folio. Paris . . 1657.

An answer to Laud's Conference, really printed in London. [Laud's *Works* II. p. [xvii].]
Bodl. Lib. Linc. C. 534.

1658 —See 1663.

1660.

225. Laudensium Apostasia : Or A Dialogue In which is shewen, That some Divines risen up in our Church since the greatness of the late Archbishop, are in sundry Points of great Moment, quite fallen

1660.

off from the Doctrine Received in the Ch. of England . . . . By Henry Hickman . . .

> 4to. London Printed by D. Max-
> well, for Sa. Gellebrand . . .
> 1660.

ll. 8 + pp. 94.
Bodl. Lib. 1242. e. 40.

226. A Just Vindication of the Questioned Part of the
Reading of E. Bagshaw Esqr. in the Middle
Temple Hall, the 24 Feb., 1639, upon the Statute
of 25 E. 3. called Statutum pro Clero, from all
scandalous aspersions whatsoever. With a true
narrative of the cause of silencing the reader by
the then Archbishop of Canterbury.   [By Edward
Bagshaw *the Elder*].

> 4to. London 1660.

Brit. Mus. E. 1019 (c).

227. England's black Tribunall.   Set forth in the Triall
of K. Charles I At the pretended Court of Justice
at Westminster . . .   Also, the Severall Dying
Speeches of the Nobility and Gentry, as were
Inhumanely put to death for their Loyalty to their
Sovereign Lord the King from 1642. to 1658.
Earl of Strafford, Arch-Bishop of Canterbury . . . .

> 8vo. London, Printed for J. Play-
> ford 1660.

ll. 4 + pp. 232.   At pp. 103-114, The Speech or Sermon of
the most Reverend Father in God, William Lord Arch-bishop
of Canterbury . . . .

Many editions of this book appeared : the following are in

1660.

the British Museum :—Twelfth Edition pp. 176, 16mo 1671,
Third Edition pp. 180, 8vo. 1680, Fourth Edition pp. 180, 8vo.
1703, Fifth Edition pp. xxxi + 258, 12mo. 1720, Sixth Edition
pp. xxxi + 308, 8vo. 1737. [Abridged Edition] pp. 12, 8vo.
1680 (?).

1663 ?

228. Labyrinthvs Cantvariensis : Or Doctor Lawd's
Labyrinth. Beeing an Answer to the late Arch
bishop of Canterbvries Relation of a Conference
between Himself & Mr. Fisher, etc. Wherein The
true grounds of the Roman Catholique Religion
are asserted, the principall Controuersies betwixt
Catholiques & Protestants thoroughly examined,
and the Bishops Meandrick windings throughout
his whole worke layd open to publique veiw [*sic*]
By T. C. [Thomas Carwell, *alias* Thorold, S. J.]

Folio. Paris. Printed John Bil-
laine 1658.

ll. 5 + pp. 415 + ll. 7. It was really printed in London,
and, according to Stillingfleet, did not appear till 1663.

229. Fair Warning : The Second Part. Or xx Prophesies Concerning the Return of Popery. By
Archbishop Whitgift, Archbishop Laud. . . .

4to. London. Printed for H.
Marsh at the Prince's Arms in
Chancery-lane. 1663.

pp. 66.

1664.

230. Of the Necessity of Reformation, In, and before
Luther's Time ; and what (visibly) hath most
hindred the Progress of it. Occasioned by some
late virulent Books, written by Papists : but
especially, by that Intituled, Labyrinthus Cantuariensis. . . . By Meric Casaubon. . . .

> 4to. London. Printed by Λ Max-
> well for Timothy Garthwait . . .
> 1664.

ll. 6 + pp. 160, with emblematical frontispiece.
Brit. Mus. 1009. c. 18 (2).

1665.

231. A Rational Account of the Grounds of Protestant
Religion ; being a Vindication of the Lord Arch-
bishop of Canterbury's [Laud's] Relation of a
Conference &c From the pretended Answer by
T. C. . . . By Edward Stillingfleet [afterwards
Bishop of Worcester] . . .

> Folio. London 1665.

ll. 11 + pp. 654.

1681.

232. [The Same] . Second Edition.

> Folio. London 1681.

1702.

233. [The Same] . Third Edition.

> Folio. London 1702.

[Reprinted in Vol. IV of his collected Works (1702),
and in two vols 8vo. Oxford, 1844] .

1668.

234. Cyprianus Anglicus: Or, the History of the Life and Death, of the most Reverend & Renouned Prelate William By Divine Providence, Lord Archbishop of Canterbury, Primate of all England, & Metropolitan, Chancellor of the Universities of Oxon. & Dublin, & one of the Lords of the Privy Council to His late most Sacred Majesty King Charles the First, Second Monarch of Great Britain. Containing also The Ecclesiastical History of the Three Kingdoms of England, Scotland, & Ireland from His first rising till His Death. By P. Heylyn D.D. Chaplain to Charles the First and Charles the Second, Monarchs of Great Britain. . . .

Folio. London for A. Seile MDCLXVIII.

ll. 2 + pp. 547.

1671.

235. [Another Edition].

Folio. London MDCLXXI.

ll. 2 + pp. 511.

1719.

236. [Another Edition.] In this edition is Added, Several Marginal Notes, & a Compleat Index to the Whole: Never before printed.

Folio. Dublin 1719.

ll. 4 + pp. 156 + 126 + 59 + v.

1668.

237. Memoires of the Lives, Actions, Sufferings &
Deaths of those Noble, Reverend, and Excellent
Personages That Suffered By Death, Sequestration,
Decimation, Or otherwise For the Protestant Re-
ligion, And the great Principle thereof, Allegiance
To their Soveraigne, In our late Intestine Wars,
From . . 1637 to . . . 1660. . . . . By Da.
Lloyd . . .

> Folio. London. Printed for Samuel
> Speed . . by John Wright . . John
> Symmes . . . and James Collins . .
> MDCLXVIII.

ll. 7 + pp. 708. Portraits of King Charles, Laud, Strafford
and many more on titlepage. At pp. 225-270 "The Life
and Death of Dr. William Laud, Lord Arch-bishop of Canterbury."

1677.

238. The Same.   [Reissued with a new
titlepage.]

> Folio. London . . . 1677.

1673?

239. A Rational Account of the Doctrine of Roman-
Catholicks concerning the Ecclesiastical Guide in
Controversies of Religion. Reflecting on the later
writings of Protestants, particularly of Archbishop
Lawd and Dr. Stillingfleet, on this subject. By
R. H. [Abraham Woodhead?] . . .

> 4to. [*s.l.* et *a.*?]

I have seen no copy of the first edition.

1673.

240. [The Same]. Second Edition with additions.

4to. *s.l.* Printed in the Year,
MDCLXXIII.

ll. 15 + pp. 448.
Brit. Mus. 3935, d. 26 (1).

1698.

241. A Sermon Preach'd in the Cathedral and Metropolitical Church of St. Peter, in York: On Friday the Fifth of November 1697 . . . . By George Halley . . . With a Postscript and Two Letters, which clearly discover the Roman Designs against the English Church and Nation.

4to. London . . . . Tho. Baxter . . .
1698.

ll. 3 + pp. 26. At p. 21 is "A Letter from Sir William Boswell to the most Reverend William Laud, late Archbishop of Canterbury, remaining with Sir Robert Cotton's Choice Papers."

1712.

242. Some Remarkable Passages Relating to Archbishop Laud, Particularly to his Affection to the Church of Rome. Beeing the Twenty Second Chapter of Gage's Survey of the West Indies, as 'twas Printed in the Folio Edition before the Restoration, but supprest in the Octavo since.

8vo. London, Printed for S. Popping at the black Raven in Pater-noster-Row. 1712. Price Three Pence.

pp. iv. + 19. Gage's *Survey* was published in 1648 and 1655 in folio, and in 1677 in 8vo.
Bodl. Lib. Pamph. 304.

1716.

243. Several Tracts By the Ever-memorable Mr. John
     Hales of Eaton-College &c. . . . . To which is
     Added, His Letter to Archbishop Laud, occasion'd
     by his Tract of Schism [i.e. his " Answer to Lord
     Say's Speech touching the Liturgy"]

> 12mo.   [London] Printed in the
> Year M.DCC.XVI.

pp. 228. With Portrait.
Brit. Mus. 3751. aa.

1721.

244. [The Same. Another Edition].

> 12mo.   [London] Printed in the
> Year M.DCC.XXI.

pp. 228. With Portrait.
Brit. Mus. 1019. c. 23.

1717.

245. The Proceedings in the Star-Chamber, against
     Henry Sherfield, Esq ; Justice of the Peace, and
     Recorder of the City of Salisbury, for breaking a
     Glass Window in the Church of St. Edmonds in
     the said City.
     Sexto die Februarii, Anno Octavo, Caroli Regis
     Termino Sancti Hillarii, Anno Domini, 1632.
     Wherein the Authority of the Bishop of the
     Diocese and the Power of Vestries, with relation
     to making any Alteration in, or Repairing of
     Churches is consider'd.

> 8vo.   London : Printed for, and
> Sold by S. Noble in Long-
> Walk, near Christ's-Hospital :

1717.

> And T. Corbett at the Corner
> of Ludgate-Hill, near Fleet
> Bridge. MDCCXVII. Price One
> Shilling.

pp. 80. With Laud's Speech.
Durham Univ. Library (Routh Collection) XLVIII. E. 7
No. 2

1718.

246. Hugo Grotius De Veritate Religionis Christianæ
Editio adcuratior ، . . quam secundùm recensuit,
notulisque illustravit Joannes Clericus . . .

> 8vo. Amstelædami CIƆIƆCCXVIII.

ll. 8 + pp. 368. At p. 364 a letter to Laud from Lord
Scudamore, on Grotius's love for Laud.
" Sanè, Domine, persuasum mihi est eum ex animo & vehe-
menter amare & revereri te & rationem quâ te geris."

1724.

247. [Another Edition].

> 8vo. Hagae-Comitis . . . CIƆIƆCCXXIV.
> ll. 7 + pp. 384.

1719.

248. Reformed Devotions Being A Collection of The
best Hymns, Prayers, and other Spiritual Exercises,
for all occasions, composed By Divines of the
Church of England And Foreign Ascetics Laud,
Featley, Duppa [etc]. The Whole Corrected, and
Improv'd by Joseph Wasse . . .

> 8vo. Oxford . . . 1719.

ll. 10 + pp. 444.
Brit. Mus. 3456. g. 36.

1722.

249. Episcopal Traytors: Or, Priests aukward Politi-
cians. Exemplify'd, In the Behaviour of the
Political Prelacy; More particularly of The
Attempts of Archbishop Laud and his Equivocal
Exit. Occasion'd, By the Commitment of the
Bishop of Rochester [Atterbury] to the Tower for
High Treason on Friday, August 24, 1722. With
Some Account, and Carracter of that Prelate.
Collected from the best historians; by a friend of
the author of Cataline, &c.,

> 8vo. London Printed for A. Moore,
> near St. Paul's MDCCXXII.

one leaf + pp 36. See Laudian Exhibition Catalogue
No. 82.
Brit. Mus. 698, g. 37.

1728.

250. A Letter To Mr. Archdeacon Eachard : Wherein
are some Remarks on the Stuart's Family and
Archbishop Laud . . . By a Country Layman.

> 8vo. London Printed for R. F.
> MDCCXXVIII.

pp 64.
Brit. Mus. 9505. bbb.

1729.

251. The Difficulties and Discouragements Which
attend the Study of the Scriptures in the Way of
Private Judgment; Represented in a Letter to a
Young Clergyman. By a Presbyter of the Church
of England [Francis Hare, afterwards Bp. of

1729.

Chichester]. 9th Edition. There is added in this Edition, corrected from the original, A Letter Written by the Reverend Mr. John Hales of Eaton to Arch-Bishop Laud, upon occasion of his Tract concerning Schism.

8vo. London MDCCXXIX.

The letter begins " May it please your grace : Whereas of late an abortive Discourse &c."

1735.

252. The Same. 10th Edition.

8vo. London 1735.

[Reprinted 1768, 1769, 1823, 1839, 1840, and 1866.]

1740.

253. New Memoirs of the Life and Poetical Works of Mr. John Milton : With An Examination of Miltons stile . . . . . By Francis Peck, M.A. . . .

4to. London Printed M,DCC,XL.

ll. 6 + pp. 437 &c.
At pp 429-437 " The Parallel, or Archbishop Laud and Cardinal Wolsey, compared ; A Vision : By Milton. London Printed MDCCXL." (See No. 127.)

1748.

254. A Supplement to some Tracts formerly published, viz. : A Defence of the Brief Account of Calvin's causing Servetus to be burned ; . . . A brief account of Archbishop Laud's cruel treatment of Dr. Leighton ; . . . . By G. Benson D.D.

8vo. London 1748.

1748.

255. A Collection of Tracts : i. A Dissertation on 2 Thess. ii. i-12 . . . . . . ix. A brief account of Archbishop Laud's cruel treatment of Dr. Leighton. x. An Essay . . . ; and a general preface. By George Benson D.D. . . .

8vo. London 1748.

1749.

256. The True Church of England-Man's Companion . . . or, a complete Manual of Private Devotions . . . Collected from the Writings of Archbishop Laud [etc] .

8vo. London 1749.

1819.

257. Another Edition.

12mo. London 1819.

1829.

258. The Life and Times of William Laud, D.D. Lord Archbishop of Canterbury. By John Parker Lawson M.A. . . . In Two Volumes.

8vo. London . . . MDCCCXXIX.

Vol. i. pp. xxix + 592. Portrait.
Vol. ii. pp. xi. + 546 + Index ll. 5.

259. The British Critic, Quarterly Theological Review and Ecclesiastical Record. Vol. vi.

8vo. London . . Rivington . . 1829.

Art. vii. The Life and Times of William Laud . . . By J. P. Lawson. pp. 412-468.

1836.

260. The Life of Archbishop Laud. By Charles Webb Le Bas M.A.

8vo. London . . . 1836.

pp. 392. Portrait. [Vol. xiii. of the Theological Library.]

261. The British Critic, Quarterly Theological Review, and Ecclesiastical Record. Volume xix.

8vo. London . . Rivington . . 1836.

Art. vi. On Le Bas' Life of Archbishop Laud. pp. 354-380.

1841.

262. Original Letters, and other Documents, relating to the Benefactions of William Laud, Archbishop of Canterbury, to the County of Berks. Edited by John Bruce Esq. F.S.A.

sm. 4to. London, Printed for the Berkshire Ashmolean Society MDCCCXLI.

pp. xix + 74. Seal of Archbishop Laud on frontispiece.

1842.

263. Archbishop Laud more than half a Papist: or, Laudism (after the lapse of two centuries) revived under the appellation of Puseyism. By the Rev. Reginald Rabett M.A. . . .

8vo. London MDCCCXLII.

One leaf + pp. vii. + 20.

1842.

264. The New York Review.   Vol. x.

8vo. New York 1842.

pp. 257-293 Life and Character of Archbishop Laud.

1845.

265. The   Christian   Remembrancer Vol IX.   Part   I
(January).

8vo.   London 1845.

pp. 201 f.   Archbishop Laud.   By. J. B. Mozley D.D.

1878.

266. Essays Historical and Theological.   By
J. B. Mozley D.D. Late Canon of
Christ Church and Regius Professor
of Divinity in the University of Oxford.   2 Vols.

8vo.   London, Rivingtons 1878.

pp. 106-228 Archbishop Laud. [Reprinted from
the *Christian Remembrancer*, Vol. IX. (No. 265)].

1884.

267. [The Same.]   Second Edition.

8vo.   London, Rivingtons 1884.

1855.

268. The Life of William Laud, Archbishop of Canterbury, and Martyr. By the Rev. John Baines,
M.A. . .

12mo.   London MDCCCLV.

pp. ix + 274.

1858 &c.

269. Catalogi Codicum Manuscriptorum Bibliothecæ
Bodleianæ Pars Secunda Codices Latinos et Mis-
cellaneos Laudianos complectens. Confecit H . .
O. Coxe . .

Oxonii e typographeo Academico
1858-1885.

pp. 534 + Index 29.

1864.

270. The Life of Archbishop Laud. By John N.
Norton, Rector of Ascension Church, Frankfort,
Ky. . . . .

8vo. Boston [U.S.A.]. 1864.

pp. 269. With Portrait.

1869.

271. Church Association Lectures 1869, delivered at
St. James' Hall, London. Revised by the Authors.
With an Introduction by the Chairman, J. C. Col-
quhoun.

8vo. London 1869.

pp. xii + 175. On pp. 138-175, Archbishop Laud and hi
Times. By the Rev. J. C. Ryle M.A.

1895.

272. Archbishop Laud and his Times. By
the Lord Bishop of Liverpool. [New
Edition] Revised and Corrected.

8vo. London 1895.

pp. 47.

1870.

273. Papers on the Doctrine of the English Church concerning the Eucharistic Presence. By an English Presbyter.
Supplement No. II, pp. 44-66 "On the 'Real Presence' of the Laudian Theology." A Postscript to Questions Suggested by the Judgment . . by Sir Robert Phillimore in the case of the Office of the Judge promoted by Sheppard *v.* Bennett.

8vo.   London, Wm. Macintosh 1870.

[The postscript also appeared separately, price sixpence : 8vo. London 1870].

274. Historical Gleanings. A Series of Sketches. Wiklif. Laud. Wilkes. Horne Tooke. By James E. Thorold Rogers. Second Series.

8vo.   London 1870.

pp. vii + 247. William Laud, pp. 65-127.

1871.

275. The American Quarterly Church Review. Vol. xxiⁱi.

8vo.   New York 1871.

The Life and Trial of Archbishop Laud, pp. 237-252.

1872.

276. The Union Review. A Magazine of Catholic Literature and Art. January to December 1872.

8vo.   London, J. T. Hayes . . .

Art. xix. Archbishop Laud, pp. 393-421.

1875.

277. Lives of the Archbishops of Canterbury by Walter Farquhar Hook D.D. . . . 12 Vols.

8vo. London 1860-76.

Vol xi. [1875] p 393.ᴵ William Laud.

1879.

278. The Home Library. Great English Churchmen : or, Famous Names in English Church History and Literature. A Series of Biographical Sketches, intended to illustrate the Annals, Character, Teaching, and Influence of the Church of England. By W. H. Davenport Adams.

8vo. London & New York, 1879.

pp. 444. William Laud, pp. 209-262.

1882.

279. Jubilee Lectures : A Historical Series delivered on the occasion of The Jubilee of the Congregational Union of England and Wales, with an Introductory Chapter. 2 Vols.

8vo. London MDCCCLXXXII.

Vol i. pp. 57-137. Laud and the Puritans. By Henry Allon D.D.

1883.

280. Pro Ecclesia Dei. Laud and Tait. An Ecclesiastical Study and Review. By A Churchman of the Diocese of Canterbury.

8vo. London 1883.

pp. 37.

1887.

281. William Laud sometime Archbishop of Canterbury. A Study. By Arthur Christopher Benson, B.A. . . .

8vo.   London 1887.

pp. xiv + 228.   With Portrait.

1890.

282. William Laud, of Reading, sometime Archbishop of Canterbury and Chief Minister of Charles I.   A Lecture Delivered to the Reading Literary & Scientific Society, April 1890. By H. M. Wallis. Now printed by Request.

8vo.   Reading 1890.

pp. 27.   With two Heliotype Portraits.

1894.

283. A Life of Archbishop Laud. By " A Romish Recusant."

8vo.   London.   Kegan Paul, 1894.

pp. xxiii + 490.   With portrait from " The Recantation of the Prelate of Canterbury " (No. 126.)

284. Waymarks in Church History.   By William Bright D.D. Canon of Christ Church, Oxford, Regius Professor of Ecclesiastical History.

8vo.   London.   Longmans, 1894.

pp. 323-354 on Archbishop Laud :—" An expansion of an article in the *Newbery House Magazine*, May, 1892."

285. Archbishop Laud's Prayer Book.   Notes on the Bibliography of the Booke of Common Prayer and Administration of the Sacraments.   And other

1894.

Parts of Divine Service for the Use of the Church of Scotland: Edinburgh 1637. By Bishop Dowden [of Edinburgh].
The Edinburgh Bibliographical Society, Session 1893-94 No. V.

4to.   Edinburgh [1894].

pp. 8.   One facsimile.   (See Nos. 76 and 77.)

286. Life and Times of William Laud Archbishop of Canterbury. By C. H. Simpkinson, M.A., ... With Portrait.

8vo.   London.   Murray 1894.

pp. viii + 307.

1895.

287. William Laud.   By William Holden Hutton, B.D., ... With a Portrait.

8vo.   London.   Methuen 1895.

pp. xi + 240.
This and Mr. Simpkinson's *Life* are reviewed by Dr. S. R. Gardiner in the *English Historical Review* for April 1895 (Vol. X. p. 372 f.)

288. Monthly Intelligencer of the Birmingham Christian Evidence and Protestant Laymen's Association. February 1895. [Consisting of a lecture on Archbishop Laud by Mr. T. H. Aston].

8vo.   Birmingham . . . 1895.

Wrapper and pp. 9-16.   Reprinted also in pamphlet form.

289. The Church Quarterly Review, Vol. XL.

8vo.   London 1895.

pp. 63-85. (April) Archbishop Laud, *Part I.*
pp. 257-282. (July) Archbishop Laud, *Part II.*

APPENDIX I.

SATIRICAL PRINTS, &c.

[It is thought well to include here such prints of Archbishop Laud as have a literary or political interest. Ordinary engraved portraits are not included ; nor are a large number of satirical prints contained in many of the books of this list.]

1895.

290. An Engraving of Archbishop Laud firing a Cannon, which bursts in the middle. Near the Archbishop stand some of the Bishops, &c. By Hollar. $8\frac{1}{4} \times 4\frac{7}{8}$.

Dec. 16, 1640.

In reference to the "Canons and Constitutions Ecclesiastical." Brit. Mus. Catalogue of Prints and Drawings, Division I. vol. I. No. 148.

291. William Laud Arch-B. of Canterbury : Prymat of England. [A portrait of Abp. Laud in prison] W[illiam] M[arshall], sculp :

$2\frac{1}{4} \times 2\frac{7}{8}$ [1641].

Used as frontispiece to " The Argument of Nicholas Fuller . . . in the Case of Tho. Lad and Rich. Mansell his Clients" 4to. 1641 [Brit. Mus. E. 156 (19)]; and reprinted on the titlepage of " Bishop Wrens Petition to the Parliament . . . 4to. London . . 1642" [Brit. Mus. E. 131 (32)].
British Museum Catalogue of Prints and Drawings Div. I. Vol. I. No. 173.

292. Portraits of Archbishop Laud and Mr. Henry Burton : Laud stands in front and vomits books ;

1895.

on the ground are more books, inscribed " Tobaco,"
" Canons and Constitutions," " Sundai No Sabath,"
" An Order Of Star Chamber." Mr. Henry Burton
is supporting the Archbishop's head. Above is
written

> " *Great was surnamed* GREGORIE *of Rome,*
>   *Our* LITTLE *by* GREGORIE comes short home."

Gregorie, otherwise Richard Brandon, being the
hangman.

$6\frac{7}{8}$ × 10 [1645].

British Museum Catalogue of Prints &c. Div. I. Vol. i.
No. 412.

293. Portrait of Archbishop Laud, speaking. With
inscription " Gull : Quondam Arch : Cant :
W [illiam] M [arshall] Sculp."

$2\frac{7}{8}$ × $3\frac{5}{8}$ [1645].

Two editions of this portrait were issued.
Brit. Mus. Catalogue of Prints &c. Div. I. Vol. i. No. 412.

294. The right Reverend Father in God Francis
Atterbury, D.D. Ld Bishop of Rochester and
Dean of Westminster . . Printed for, and sold
by Eman. Bowen . . London. [Bishop Atterbury in a Window of the Tower, behind prison
bars, holding a portrait of ," William Laud, Arch
Bishop of Canterbury Suffer'd martyrdom Janu.
10. 1644 "]

11 × 8 [1722].

Laudian Exhibition Catalogue No. 82.

APPENDIX II.

[*This list is probably far from complete, but no more have been found hitherto.*]

1624.

295. The New Art of Lying, Covered by Iesvites vnder the Vaile of Eqvivocation, Discovered and Disproved By Henry Mason.

> 4to. London: Printed by George Purslowe for Iohn Clarke . . 1624.

ll. 26 + pp. 106. The dedication, to the Archbishop of Canterbury, begins "The first newes that I heard of the Equiuocating Arte, was that which I learned out of your Graces writings. And well might this be to me the first newes. For, if I mistake not, you were the first Writer, that published those trickes in print to the World." This would seem to refer to Laud's Third Conference. But Laud was not Archbishop in 1624; and the book was certainly first published then, as it occurs in the Register of the Stationers' Company on Jan. 18, 1623-4 [Arber, *Transcript* IV. 73]. Yet the dedication must refer to him rather than to Archbishop Abbott, as it is repeated in the Edition of 1634 (*post*). The probability, therefore, is that the Dedication (together with some other matter) was only issued with the latter part of this edition. At the same time, I have seen no copy without it.

Brit. Mus. 3938. aaa. 54.

1634.

296. [The Same. Another Edition].

> 12mo. London, Printed for John Clark . . 1634.

ll. 26 + pp. 347 + one leaf.
Brit. Mus. 852. c. 1.

1634.

297. Marcvs Aurelivs Antoninvs The Roman Emperor,
His Meditations Concerning Himselfe Treating of
a Naturall Mans happinesse ; Wherein it consisteth
and of the means to attaine unto it. Translated
ovt of the Originall Greeke ; with Notes : By
Meric Casavbon.

> 8vo. London. Printed by M.
> Flesher for Richard Mynne . . .
> M DC XXXIV.

ll. 5 + pp. 210 of Text + pp. 46 of Notes.
Brit. Mus. C. 45. e. 2. This copy is profusely annotated
in the handwriting of Meric Casaubon.

1636.

298. [Greek Title.] Theophylacti Archiepiscopi Bul-
gariæ in D. Pauli Epistolas Commentarii : Studio
& Curâ Reverendissimi Patris, Domini Augustini
Lindselli, Episcopi Herefordensis . . .

> Folio. Londini, E Typographeo
> Regio M.DC.XXXVI.

ll. 3 + pp. 1041.
Brit. Mus. 9. d. 9.

1638.

299. [Greek Title]. Liber Precvm Pvblicarvm Ac
Celebrationis Sacramentorum reliquorumq ;
Rituum & Cæremoniarum in Ecclesiâ nostrâ
Anglicanâ, in Studiosæ juventutis gratiam nunc

1638.

primùm græcè editus.   Operâ & Studio Eliæ Petili [Petley] Presbyteri.

>   8vo.   Londini Typis Tho. Cotes[i] pro Ricardo Whitakero . .
>   MDCXXXVIII.

Brit. Mus. 683. c. 13.

1639.

300. Fabulæ Pontificæ Evangelicæ Veritatis radiis dissipatæ.   Autore Martino Wescombe . . .

>   12mo.   Oxoniæ, Excudebat L. Lichfield M.DC.XXXIX.

ll. 15 + pp. 85.
Brit. Mus. 1225. a. 16.

301. Grounds of Grammar Penned and Pvblished. By Iohn Bird Schoolemaster in the Citty of Glocester . . .

>   12mo.   Oxford, Printed by Leon. Lichfield Printer to the Vniversity.   M.DC.XXXIX.

ll. 4 + pp. 184.

1641.

302. [The Same.   With another Titlepage].

>   12mo.   Oxford, Printed by L. Lichfield, for Humphery (*sic*) Mosley, at the Princes Armes in St. Paul's Churchyard. M.DC.XXXXI.

ll. 4 + pp. 184.

1640.

303. Grammatices Latinæ Compendivm, Anno 1637
E Grammaticis tum veteribus, tum neotericis,
summa judicii lima nobilitates, excerptum, & in
unum corpus methodo accuratiore & faciliore
redactum, & ad tenellæ ætatis captum, confor-
matum . . . . [By Thomas Hayne].

> 12mo. Londini, Excusum typis
> Ed. Griffini . . 1640.

ll. 6 + pp. 144.

Brit. Mus. 12934. a. 14. This copy does not contain the
Dedication to Archbishop Laud ; but I insert the book on the
authority of Hazlitt, *Bibliographical Collections and Notes* III.
107.

304. Psalterium Davidis Latino-Saxonicum vetus. A
Johanne Spelmanno D. Hen. fil. editum. E
vetustissimo exemplari MS in Bibliotheca
ipsius Henrici, & cum tribus aliis non multo
minus vetustis collatum . .

> 8vo. Londini, Excudebat R
> Badger . . . 1640.

Brit. Mus. 1008 b. 6.

[Vossius had proposed to dedicate his book on idolatry
(*De Idolatria Gentili*) to Laud, but desisted on account
of the troubles of 1641.—Vossii *Epistolæ* (1690) p. 377 b.]

ADDITIONAL NOTE.

There are Biographies of Archbishop Laud in the *Biographia Britannica*, Lodge's *Portraits, Lives of Eminent and Illustrious Englishmen* (Vol. iii. pp. 103-111, 1836), Rose's *Biographical Dictionary, Dictionary of National Biography* (Vol. xxxii, pp. 185-194, by Dr. S. R. Gardiner), &c. &c.

S. John's College Oxford was at one time collecting materials for a biography of Laud. See *Clarendon Papers* Vol. II. 328 (1772). Sir E. Hyde to Dr. Steward :— " The College does well to recollect his life ; I pray God they proceed in it, or do anything else worthy the memory of that man." They may have ceased owing to the publication of Heylin's work.

Sancroft first planned the publication of Laud's *Diary*, when he was Dean of S. Paul's, at the instigation of Archbishop Sheldon ; and he continued working at it after his retirement to Fresingfield. Judging from the extent of his MS. collections, he would seem to have projected a new life of Laud also ; but of this there is no proof. The former plan was carried out after his death by his chaplain, Henry Wharton (see No. 66) ; the latter, if made, was never carried out.

See also the following :—

Notes and Queries—

Series 1. Vols. iii. pp. 158, 199, 224 ; iv. 87 ; v. 179, 314.

Series 2. Vols. i. 119, 456 ; iii. 425 ; vii. 252 ; viii. 309, 389, 437, 540 ; ix. 419 ; x. 110, 495 ; xi. 386.

Series 3. Vols. ii. 342 ; iii. 3 ; v. 1 ; vii. 146.

Series 8. Vol. ii. 522.

Historical MSS. Commission Reports—

Vol. IV. pp. 124-148.   Archbishop Laud's Visitations.

&c. &c.

Transactions of the Royal Society of Literature—

Vol. II. p. 205 f. (1834).   A Paper by Archdeacon Todd on Laud's services to General Literature.

European Magazine—

September 1792.   Some curious facts with regard to the fee given by Archbishop Laud to John Herne, one of his Counsel in his Trial, contained in a letter from Herne's grandson (dated 1701).

&c. &c.

WRITINGS OF ARCHBISHOP LAUD

HITHERTO UNPUBLISHED OR BUT LITTLE KNOWN.

A.—*The Instrument of resignation of the Chancellorship of Oxford University.*

B.—*Verses on Various Occasions.*

[*The Instrument of Resignation has never been published before : the Verses were published in 1612 and 1613, and have, apparently, never been reprinted.*]

A.—THE RESIGNATION OF THE CHANCEL-LORSHIP OF OXFORD UNIVERSITY.

[Wood MS. C. 53.]

In Dei Nomine Amen. Coram vobis Testibus fidedignis hic præsentibus, Ego Gulielmus Providentia Divina Cantuariensis Archiepiscopus, totius Angliæ Primas et Metropolitanus ac Cancellarius Academiæ sive Vniuersitatis Oxoniensis, volens et affectans ex certis Justis et legitimus causis me et animam meam ad id moventibus ab onere, Officio et munere dicti Cancellaria-tus exui penitus et exonerari dictum Cancellariatum sive munus et Officium Cancellariatus Academiæ sive Vniuersitatis Oxoniensis præadictæ Procancellario, Ma-gistris et scholaribus Academiæ sive Vniuersitatis præadictæ seu alij personæ sive alijs personis quibuscunque hanc meam renunciacionem et resignacionem admittendi potestatem habentibus seu habituris, non vi vel metu coactus nec dolo malo ad hoc inductus aut aliqua alia sinistra machinacione circumventus sed ex mera mea et certa scientia meroque motu et spontanea voluntate pure, sponte, simpliciter et absoluté resigno ac renuncio ac re et verbo vacantem dimitto, Jurique Titulo et possessioni meis in Cancellariatu præadicto præahabitis et mihi com-petentibus renuncio ac ab eisdem cum suis Juribus et pertinentijs vniuersis totaliter et expresse recedo in hijs scriptis. In Cuius rei Testimonium sigillum meum

T

præsentibus apposui.   Datum apud Turrim Londonien-
sem Vicesimo secundo die Mensis Junij Anno domini
Millesimo sexcentesimo quadragesimo primo.

[*Signed*] W. CANT.

[*The following endorsements are in different hands.*]

(1) Resignacio Cancellariatus Vniuersitatis Oxoniensis per
Gulielmum Archiepiscopum Cantuariensem.

(2) Archbishopp of Canterbury his Resignacion of his Chancellorship of the Vniversity of Oxon, 1641.

(3) This instrument was read, inscribed, sealed and deliuered as
his acte & deede in the presance of vs whose names are
hervnder written by the within named most reuerend father
William, lord Archbishop of Canterbury.

WILLIAM MERICKE

THOMAS . . . ERS (?)* senior notary publique.

WALTER DOBSON notary publique

EDWARD LATHAM notary publique

(4) Given to me by Robert Whorwood of Oxoñ Gent. 29 Feb.
1679.   A. WOOD.

---

* Name indistinct.

B.—LATIN VERSES WRITTEN BY LAUD WHILE AT OXFORD.

I. In Memory of Henry Prince of Wales.

[In *Justa Oxoniensium.*—See *Bibliography* No. 1.]

Henricus fulcrum Patris, Patriaeq : columna,
    Relligionis honor, Nobilitatis Amor.
Lumen amicorum, Magnae spes altera *Troiæ*,
    Mundi Sol oriens, occidit ante diem.
Si quid in humanis certum, dum viueret ille
    Anglica terra satis tuta, potensq : satis.
At iam quassa tremit, quasi Fundamenta laborent,
    (Nam Fundamentum Regia progenies)
Ducite quin pompam, sed quid iam Pompa valebit ?
    Hoc funus planctus & lachrymae celebrent.
Et quonian meruit longam traducere vitam,
    Det vitam serę posteritatis Amor.

Sunt splendor Orbis, *Insulae Brittanicae*
Britanniarum splendor est haec Anglia ;
Iacobus, ille est *Angliae* splendor suae.

Henricus, vnus ille, (dum vixit) simul
Virtute, Meritis, Famâ, adornauit sua,
Iacobum & *Angliam, Insulasq̄ Britannicas.*

Quin ergo possunt raptum, (& ad superos) piè
Non flere, Natum, Principem, summus Decus,
Iacobvs, *Anglia, Insulae Brittannicae ?*

      Gvliel. Lavd, Doct. Theol. Col. D. Iohan.
      Bapt. Præses.

II. IN MEMORY OF SIR THOMAS BODLEY.

In *Ivsta Funebria*, p. 6.

Si sint vivaces hominum monumenta libelli,
　Nomine si dignos Musa perire vetet :
Quàm famę (BODLEIE) tuę monumenta supersunt
　Plurima ?　quamq ; tibi est debita longa dies !

Nec justum reor, vt Mors, quæ tamen omnibus vna
　Dicitur, aequali sit tibi lege data.
Ergo Mortalis quod vitae Fata negârunt,
　Concedet serae Posteritatis Amor.
Et nova consurgens olim testabitur aetas,
　Quàm dignus fueris non potuisse mori.

Gvliel.　Lavd.　Sac.　Theol.　Doct.　et　Coll.
Iohan.　Præses.

III.   IN HONOUR OF THE MARRIAGE OF PRINCESS ELIZABETH OF ENGLAND WITH THE COUNT PALATINE FREDERICK.

In *Epithalamia*, leaf 7 b.

Non homo, non gentes, non *separet* vlla Potestas,
    Quos voluit vnire Deus.
At quos Nobilitas, Pietas quos junxit, & ætas,
    Hos voluit vnire Deus.
Nobile *Par*, Mundo sub fausto sydere Natum,
    Ad hoc beandum sæculum.
Vivite fœlices, numerosâ prole Beati :
    Amore constantes Pio.
VXOREM *Thamesis* celebret, *Rhenusq̄* MARITVM ;
    Vtrumq̄ ; Posteritas colat.

        Gvliel. Lavd Sacræ Theol. D. Coll.
        Ioan. Prœses.

Archbishop Laud Commemoration, 1895

CATALOGUE

OF THE

Exhibition of Laudian Relics

and other Objects of Interest.

Held in the Schoolroom over the Porch of the

Parish Church of Allhallows Barking, E.C.

January 10-31, 1895.

PATRON.

THE PRESIDENT OF S. JOHN'S COLLEGE, OXFORD.

COMMITTEE.

THE LORD BISHOP OF S. DAVID'S.

THE LORD BISHOP OF OXFORD.

THE LORD BISHOP OF PETERBOROUGH.

THE REV. W. BRIGHT, D.D., Canon of Christ Church, Professor of Ecclesiastical History in the University of Oxford.

THE REV. G. F. BROWNE, B.D., Canon of S. Paul's.

THE REV. A. J. MASON, D.D., Vicar of Allhallows Barking, E.C.

THE REV. R. W. DIXON, Hon. Canon of Carlisle.

THE REV. W. H. HUTTON, B.D., Fellow and Tutor of S. John's College, Oxford.

THE REV. C. H. SIMPKINSON, Rector of Farnham.

THE REV. J. L. FISH, Rector of S. Margaret Pattens, E.C.

HIS GRACE THE DUKE OF NEWCASTLE.

D. S. MARGOLIOUTH, ESQ., Laudian Professor of Arabic in the University of Oxford.

H. O. WAKEMAN, ESQ., Fellow of All Souls' College, Oxford.

A. C. BENSON, ESQ., Assistant Master of Eton College.

THE REV. W. E. COLLINS, Professor of Ecclesiastical History at King's College, London (*Secretary*).

THE MEMBERS of the Laud Commemoration Committee desire most heartily to thank all those who have so generously placed their treasures at their disposal, thus giving to the Exhibition the interest which must attach to a collection of objects of such unique historical and intrinsic value.

INDEX OF EXHIBITORS.

CATALOGUE OF EXHIBITS.

A.—Personal Objects belonging to, or connected with, the Archbishop.

1. Chalice given to the Church of Holy Trinity, Knightsbridge, by Laud when Bishop of London. Silver-gilt, with inscription, " Sanctæ et Individuæ Trinitati " on the bowl; and " The guift of the right Hon^hl. and right reverent Father in God Willm. Lord Bishop of London " on the foot.

There was an ancient hospital at Knightsbridge with a chapel, to which the inhabitants of the village of Knightsbridge used to resort for Divine Service. In 1629, the chapel being ruinous, they petitioned Laud, then Bishop of London, for leave to rebuild it. This was granted, and (subject to the rights of the parishes of S. Martin-in-the-Fields, S. Margaret Westminster, and Kensington), they were allowed to have the services of a licensed curate. It was under those circumstances, doubtless, that the chalice was given.

Lent by the Vicar and Churchwardens of
Holy Trinity, Knightsbridge.

2. Bishop Launcelot Andrewes' Devotions in Greek, being the copy given by him to Laud. In Andrewes' own handwriting; perhaps the copy described by Drake as " happy in the glorious deformity thereof, being slubbered with his pious hands, and watered with his penitential tears."

186 pages; size, 5 × 3; bound in white vellum, and fastened with green silk ribbons. With inscription on the front cover in Laud's writing (almost obliterated), " My reverend Friend Bishop Andrewes gave me this Booke a little before his death. W: Bath. et Wellen."

Lent by the Rev. R. G. Livingstone

2a. Another MS. of Bishop Andrewes' Devotions, in the handwriting of his secretary, Samuel Wright. Given by Wright to Richard Drake, Fellow of Pembroke College, Cambridge.

168 pages, preceded by 6 blank. $6\frac{1}{2} \times 3\frac{7}{8}$; bound in brown calf. With an inscription on the second blank page, "*Amicissimus meus Samuel Wright Lancelot Wintoniensi Epo olim à Chartis, nunc autem Matthaeo Eliensi à Registris, pretiosum hoc* κειμήλιον *suâ manu accuratè descriptum dono dedit mihi.*—Ricardo Drake."

Lent by the MASTER AND FELLOWS OF PEMBROKE COLLEGE, CAMBRIDGE.

2b. A Manual of the Private Devotions and Meditations of The Right Reverend Father in God, Lancelot Andrews, late Lord Bishop of Winchester. Translated out of a fair Greek MS. of his amanuensis. By R. D[rake], B.D. London, Printed by W.D., for Humphrey Moseley, at the Prince's Arms in S. Paul's Church-yard, MDCXLVIII.

The first complete edition in English. 321 pages. $4\frac{1}{2} \times 2\frac{1}{2}$, original brown calf.

Lent by the MASTER OF PEMBROKE COLLEGE, CAMBRIDGE.

3. Red Skull-cap, worn by the Archbishop at his execution, January 10, 1645.

It is much worn on one side, and elsewhere pieces have been snipped off,—doubtless to be kept as relics.

Lent by the PRESIDENT AND FELLOWS OF S. JOHN'S COLLEGE, OXFORD.

4. Walking-stick, which belonged to Archbishop Laud.

Of ebony, with ivory head and long iron ferule. The case containing it bears the inscription —" Hoc baculo dextrans subeunte | Gressus suos firmavit | Gulielmus Laud | Archiepiscopus Cantuar. | idemque hujus collegii Benefactor | insignis, cum ad mortem | immeritam ductus esset. | Præsidenti et sociis | Coll. Divi Johannis Baptistæ | d.d. | Gul. Aubrey Phelp, A.M. | Ecclesiæ de Stanwell | in Com. Middlesex Vicarius. | A.D. MDCCCXV."

Lent by the PRESIDENT AND FELLOWS OF
S. JOHN'S COLLEGE, OXFORD.

5. Chair, which once belonged to Archbishop Laud, formerly in the possession of S. John's College, Oxford.

Carved in oak, somewhat mutilated and repaired, and upholstered in crimson figured velvet.

Lent by MISS WHITMORE-JONES.

6. The Shell of Archbishop Laud's Tortoise. When found in a lumber room some years ago, there was a label pasted upon the shell which stated that the tortoise was put into the garden at Lambeth in 1633, where it remained till the year 1753, when it was unfortunately killed by the negligence of the gardener. Since then it has been preserved in the Muniment Room at Lambeth.

There were two other old labels with the shell, to much the same effect : and it is mentioned also in " *Experimental Researches on the Light and Luminous matter of the Glow-worm, and the Torpidity of the Tortoise, &c.*" by John Murray, F.S.A., F.L.S. (Glasgow, 1826), p. 168.

There is a memorandum on the history of this Tortoise, dated May 16, 1889, by Prof. Sir W. H. Flower, in Lambeth Palace Library. After examining the evidence of the labels and Murray's

Experimental Researches, he comes to the conclusion that the tortoise was probably " placed by Laud in the garden at Fulham, when he went there in 1628, removed by him to Lambeth in 1633, and died through the gardener's carelessness either in 1730 or 1753. The animal is the common Land Tortoise of North Africa and Asia Minor, so frequently brought to this country, *Testudo græca* of most authors, *T. ibera*, Pallas, of the recently issued British Museum Catalogue of Chelonians."

Lent by His GRACE THE ARCHBISHOP OF CANTERBURY.

7. Bookcase Doors, formerly belonging to Archbishop Laud, of oak and gilded metal, carved in handsome open-work panels containing Laud's Arms, the same impaled with the Arms of Canterbury, his crest, the Episcopal mitre, &c   Formerly in the possession of S. John's College, Oxford.

Lent by the REV. T. ARTHUR CURTIES.

B.—AUTOGRAPH MANUSCRIPTS.

8. " The Diary of the Most Reverend Father in God, William Laud, Archbishop of Canterbury." The original MS., a long, narrow volume, closely written.

It was this " little book or diary, containing all the occurrences of my life," which was carried off by Prynne when he searched the Archbishop's chamber in the Tower for papers. And from this, with much garbling and mutilation, Prynne prepared his *Breviate*.

The narrowness of the inner margin proves that the Diary has been rebound since it was first written.

Lent by the PRESIDENT AND FELLOWS OF
S. JOHN'S COLLEGE, OXFORD.

9. " The History of the Troubles and Tryal of William Laud, Archbishop of Canterbury." The original MS., a small folio volume.

Written by the Archbishop during his imprisonment in the Tower.

Lent by the PRESIDENT AND FELLOWS OF S. JOHN'S COLLEGE, OXFORD.

10. The Coronation Service of King Charles I. Laud's own copy, used by him as Master of the Ceremonies, or " Vice-Dean of Westminster," in the place of Williams, Bishop of Lincoln, the Dean of Westminster. Partly in Laud's hand-writing, with added notes by Sancroft, Thomas Baker and others. MS. L. 12, S. John's College Library. 119 pages numbered, and many blank; $5\frac{5}{8} \times 3\frac{1}{8}$, bound in old brown calf gilt, gilt edges. Written in black, with rubrics in red and titles in gold. Largely annotated by Laud (his autograph as Bishop of S. David's occurs on page 52).

Formerly in possession of Bishop Dolben, of Rochester (afterwards Archbishop of York) ; then it belonged to Sancroft, by whom it was left to Bishop Lloyd, of Norwich, who gave it to Thomas Baker, in trust for S. John's College.

Lent by the MASTER AND FELLOWS OF S. JOHN'S COLLEGE, CAMBRIDGE.

11. A Collection of Papers and Letters formerly be-longing to Abp. Laud ; many of them written by his own hand and most of them endorsed by him. Together with some papers of Arch-

U

bishops Sheldon and Sancroft, and many of
Mr. Chillingworth. Bound in one volume and
lettered Cod. Miscel. 943. Lambeth Palace
Library.

MS note on first page " This MSS was happily recovered by
Abp. Herring from Mrs. Ibbott Widow of Dr Ibbott formerly
Librarian at Lambeth. This MS it seems with some money
and papers was in a Box which Abp. Tenison directed his Executors to burn wit:.out opening; but the Box bursting in the fire,
the money and this Book which they supposed was forgot by
the Abp. was taken out and preserved. Abp. Herring made
Mrs Ibbott a present of five guineas for this book." And in a
later hand " This information I received from the Revᵈ Mr
Henry Hall, Librarian to Abp. Herring, my immediate predecessor in that Office. And : Coltee Ducarel. Lambeth Librarian
Oct 15. 1757."

A most interesting collection, containing autograph papers of
King Charles I., Abps. Abbott, Laud, Juxon, Mountain,
Williams, Sheldon, Sancroft, Bishops Wren and Montague,
Clarendon, Noye, Bastwick, and others. Among them are the
Earl of Devonshire's Apology on his Marriage to James I.,
Charles I.'s letter missive for the translation of Laud to
Canterbury, Laud's transcript of some notes written in his
Prayer Book by Bishop Andrewes, and Laud's Accounts of his
Province to Charles I., with the King's notes in the margin.

Lent by HIS GRACE THE ARCHBISHOP OF CANTERBURY.

12. A Volume of Original Letters between Archbishop
Laud and Bishop Williams of Lincoln, numbered 1030. Lambeth Palace Library.

All Bishop Williams' letters are endorsed in Laud's own hand.
Preceded by a note from Mr. John Chamberlain to Abp.
Tenison, give an account of his receiving these letters from
Mr. Petyt, Keeper of the Records in the Tower.

Lent by HIS GRACE THE ARCHBISHOP OF CANTERBURY.

13. The Sixth Accompt of Robert Bateman: Esquire Chamberlein of the City of London for the mony received and paid for repaireing of y^e Cathedrall Church of St Paul in London : for one whole yeare vizt from Mich^{as} Anno Dom. 1636 : unto Mich^{as} Anno Dom. 1637 :

Parchment leaves $17\frac{1}{2} \times 12\frac{1}{8}$; bound in vellum. With the autograph signatures of (among others) Laud and Juxon. See Nos. 113-115.

Lent by the DEAN AND CHAPTER OF S. PAUL'S.

14. Warrant of the Privy Council to the High Sheriff of the County of Rutland for the Collection of Ship-Money, dated Whitehall, November 9th, 1638, with fourteen Autograph Signatures, including Archbishop Laud, Bishop Juxon, Sir Thomas Coventry Lord Keeper, the Earls of Lindsey, Arundell, and Manchester, &c.

Lent by the REV. E. FIELD.

15. Letter of Archbishop Laud, with Autograph Signature, to the City of Edinburgh.

This letter, which was unknown to the Editors of Laud's works, was published in the *English Historical Review*, October 1892.

Lent by the REV. W. H. HUTTON.

16. Letter of Archbishop Laud (in Latin) to Hugo Menard, with Autograph (?) Signature ; concerning the *Epistle of Barnabas.* (Laud's *Works*, vi. 568.)

Arc. v. 11. Sion College Library. In a volume with 19 other letters, &c., including one in the handwriting of Lord Chancellor Bacon.

Lent by the PRESIDENT AND FELLOWS OF SION COLLEGE.

17. Holograph Letter of Archbishop Laud to the Countess of Leicester, endorsed by the Earl "Lord of Canterbury to my wife, 18th Nou., 1636." (Laud's *Works*, vii. 297.)

Lent by ALDERMAN SIR JOSEPH C. DIMSDALE.

18. Holograph Letter of William Juxon, Bishop of London, afterwards Archbishop of Canterbury.

Lent by ALDERMAN SIR JOSEPH C. DIMSDALE.

19. Holograph Warrant of W. Juxon as Lord Treasurer.

"Sʳ Robert Pye. These are to pray you to cause payment to be made unto the Lady Young, and Mr. Weymis, of half a yeares Pay of their severall Pencions. And for soe doing this shal be yʳ Warranty.—Guil: London."

Lent by MR. W. V. DANIELL.

C.—SPECIMEN BOOKS WHICH BELONGED TO ARCHBISHOP LAUD.

20. Little Gidding Book. A Harmony (or Concordance) of the Moral and Ceremonial Law, dated 1640. Large folio. Formed of cuttings from Bibles, &c., carefully arranged and mounted. Profusely illustrated, and bound in purple velvet, stamped in gold.

See the *Lives of Nicholas Ferrar* [ed. Prof. Mayor] for an

account of the community of Little Gidding, which was under Laud's sanction, and for the visit of the Ferrars to him.

A list of the known Little Gidding Books is given in *Nicholas Ferrar*, edited by T. T. Carter, chap. viii. This volume is numbered XI.

Lent by the PRESIDENT AND FELLOWS OF
S. JOHN'S COLLEGE, OXFORD.

21. A Relation of the Conference between William Lawd, Then, L^rd Bishop of St. David's, Now Lord Arch-Bishop of Canterbury: and Mr Fisher the Jesuite, by the Command of King James of ever Blessed Memorie. By the sayd Most Reverend Father in God, William Lord Arch-Bishop of Canterbury. London. MDCXXXIX.

The First Edition ; very large paper ; with Laud's Autograph Notes, and his Arms on cover.

" I do remember, that being Chaplain to the Honourable Sir Lionel Tolmach, Baronet, about the year 1666, I heard him relate . . . how that in his younger days he was at Rome, and well acquainted with a certain Abbot ; which Abbot asked him, Whether he had heard any news from England ? He answered, No. The Abbot replied, I will tell you then some ; Archbishop Laud is beheaded. Sir Lionel answered, You are sorry for that, I presume. The Abbot replied again, that they had more cause to rejoice, that the greatest enemy of the Church of Rome in England was cut off, and the greatest CHAMPION of the Church of England silenced ; or words to that purpose. In witness whereof, I have hereunto set my hand, this 28th day of September, 1694. JONA. WHISTON, Vicar of Bethersden in Kent."

" His own book against the Jesuit will be his lasting epitaph."—SIR EDWARD DERING.

Lent by HER MAJESTY THE QUEEN.

22. Virgilii Evangelissantis Christiados.   Libb. xiii.
8vo.   1638.

With the Archbishop's Arms on cover.

Lent by HIS GRACE THE ARCHBISHOP OF CANTERBURY.

23. Hippocratis, Aphorismi (Graece, Latine).   8vo.
1609.

With the Archbishop's arms on the cover, his Autograph
Signature, *William Laud*, on the title page, and Autograph
Notes.

Lent by HIS GRACE THE ARCHBISHOP OF CANTERBURY.

24. Gospels of the four Evangelists in Saxon, out of
Latin.   4to.   1571.

With the Archbishop's Arms on the cover, his Autograph
Signature, *G. Cant.*, on the title page, and Autograph Notes.
Fly-leaf has " Archbishop Laud, owner of this book."

Lent by HIS GRACE THE ARCHBISHOP OF CANTERBURY.

25. The Statutes (X Anno Caroli Regis).   4to.   1636.

With the Archbishop's Arms on both covers.

Lent by HIS GRACE THE ARCHBISHOP OF CANTERBURY.

26. Junius de Picturâ Veterum.   4to.   Amstelædami
MDCXXXVII.   Bound in crimson velvet.

With the Archbishop's arms on both covers and inscription
(possibly Autograph). Given by him to the College on June 28,
1639, as we learn from the Postscript to Letter ccccxxxi. [*Works*,
vii. 582.]

Lent by the PRESIDENT AND FELLOWS OF
S. JOHN'S COLLEGE, OXFORD.

27. Theatri Geographiæ Veteris. Folio. Amstelodami 1618.

With the Archbishop's Arms on both covers.

> Lent by the PRESIDENT AND FELLOWS OF
> S. JOHN'S COLLEGE, OXFORD.

28. Book of Common Prayer. Black Letter. 4to. 1633. Bound in old calf.

With the Archbishop's arms on both covers.

> Lent by the TEALE LIBRARY, S. CUTHBERT'S
> KENSINGTON.

D.—OTHER OBJECTS OF INTEREST.

29. Shirt of King Charles I. One of two worn upon the Scaffold.

> "He then appointed what Cloaths he would wear. '*Let me have a Shirt on more than ordinary,*' said the King, '*by reason the season is so sharp as probably may make me shake, which some Observers will imagine proceeds from Fear. I would have no such Imputation. I fear not Death! Death is not terrible to me! I bless my God I am prepared.*'"—Herbert's *Memoirs*.

> Lent by BEWICKE BLACKBURN, ESQ.

30. Bowl or Caudle Cup, said to have been used for the last Communion of King Charles I. Of mother-of-pearl without and silver-gilt within; with silver handles.

> The chalice used on this occasion is in the possession of the Duke of Portland. But it is possible that this bowl may have been used instead of a paten.

> Lent by H. JOHNES FIELDING, ESQ.

31. Register of Archbishop Laud's Burial.   From the
registers of Allhallows Barking Church.

Burialls, Ano D⁰ : 1644 and 1645.

	Died	Buried	William Laude Archbishup of
January	10	11	Canterbery beheaded . . .

After *beheaded* there is a word erased, which doubtless was
traitor.

Lent by the VICAR AND CHURCHWARDENS OF
ALLHALLOWS BARKING, E.C.

32. MS. Poem in honour of Archbishop Laud, in the
Vestry Minute Book of Allhallows Barking
Church for July, 1663.

"Upon the Remoue of ye most Revend
William
Lord Arch-Bishop of Canterburie his bodie from
Allhallowes Barking London, to St John's
Colledg in Oxford, July ye 21th, 1663.

When first Injustice Pack't up his High-Court,
When Vsurpation grau'd a Broad Seale for't,
When Death, in Butchers : dres did th' axe advance,
And Tragique : purpose with all Circumstance
Of Fright & Feare tooke up the fatall Stage
To act Rebellion in it's Rule, and Rage
When Friendship fainted, and late : Love stark dead,
When few own'd him, whom most men honored,
Then BARKINGE home, then (thus by th' world forsooke)
The butcherd Bodie of ye Martyre tooke,
Tore up her quiett Marble, lodg'd him sure
In ye cheife Chamber of her Sepulture ;
Where he intire, and undisturb'd hath bin,
Murther'd & mangl'd tho at's laying in,
Where he's vntainted too, free from distrust
Of a vile mixture with Rebellious dust ;
To make that sure, Braue Andrew's begg'd it meet
To Rott at's Coffin, and to rise at's Feet,
But now our Learned Lawd's to Oxford sent,
St. John's is made St. WILLIAM's Monument,

Made so bym'self ; This pious Primate's knowne
Best, by the Bookes, and Buildings of his owne,
Whome, though th'accursed age did then deny
To lay him, where ye Royall Reliques lye,
Which was his due ; At's Bodies next Remoue
Hee'l Rise, and Reigne amongst ye blest aboue."

Lent by the VICAR AND CHURCHWARDENS OF
ALLHALLOWS BARKING, E.C.

33. Notes of charges against Archbishop Laud, believed to be the autograph notes of William Prynne used against the Archbishop in his Trial.

Consisting of six closely-written sheets of large brief-paper, $18\frac{1}{2} \times 14$, and fragments of two others, carefully repaired, mounted, and half-bound in parchment, lettered " Mr. Prynne's Observations," with marginal notes, some by another hand.

The last sheet bears the endorsement " Mr. Prynne's Notes agst Archbishop Laud, given me by Geo. Clarke, Esq., A.D. 1740, out of Mr. Prynne's Library at Swanswick, near Bath. N.B. Mr. Prynne's estate there now belongs to y^e s^d Mr. Clarke. And. Coltee Ducarel."

Lent by the DEAN AND CHAPTER OF CANTERBURY.

34. Medal struck in honour of Archbishop Laud. Three examples, two in silver, one in brass, $2\frac{1}{2}$ inches in diameter. *Obv.* Portrait of Archbishop Laud, profile, in square cap, with inscription GVIL : LAVD . ARCHIEPISC . CANTVAR . X . IAN . 1644. *Rev.* An Angel holding a mitre ; two Angels beneath holding a crown : at the base, view of London and the Thames, with old S. Paul's and S. Saviour's, Southwark, with inscription SANCTI CAROLI . PRÆCURSOR.

Lent by the PRESIDENT OF S. JOHN'S COLLEGE,
OXFORD, the REV. W. H. HUTTON, and the
REV. DR. SPARROW-SIMPSON respectively.

35. Bust of Archbishop Laud, probably by Herbert le Sueur, dated 1633.

In bronze, undraped. From the Library of S. John's College.

Lent by the PRESIDENT AND FELLOWS OF
S. JOHN'S COLLEGE, OXFORD.

36. Photographic Specimens of MSS. given by Archbishop Laud to the Bodleian Library.

LIST OF MSS. PHOTOGRAPHED.

HEBREW : Compendium of Ritual decisions by R. Asher, Son of Yehiel.

Translation of Maimonides' Guide of the Perplexed.

Commentary on Liturgies collected by Ahron Ben Hayyim.

Hebrew Poems.

SPANISH IN HEBREW CHARACTERS : Libri di Magica, by Gil de Burgos.

ARABIC : The Pentateuch.
History of Ibn Sasarri.
El-Ghazzali's Revival of the Religious Sciences.
Arabic Chronicle (anonymous).
Biographical Dictionary of El-Dhahabi.
Specimens of Calligraphy.

GREEK : MS. E of the Acts of the Apostles.

LATIN : Aegidii Poema de Re Medica.

SAMARITAN : The Pentateuch.

ETHIOPIC : Organon Mariae.

PERSIAN : Sa'di's Gulistan.
Apophthegms.

CHINESE : Log-book.

CHURCH-SLAVONIC : New Testament.

BOHEMIAN : New Testament.

IRISH: New Testament.

FLEMISH: Paradisus Animae.

ITALIAN: Laude de la Caritade.

SPANISH: Letter from Don Pedro Franquesa to Don Juan de Aquila.

FRENCH: Froissart's Chronicle.
Quintus Curtius.

ANGLO-SAXON: Chronicle.

Diary, 1639, June 28th. "I sent the remainder of my manuscripts to Oxford, being in number 576. And about an hundred of them were Hebrew, Arabic, and Persian. I had formerly sent them about 700 volumes." See also *History of his Chancellorship (Works*, v. 225 f.*)*.

Things projected. No. 12. "To set up a Greek press in London and Oxford, for printing of the Library Manuscripts ; and to get both letters and matrices. Done for London."

Lent by D. S. MARGOLIOUTH, ESQ.,
Laudian Professor of Arabic in the
University of Oxford.

37. A Display of Heraldry. By "Master GVILLIM:" 4to, London, Ralph Mab, 1632.

Showing on page 382, the Arms of " The Rgᵗ Rᵉᵛ Father in God Wᵐ Laud, Lᵈ Bishop of London, Chancellour . . . Un: Ox: Dean of the Chap: Royal " &c.

Lent by the REV. J. W. KENWORTHY.

38. The History and Antiquities Ancient and Modern of the Borough of Reading. By John Man. 4to, Reading, 1816.

Showing on page 48, the house in Broad Street in which William Laud was born.

Diary. " I was born October 7, 1573, at Reading."

Lent by the REV. C. W. PENNY.

39. The History of the Municipal Church of St. Lawrence, Reading. By the Rev. Charles Kerry. 8vo, Reading 1883.

Showing the Font, in which Laud was christened.

Lent by H. C. BOND, ESQ.

40. Rubbing of Memorial Brass to Archbishop Laud, in the Chapel of S. John's College, Oxford.

With inscription " In hac Cistvla condvntvr exvviæ Gvlielmi Lavd Archiepiscopi Cantvariensis qvi secvri percvssvs immortalitatem adijt, die decimo Ianvarij An° Dⁿⁱ 164⅘ Ætatis avtᵉ svæ 72, Archiepiscop. 11."

As Henry Wharton tells us, this was the inscription placed upon the coffin itself:—" On the Arch-Bishop's Coffin was nailed a little Brass-Plate, with his Arms, and this Inscription engraven thereon, &c." (*Hist. of Tryal* p. 453.)

Lent by the REV. W. H. HUTTON.

41. Rubbing of Memorial Brass to Archbishop Laud's Auditor, at the W. end of the North Aisle of Allhallows Barking Church.

" Here lyeth the body of Geo. Snayth, Esqʳ, sometime Auditor to Willᵐ Laud, late Arch Bishop of Canterbury," &c.

Presented by MISS JOHNSON.

42. Laud blessing Strafford on his way to Execution. From the picture by De La Roche, in the possession of the Duke of Sutherland.

" The next morning at his coming forth he drew near to the Archbishop's lodging, and said to the Lieutenant ' Though I do not see the Archbishop, yet give me leave, I pray you, to do my last observance towards his rooms.' In the meantime the Archbishop, advertised of his approach, came out to the window. Then the Earl bowing himself to the ground, ' My

Lord ' said he, ' your prayers and your blessing.' The Archbishop lift up his hands and bestowed both ; but overcome with grief, fell to the ground in animi deliquio."—Heylin's *Cyprianus Anglicus*, p. 481.

Lent by Mr. W. V. DANIELL.

43. Leaves of a maple-tree planted by Laud at Ibstock (?) in Leicestershire.

These were given to the Rev. T. Arthur Curties 20 years ago by an old clergyman, the Rev. E. Dodds, then Rector of Great Glen, Leicestershire.

Lent by the REV. T. ARTHUR CURTIES.

44. Trial of Archbishop Laud. Engraving by Hollar.

Lent by Mr. H. A. J. BREUN.

45. Photograph of Laud's Instrument of Resignation of the Chancellorship of the University of Oxford.

This, the formal letter of resignation, is hitherto unprinted. It will be found at p. 273 of this volume.

Lent by Professor MARGOLIOUTH.

46. Protection for the Archbishop's Ferrymen at Lambeth. With Admiralty seal and signatures of Admiral Sir George Rooke and others. Dated March 10, 1701.

The Ferry-boat held an important place in the life of an Archbishop in those days.

Diary, 1633, Sept. 19. "The day . . . when I first went to Lambeth, my coach, horses, and men sunk to the bottom of the Thames in the ferry-boat, which was overladen ; but I praise God for it, I lost neither horse nor man."

Lent by HIS GRACE THE ARCHBISHOP OF CANTERBURY.

E.—CONTEMPORARY BOOKS AND TRACTS.

*(Only such as contain Portraits, or are otherwise specially interesting,
are exhibited).*

47. Fragments of leaves of the suppressed edition of
Archbishop Laud's Scottish Prayer Book.

A contemporary writer, Robert Baillie, says "It is now
perceived, by the leaves and sheets of that booke, which are
given out athort the shoppes of Edinburgh to cover spyce and
tobacco, one edition at least was destroyed." These fragments,
which were discovered in the binding of a copy of the Edition
of 1637, differ from the corresponding parts of the published
work, and are probably portions of the destroyed edition.
They are the only known specimens that have survived.

Lent by the LORD BISHOP OF EDINBURGH.

48. The Booke of Common Prayer and Administration
of The Sacraments. And other parts of Divine
Service for the use of the Church of Scotland.
Folio. Black Letter. Edinburgh, 1637.

Prepared by Ab^p Laud. Two copies, to show the variation
from the English Prayer Book in the Prayer of Consecration, &c.

Lent by the LORD BISHOP OF EDINBURGH.

49. The History of the Troubles and Tryal of The
Most Reverend Father in God, and Blessed
Martyr, William Laud, Lord Arch-Bishop of
Canterbury. . . . To which is prefixed
The Diary of His Own Life. *First Edition.*
Folio. London, MDCXCV.

With a fine portrait.

Lent by the REV, PROF. COLLINS,

50. A Summarie of Devotions, compiled and used by Dr. William Laud, sometime Ld Arch-Bishop of Canterbury. *First Edition.* 8vo. Oxford, 1667.

With an interesting portrait of Laud inserted.
Formerly in the possession of Dr. Routh, President of Magdalen College, and of Dr. Hawkins, Provost of Oriel College.

Lent by MISS HAWKINS.

51. A Summarie of Devotions compiled and used by Dr. William Laud, &c. 5⅛ × 3⅛. London, 1667.

Lent by the REV. T. ARTHUR CURTIES.

52. A Speech in the Starr Chamber, at the censure of J. Bastwick, H. Burton, and W. Prinne. 4to. London, 1637.

Lent by the REV. DR. SPARROW-SIMPSON.

53. The Arch-Bishop of Canterbury's Speech or His Funeral Sermon, preached by Himself on the Scaffold on Tower-hill Two Copies, 4to. London, 1644, and one 4to. London, 1709.

Lent by the REV. DR. SPARROW-SIMPSON, MR. ALDERMAN DIMSDALE, and His Grace the ARCHBISHOP OF CANTERBURY respectively.

54. The True Copie of a Letter sent by . . . Laud . . . to the University of Oxford when he resigned the office of Chancellor . . . 4to. Oxford, 1641. Bound up with

The Copie of a Letter sent from William Lavd

Archbishop of Canterbury the 28 of June
MDCXLI unto the Vniversitie of Oxford, 1641.

The latter is a forgery.
With portrait inserted.

Lent by the PRESIDENT AND FELLOWS
OF SION COLLEGE.

55. A Breviate of the Life of William Laud Arch-
Bishop of Canterbury.   By William Prynne of
Lincoln's Inn, Esquire.   Folio.   London, 1644.

With Hollar's print of the Trial.

Lent by Mr. W. V. DANIELL.

56. Canterburies Doome, or The First Part of a Com-
plete History of the Commitment, Charge,
Tryal, Condemnation, Execution of William
Laud, late Arch-Bishop of Canterbury.   .   .   .
By William Prynne, of Lincolns Inn, Esquire.
Folio.   London, 1646.

With Hollar's print of the Trial, and portraits of Prynne
and Laud—the latter very curious, and probably not authentic.
See No. 81.

Lent by the REV. DR. MASON.

57. Ecclesiæ Anglicanæ Suspiria ; the Tears, Sighs,
Complaints and Prayers of the Church of
England.   .   .   .   By John Gauden, D.D.
Folio.   London, 1659.

With curious emblematical frontispiece.

Lent by Mr. W. V. DANIELL,

58. Cyprianus Anglicus: Or, The History of the Life and Death of The most Reverend and Renouned Prelate William By Divine Providence Lord Archbishop of *Canterbury.* . . . By P. Heylin, D.D. and Chaplain to *Charles* the First and *Charles* the Second, Monarchs of *Great Britain.* Folio, London MDCLXXI.

Lent by the REV. PROF. COLLINS.

59. Scrinia Reserata : a Memorial Offered to the Great Deservings of John Williams D.D. . . . Ld Keeper of the Great Seal of England and L^d B^p of Lincoln . . . By John Hackett D.D., Late L^d B^p of Litchfield and Coventry. Folio. London, 1693.

With fine portrait of Bishop Williams.

Lent by the REV. PROF. COLLINS.

60. The Pope's Benediction, or His generall pardon, . . . sent into England by *Ignatius Holy-Water,* a *Jesuit,* to the Arch-Bishop of *Canterbury* and to the rest of his subjects there. 4to. London, 1641.

Two satirical cuts. Begins "All haile to our Laud of little grace."

Lent by the PRESIDENT AND FELLOWS OF SION COLLEGE.

61. Rome for Canterbury; or a true relation of the Birth and Life of W. Laud, 4to. *s.l.* 1641.

With portrait.

Lent by the PRESIDENT AND FELLOWS OF SION COLLEGE.

62. The Recantation of the Prelate of Canterbury: Being his last *Advice* to his Brethren the Bishops of England : *To consider his Fall, observe the Times*, forsake their Wayes, and to joyne in this good work of REFORMATION. 4to. London, 1641.

With curious portrait of Laud falling.
A presentation copy from " A Romish Recusant."

Lent by the REV. W. H. HUTTON.

63. Mercuries Message or The Coppy of a Letter sent to William Laud late Archbishop of Canterbury now prisoner in the Tower. 4to. London, 1641.

With portrait.

Lent by the REV. PROF. COLLINS.

64. An Answer to the most Envious, Scandalous, and Libellous Pamphlet, Entitled Mercuries Message. 4to. London, 1641.

With very curious portrait.

Lent by the REV. PROF. COLLINS.

65. A Second Message to Mr. William Laud, now prisoner in the Tower on behalf of Mercurie. 4to. London, 1641.

With portrait and MS. addition, " A Canterbury Tale."

Lent by the PRESIDENT AND FELLOWS OF SION COLLEGE.

66. A true Description, or rather a Parallel betweene Cardinall Wolsey, Arch-Bishop of York, and William Laud, Arch-Bishop of Canterbury. 4to. *s.l.*, 1641.

Bound up with the " Speech in the Starr Chamber," " Divine and Politike Observations," and the " Speech *or* Funerall Sermon."

Lent by J. M. BARTON, ESQ.

67. " Former Ages never heard of
and
After Ages will admire."

4to. London, 1654.

A very interesting pamphlet, with many curious cuts, including "The rising of Prentises and Sea-men on the Southwark side to assault the Arch-bishop of Canterburys House at Lambeth," and " Execution of Archbishop Laud." Bound up with other curious tracts.

Lent by the RIGHT HON. LORD NORTHBOURNE.

F.—PORTRAITS (OILS AND ENGRAVINGS).

OIL PAINTINGS.

68. William Laud, Archbishop of Canterbury. By Van Dyck.

See W. H. Hutton's *Laud*, p. 37, *note* 3.

Lent by the PRESIDENT AND FELLOWS OF
S. JOHN'S COLLEGE, OXFORD.

69. King Charles I.   Artist unknown.

> Lent by the PRESIDENT AND FELLOWS
> OF SION COLLEGE.

70. Sir Thomas Wentworth, Lord Strafford.   Copy of a portrait by Van Dyck, in the Egremont Collection.   Given by the late Earl of Egremont to S. John's College.

> Lent by the MASTER AND FELLOWS OF
> S. JOHN'S COLLEGE, CAMBRIDGE.

71. William Juxon, Bishop of London 1633-1660, Lord Treasurer of England (afterwards Archbishop of Canterbury 1660-1663).   Artist unknown.

> Lent by the VERY REV. THE DEAN OF WORCESTER.

72. John Williams, Bishop of Lincoln 1621-1641, Dean of Westminster and Lord Keeper of England (afterwards Archbishop of York 1641-1644).

> Lent by the DEAN AND CHAPTER OF WESTMINSTER.

73. Edward Pococke, 1st Laudian Reader in Arabic in the University of Oxford.   Copy of a picture in the Bodleian Library, made for Dr. Pusey during his tenure of the Regius Professorship of Hebrew (1828-1882).

> With Inscription, " Edv. Pocock, S.T.P. | Nat. A.D. 1604 |
> Ling. Arab. Prof. Laud. 1636 | Ling. Heb. Item Prof. 1648 |

Ex utroque officiis ejectus 1650 | Restitutus, nullo ei pari invento 1651 | Ob. A.D. 1691."

Things projected, No. 17. "To erect an Arabic Lecture in Oxford, at least for my lifetime, my estate not being able for more. . . . Done. I have now settled it for ever. The Lecture began to be read August 10th, 1636."

Lent by the REV. DR. DRIVER, Regius Professor of Hebrew in the University of Oxford.

74. Miniature Portrait of Archbishop Laud on ivory, painted in 1858, by Mrs. Davis Cooper, from the portrait by Myttens, now in the possession of Charles W. Wood, Esq.

An Autotype reproduction of the original portrait forms the frontispiece to this Volume.

Lent by MRS. DAVIS COOPER.

ENGRAVINGS, ETC.

75. William Laud, Archbishop of Canterbury. Engraved by James Watson from the portrait by Van Dyck now in the Hermitage Gallery at S. Petersburg.

This painting was once in the possession of Sir Robert Walpole at Houghton Hall, and was sold thence to Catherine II. of Russia.

Lent by DR. N. EVANS.

76. Archbishop Laud. Autotype Reproduction of the Portrait by Van Dyck at S. Petersburg.

Lent by the REV. DR. MASON.

77. Archbishop Laud. Engraved by Loggan from the portrait by Van Dyck at S. John's.

> Lent by the PRESIDENT AND FELLOWS OF
> S. JOHN'S COLLEGE, OXFORD.

78. Archbishop Laud. After Van Dyck.

Framed in the wood of the Inner Quadrangle of S. John's College Oxford, built by Laud.

> Lent by the REV. T. ARTHUR CURTIES.

79. Archbishop Laud. A very curious engraving by Benedictus Audran, after a portrait by Wan der Werff.

> Lent by the REV. T. ARTHUR CURTIES.

80. Collection of Engravings of Archbishop Laud, including one printed in France, one in the Low Countries, and one in Germany.

> Lent by MR. H. A. J. BREUN.

81. Archbishop Laud. A Portrait of a Bishop in a Geneva Cap, quite unlike Laud, but found in several contemporary tracts, and in some copies of Prynne's *Canterburies Doome*.

Apparently the printer, being unable to get a true picture, utilised an old wood block of rather earlier character.

> Lent by MR. W. V. DANIELL.

82. Bishop Atterbury in prison in the Tower, holding a portrait of Archbishop Laud. Printed for Eman. Bowen, the corner of Bolt Court, in Fleet Street, London [1722].

"He [Atterbury] was publicly prayed for in most of the Churches of London and Westminster ; and there was spread among the people a pathetic print of the Bishop looking through the bars of a prison, and holding in his hand a portrait of Archbishop Laud ".—Mahon, *History of England from 1713 to 1783*, ch. xii.

See *Bibliography*, No. 249.

Lent by MR. H. A. J. BREUN.

83. King Charles I. After the Portrait by Van Dyck in the Pembroke Collection.

Lent by MR. W. V. DANIELL.

84. King Charles I, Queen Henrietta Maria, Abp. Laud, and the Earl of Strafford. Four contemporary woodcuts on two sheets.

Lent by the REV. F. A. H. VINON.

85. George Abbot, Archbishop of Canterbury 1610-1633. From a portrait in the possession of the Earl of Verulam.

Laud's Calvinistic predecessor. On August 6, 1633, Laud (then Bishop of London) came to visit the King at Greenwich, not having heard that Abbot was just dead. "My Lord's Grace of Canterbury," said the King, "you are very welcome."

Lent by MR. W. V. DANIELL.

86.   Launcelot Andrewes, Bishop of Winchester 1619-
1626.   Dated 1618.   (*Very rare.*)

Lent by Mr. W. V. DANIELL.

87.   Bishop Andrewes.   Dated 1635.

Lent by the MASTER OF PEMBROKE COLLEGE,
CAMBRIDGE.

88.   Bishop Andrewes, in Geneva Cap.   By Hollar;
dated 1643.

Lent by MR. W. V. DANIELL.

89.   William   Juxon,   Bishop   of   London   (afterwards
Archbishop of Canterbury).   Two engravings,
one of which is the other reversed.   After the
portrait at Longleat.

Lent by MR. W. V. DANIELL.

90.   Bishop Juxon.

Lent by the DEAN AND CHAPTER OF S. PAUL'S.

91.   George Villiers, Duke of Buckingham (1592-1628).
After the portrait by C. Johnson.   Engraved by
Houbraken.

Diary, June 15, 1622, "I became C[onfessor] to my Lord of
Buckingham."

Lent by MR. W. V. DANIELL.

92. Sir Thomas Wentworth, Earl of Strafford, 1593-1641. After the portrait by Van Dyck in the possession of Sir F. Child.

> Lent by REV. PROF. COLLINS.

93. William Prynne, John Bastwick, and Henry Burton. Set in the pillory by authority of the Star Chamber, June, 1637. Three woodcuts.

Diary, June 14, 1637. "This day Jo. Bastwick, Doctor of Physic, Henry Burton, Bachelor of Divinity, and William Prynne, Barrister-at-Law, were censured for their libels against the hierarchy of the Church, &c."

> Lent by Mr. W. V. DANIELL.

G.—ENGRAVINGS, &C., OF PLACES.

94. The house in Broad Street, Reading, in which Laud was born.

See No. 38.

> Lent by MR. E. HILL.

95. St. Laurence's Church, Reading, in which Laud was christened.

See No. 39.

> Lent by H. C. BOND, ESQ.

96. The Grammar School, Reading: in which Laud probably received his earliest Education, and of which he was a generous benefactor in later years.

Lloyd, *Memoirs,* p. 225, tells how Laud's schoolmaster used to say to him " When you are a little great man, remember Reading School."

Letter CXXVII. To the Corporation of Reading. " I pray leave to put you in mind that you have no preferment for your school, but only for two places into Saint John's College in Oxford ; and by God's blessing, of later times some of your sons have thrived extraordinarily well there."

Lent by MR. W. V. DANIELL.

97. Two Views of S. John's College, Oxford, by Loggan.

Things Projected, No. 2. " To build at S. John's in Oxford, where I was bred up, for the good and safety of that College. Done."

Diary, 1631, July 26th. " The first stone was laid of my building at S. John's."

1635, September 3rd. " I went privately from the Bishop of Oxford's house at Cuddesdon, to S. John's in Oxford, to see my building there, and give some directions for the last finishing of it."

See *Letter* CCXCI for Laud's wishes as to the arrangement of the New Buildings.

Lent by the REV. W. H. HUTTON, B.D.

98. Inner Quadrangle of S. John's College, Oxford (built by Archbishop Laud), with a Procession of Founders and Benefactors. Being the plate of the Oxford Almanac for 1734.

Lent by the REV. T. ARTHUR CURTIES.

99. The Chapel of Gray's Inn, before restoration, of which Inn Laud was a Student.

Hart MSS. No. 1912. " Arch-bishopps of Canterbury admitted of this Society. . . . .

Lawd, William,
admitted 1 November, 1615."

Lent by H. C. RICHARDS, ESQ.

100. Parish Church of North Kilworth, Leicestershire, of which Laud was Rector from 1608 to 1609. Engraving and three photographs.

Diary, 1608, April. "The Advowson of North Kilworth, in Leicestershire, given to me."

Lent by the REV. C. W. BELGRAVE, Rector of
North Kilworth.

101. Parish Church of West Tilbury, Essex, of which Laud was Rector from 1609 to 1616. Photographs.

Diary, 1609. " I changed my Advowson of North Kilworth, for West Tilbery, in Essex ; to which I was inducted October 28th, to be near my Lord of Rochester, Dr. Neile."

1616, November. " I resigned my Parsonage of West Tilbery."

Lent by the REV. J. B. DOBREE, Rector of
West Tilbury.

102. Parish Church of Norton, Kent, of which Laud was Rector from 1610 to 1617. Photographs.

Diary, 1610. " I left Cuchstone, and was inducted into Norton, November, by proxy."

Lent by the REV. W. CROWTHER, Rector of Norton.

103. Parish Church of Ibstock, Leicestershire, of which Laud was Rector from 1617 to 1626. Photographs.

Diary, 1617. " I was inducted to Ibstock, in Leicestershire, August 2nd, in my return out of Scotland : and left Norton."

1626, March 6th. " I resigned the Parsonage of Ibstock, which I held in Commendam."

Lent by the REV. SAMUEL FLOOD, Rector of Ibstock.

104. Parish Church of Crick, Northamptonshire, of which Laud was Vicar from 1622.

Diary, 1622, January 27th. " I went out of London about the Parsonage of Creeke, given me into my Commendam. January 29th. I was instituted at Peterborough into the Parsonage of Creeke. January 31st. I was inducted into Creeke. February 2nd. Being Sunday and Candlemas Day, I preached and read the Articles at Creeke."

1624, July 23rd, Friday. " I went to lie and keep house, and preach at my Livings, held in Commendam, Creeke and Ibstock."

Lent by the REV. J. B. GRAY, Vicar of Crick.

105. The Chapel of Abergwili Palace, Caermarthen, rebuilt by Laud when Bishop of S. David's. Photograph.

A modern brass in the Chapel bears the inscription " ✠ Capellam propriis sumptibus exstructam Willelmus Laud episcopus Meneviensis in nomine Sancti Joannis Baptistæ die vigiliæ decollationis consecravit m. Augusti d. xxviii^{vo}. A.D. mdcxx^{to}."

Diary, August 20th, 1625. " I consecrated the chapel, or oratory, which I had built at my own charge in my house, commonly called Abergwilly House. I named it the chapel of S. John Baptist, in grateful remembrance of S. John Baptist's College, in Oxford, of which I had been first Fellow, and afterwards President."

Presented by the LORD BISHOP OF S. DAVID'S.

106. Church of S. Katherine Cree, E.C. Engraving.

Rebuilt (excepting the Tower) 1628-30, and consecrated by Laud (as Bishop of London). The consecration of this Church, and the ceremonies on the occasion, formed one of the charges against the Archbishop at his Trial. *Hist. of Troubles.* pp. 339, 340.

Diary, 1630-1, Jan. 16, Sunday. " I consecrated S. Catherine Creed Church in London."

Lent by MRS. GARRETT.

107. Parish Church of Great Stanmore, consecrated by Laud (as Bishop of London) on July 17, 1632. Photograph.

Diary, 1632, July 17, Tuesday. " I consecrated the Church at Stanmore Magna in Middlesex, built by Sir John Wolstenham."

Presented by the REV. F. C. JACKSON, Rector of Great Stanmore.

108. A Bird's-eye View of Lambeth Palace. Engraving, dated 1697.

Lent by MR. W. V. DANIELL.

109. Lambeth Palace Chapel, as it was in the Seventeenth Century. Engraving.

The ceiling, mouldings, &c., are by Laud ; the stalls and screen by Juxon after the Restoration.

Lent by Mr. W. V. DANIELL.

110. Lambeth Palace Chapel. Engraving of the Crypt.

Lent by Mr. W. V. DANIELL.

111. Church of S. Mary the Virgin, Oxford. Restored by Laud and others. Engraving.

Lent by Mr. W. V. Daniell.

112. Church of S. Mary the Virgin, Oxford. Engraving of the South Porch, the statue of the Blessed Virgin Mary in which was charged against Laud at his Trial. (**Prynne**, *Cant. Doome*, p. 71.)

Diary, 1637. "In this year the Porch of S. Mary's was finished at the cost of my Chaplain, Dr. Morgan Owen, which was £230."

Lent by Mr. W. V. Daniell.

113. Old S Paul's Cathedral, West Front, built by Inigo Jones. Engraving by Hollar, dated 1643.

The Cathedral was restored within and without mainly through the exertions of Laud, once its Bishop. He invited the King to the City on a State visit. After service he went over the Cathedral, and the inspection revealed the great need of restoration. The work was at once taken in hand, beginning with the disused and dilapidated choir; and under Laud's auspices it went on vigorously. He himself guaranteed £100 a year, and gave far more. The King gave Inigo Jones's new West Front—greatly admired at the time—and within about ten years over £100,000 had been spent upon the work, which was nearly finished at the time of Laud's impeachment. In the changes which followed, it need hardly be said, nothing more was done.

Things projected. No. 5. "To set upon the repair of S. Paul's Church in London. Done."

"Thus fell Laud, and S. Paul's with him: The yearly Contribution toward whose Repair, *Anno* 1641, when he was plunged into his Troubles, fell from the sum of 15000*l.* and upward, to somewhat less than 1500, and afterwards by degrees to nothing."—Heylin, *Cypr. Ang.* p. 504.

Lent by the Rev. Dr. Sparrow-Simpson.

114. Old S. Paul's Cathedral, South Side, showing the new South Transept. Engraving by Hollar.

Lent by the REV. DR. SPARROW-SIMPSON.

115. Old S. Paul's Cathedral, Interior of the Nave. Engraving by Hollar.

Laud's friend, Sir Paul Pindar, gave £10,000 for the decoration of the interior.

Lent by the REV. DR. SPARROW-SIMPSON.

116. Parish Church of Tadlow, in Cambridgeshire.

"There happened also in the Town of Tadlow a very ill incident on Christmas Day 1638 by reason of not having the Communion Table railed in, that it might be kept from profanation. For in Sermon time a dog came to the Table and took the loaf of bread, prepared for the Holy Sacrament, in his mouth and ran away with it. Some of the parishioners took the same from ,the dog, and set it upon the Table. After the Sermon the Minister cd. not think fit to consecrate the bread ; and other fit for the Sacrament was not to be had in that town ; and the day so far spent that they could not send for it to another town ; so there was no communion. And this was presented by four sworn men of the town aforesaid." Laud's Account of his Province, 1639 *(Works* v. 367*)*. It was the danger of profanation such as this which led to Laud's directions for the railing in of the Holy Table.

Lent by the REV. H. W. P. STEVENS,
Vicar of Tadlow.

117. The Parish Church of Allhallows Barking, E.C., in which Laud lay buried, 1645-1663. Engraving, dated 1736.

The brick Tower is an almost unique specimen of the Ecclesiastical architecture of the Commonwealth period.

Of this Church Dr. Edmund Layfield, Laud's nephew, was Vicar. At the time of Laud's death he was in prison and sequestrated by order of the Parliament ; and the use of the Book of Common Prayer had been prescribed on the very day upon which the Ordinance for the Archbishop's death was passed. Nevertheless, an intrepid priest named Fletcher was found who was willing to use the Book, and Laud was buried in the vault under the Altar, with the Burial Service of the Church for which he died.

Calendar of State Papers (Domestic), 1663–64, *p.* 320.

Oct. ? Petition of Thomas Fletcher to the King for the living of Boxford, Suffolk, void by death of Jas. Wharwell.

Has been constant 22 years in preaching and reading the book of Common Prayer ; buried Archbishop Laud with that book when others dared not ; kept Christmas Day at S. Giles's Cripplegate, London, when other churches were shut ; and hazarded his life by going into Kent four Sundays, to animate the people then in arms for His Majesty. Has only supplied the cure at Stratford-le Bow on a contribution of the inhabitants.

Endorsed is—

Sir John Robinson to Sec. Bennet. Certifies at request of many persons of quality that the petitioner was a confident reader of the Common Prayer book in times of danger, a bold asserter of the King's cause, animating his audience to loyalty. "And true it is he buried that most reverend prelate mentioned in the petition when many would not have undertaken it."

October 2, 1663.

[He seems never to have received the living.]

Lent by the REV. DR. MASON.

118. A True and Exact Draught of the Tower Liberties : survey'd in the year 1597 by *Guillelmus Haiward* and *J. Gascoigne.*

Showing the site of the Scaffold.

Lent by the REV. DR. MASON.

INDEX.

[The names of books &c. are printed in *italics*. The asterisk * is prefixed to the names of printers and booksellers &c.]

z